Tax and Business Planning for High Technology Businesses

by
Anne and Henry Fairpo

Dan
As promised!
A + H.

Tolley
LexisNexis™

Members of the LexisNexis Group worldwide

United Kingdom	Butterworths Tolley, a Division of Reed Elsevier (UK) Ltd, Halsbury House, 35 Chancery Lane, London, WC2A 1EL, and 4 Hill Street, Edinburgh EH2 3JZ
Argentina	Abeledo Perrot, Jurisprudencia Argentina and Depalma, Buenos Aires
Australia	Butterworths, a Division of Reed International Books Australia Pty Ltd, Chatswood, New South Wales
Austria	ARD Betriebsdienst and Verlag Orac, Vienna
Canada	Butterworths Canada Ltd, Markham, Ontario
Chile	Publitecsa and Conosur Ltda, Santiago de Chile
Czech Republic	Orac sro, Prague
France	Editions du Juris-Classeur SA, Paris
Hong Kong	Butterworths Asia (Hong Kong), Hong Kong
Hungary	Hvg Orac, Budapest
India	Butterworths India, New Delhi
Ireland	Butterworths (Ireland) Ltd, Dublin
Italy	Giuffré, Milan
Malaysia	Malayan Law Journal Sdn Bhd, Kuala Lumpur
New Zealand	Butterworths of New Zealand, Wellington
Poland	Wydawnictwa Prawnicze PWN, Warsaw
Singapore	Butterworths Asia, Singapore
South Africa	Butterworths Publishers (Pty) Ltd, Durban
Switzerland	Stämpfli Verlag AG, Berne
USA	LexisNexis, Dayton, Ohio

A CIP Catalogue record for this book is available from the British Library.

ISBN 0 7545 1256 8

Typeset by M Rules, London
Printed and bound by Antony Rowe Ltd., Chippenham, Wiltshire

Visit Butterworths LexisNexis *direct* at www.butterworths.com

Preface

What a time!

Five computers were used in writing this book: two laptop PCs, two Apple iBooks and an Apple G4. Software allowed us to communicate with colleagues, Butterworths Tolley and each other through e-mail and meant that we could swap the manuscript between the computing platforms without (too many) problems. It checked our spelling, helped us create the graphics and ruthlessly questioned parts of our grammar.

Broadband access to the Internet came through cable and across a wireless network to the Apple computers. Less broadband access came through mobile phones. Search engines helped us with data gathering and checking facts.

That is just the home computing end of the technology that surrounded us during the writing process – and most of this technology has been developed or launched in the last five years.

Technology businesses are not so much a breed apart as a breed aside – they have many of the same issues and challenges to face as other businesses but have additional ranges of mountains to climb.

We have both worked with or for technology businesses; businesses that aim to deliver products and services and make money out of intellectual property. Growing up in a world where technology has become ever more the norm we have benefited from watching the businesses experiment, challenge boundaries and make the unbelievable everyday.

We have seen the digital age arrive and the worlds of commerce and the consumer wonder what to do with it. We have witnessed the rise of the dot.coms and their fall just as we observed the rollercoaster of the biotech sector in the 1990s. In both cases the sectors, paradoxically, must be the stronger for the experience both in terms of having weeded out some of the weaker players and from the point of view of strategic thinking.

Strategy, plan and solutions

Our work is about helping companies succeed, be it through rolling out the right e-business underpinnings for their business or through flotation on the stock market. We have learned that the successful businesses:

- know where they want to be;
- have a long-term strategy – they know how they want to get there;
- they have a plan of action; and
- they are not looking for stock answers, they want solutions.

The concepts in this book and the technical considerations that go with them are distillations of what we have seen and the solutions that we have seen used to avoid the pitfalls. They are not intended to be rigid rules nor are we setting out to create new ways of running businesses. They are simply what we have seen working in practice and ideas to provoke thinking and help ensure that key areas are not overlooked.

Help and assistance

We could not have undertaken writing this book without the enthusiastic support of the partners at both the firms where we work. Our thanks goes to them, and particularly to our heads of department, Ian Latter at KPMG and Nick Whitaker at PKF, for indulging us. In addition, we owe significant thanks to all those colleagues past and present, clients and contacts who have, perhaps unknowingly, taught us, helped us and opened our eyes to the range of ways that things can be done in technology businesses. To our families and friends for introducing us to technology and letting us learn about it at first hand, we owe a debt we cannot begin to repay – even if sometimes we wonder what all the bits of technology around the house are actually for!

In creating this book we have had the invaluable help and support of Alison Lovejoy, Stephen Mullaly and our editor, Howard Cruthers from our publishers. Alongside them colleagues in both firms deserve our thanks for help in answering questions and providing examples. In particular our thanks go to Judith Finch at KPMG for her enthusiastic support and suggestions across the gamut of topics and Jason Homewood and Hugh Mathew-Jones at PKF for insight and input into the technical chapters on accounting issues and valuation. Chris Yates-Smith from Teem Co, with his thoughts on the branding issues, and Gavin Fairpo, reviewing the book generally, also gave generously of their time and wide experience.

Any errors or misconceptions that remain after their efforts are entirely our responsibility.

Anne and Henry Fairpo
September 2001

Contents

Contents

Part II – Forming Your Strategy

Part III – Technical Considerations

Practical Issues

Introduction

Introduction

1

OBJECTIVES

- To define Technology businesses.
- To explain the objectives of the book.
- To explain the parameters of the book – what it is not designed to cover as well as what it is.

Technology businesses

1.1 Defining technology businesses sounds very easy – but in practice it isn't. Everyone has a slightly different view of what a technology business is or, often, more strongly held opinions on what a technology business is not.

The authors have grappled with this for a long time and produced a definition which is still a compromise – as in so many areas the Internet both threw a spanner in the working of an otherwise successful definition and helped to refine it into something more specific.

So first of all the simple answer:

DEFINITION

A *technology business* is one that generates its revenues by providing customers with the ability to address needs or wants through offerings built on the application of intellectual property held in house.

Unfortunately, this in turn raises the question of what is meant by intellectual property.

Intellectual property (IP)

1.2 Most people see IP as being a sub-set of business knowledge and therefore only part of the goodwill of a business.

> **DEFINITION**
>
> *Goodwill* is the intangible element of the value of a business that accounts for the value of the whole business exceeding the value of the simple sum of the business's financial assets less its financial liabilities.

However, in general conversation, one often hears the term used to cover a broad range of commercial knowledge and know-how which leads to a general confusion over the boundaries between IP, know-how and knowledge.

What is clear is that for technology businesses IP is different from scientific knowledge in a number of respects. Most importantly, technology IP has a potential real world application whereas certain elements of science are focused on adding to the sum of human knowledge rather than addressing a specific need.

Although the authors are aware that this is still vague they think of IP as ideas, concepts or mechanisms that lead to some *thing* that is useful (and is physical in nature or at least having some outward manifestation such as the output of a computer programme) being *created*.

The act of creation may be the direct or indirect outcome of applying the IP in the real world. An example of an indirect outcome is drug delivery IP. Something that helps deliver a drug to the required site of action does not, of itself, treat the patient. But if the drug delivery IP can protect a drug that would otherwise be attacked and broken down by the body's immune system before it reached the required site of action the IP is useful in treating the disease. The creation of a drug that uses the delivery IP is therefore an indirect creation of something useful that uses the drug delivery IP.

This concept of IP therefore rules out certain areas that could even be theoretically patentable including:

- Concepts or products with no known real world application or applications where it is unclear that the concept/product really makes a difference (as in certain patent claims for natural proteins seen in the US that cite their addition to shampoo as an application).
- Commercial knowledge, such as who produces a certain product and where to source products.
- Commercial standing, as in the fact that certain suppliers will only supply certain businesses or that certain customers will only buy from businesses with certain qualifications (such as ISO 9000 certification).
- Simple knowledge (even if technical in nature) such as how to use a lathe to cut metal.
- An idea that is so broad in potential application that it is unspecifiable or is really just an observation (such as the theory that on the Internet you can get from any one place to any other place in six clicks).

Hence, this rules out of this definition of technology companies a range of businesses including:

- Pure retailers (even if they sell technology products).
- Pure E-commerce players (so called e-tailers or businesses that exist to sell services and use the internet as their sole conduit for doing business).
- Manufacturing activities with no design element or where the manufacturing is really just assembly (such as many computer manufacturers).
- Businesses that use technology or IP but don't create it themselves (such as airlines who use very sophisticated technology on their planes and in their back office systems but, generally, buy that technology in).

Why 'held in house'?

1.3 Again, this has more to do with trying to ensure that certain businesses fall outside the definition than about technology itself.

Technology businesses can and often do license in IP. They purchase or license technologies for a series of reasons and two complementary business models exist purely on this basis:

- the in-licensing developer; and
- the outlicensing discoverer.

This is a simple corollary of the rule that you cannot benefit commercially from work done by others without paying some due for the right to use that work. Hence the concept of the outlicensing discoverer whose revenue model is based on selling discoveries to others and receiving access fees and royalties in return – a model widely used by biotechnology businesses.

In turn, including the requirement for the revenues to be generated from offerings built on IP held in-house ensures that the businesses that fall within the definition undertake at least some development on the technology they sell. Otherwise they become either distribution agents or simple retailers, even if they arrange and source the manufacturing themselves.

Again, this excludes certain suppliers of items such as computer peripherals which, while badged with a corporation's name, may not include any technology that is proprietary to that corporation.

So what businesses are included?

1.4 The following is a list of some of the generic types of business that are considered to be technology businesses for the purposes of this book:

- Software developers and systems integrators (including developers of applications used on or to support the Internet).
- Component developers (including integrated circuit and other component designers).
- Hardware design and development businesses working at the circuit board level (such as hi-fi equipment design) or in radical engineering solutions (as in areas of the automotive industry).
- New materials research and development businesses.
- Researchers and developers of new motive or static power sources or power transmission mechanisms.
- Developers of optics and optical systems.

- Research and development based pharmaceutical and biopharmaceutical companies (including diagnostics and medical device companies but excluding distributors and certain generics businesses).
- Genomics and proteomics companies (including analytical companies).
- Developers of genetically modified organisms (for food, environmental or other uses).
- Developers of environmental analysis, remediation or containment technologies.
- Nanotechnology businesses.
- Telecommunications businesses developing hardware and transmission mechanisms (but not resellers either switched or switchless or ISPs).
- Imaging or display technology development businesses.
- Developers of technologies for testing other products (but not simple certifiers even if they develop their own certification regimes) and developers of analytical techniques and technologies (so long as they have real world applications).
- Developers of instrumentation technologies for monitoring of processes (but not simple instrumentation manufacturers).
- Developers of process technologies (but not simple manufacturers or suppliers of processing equipment even if only used in technology businesses) and new product formats.
- Some chemical companies (those with significant research and development activities leading to new products or new techniques for manufacture or synthesis of compounds) and agrochemical businesses.
- Agricultural biotechnology businesses.
- Certain businesses based on developing new structures or structural applications (but not civil engineering businesses doing pure design and construction management work).
- Convergence businesses involved in integrating different existing technologies to improve or make use by the customer easier.
- Solutions providers and consultants on problem solving for processes, products and convergence (but not lawyers, accountants and patent agents).

No doubt there are and will be many others that fit the authors' definition but this list is intended to be illustrative rather than in any way proscriptive.

The objectives of this book

1.5 This book is designed as a guide. It is therefore generic by design and high level in nature. The key objectives of the guide are:

- To set out the stages that technology businesses go through and highlight what elements of the business change along the way.
- To help those who run technology businesses ensure they have considered all the key areas of their businesses.
- To help them look forward rather than just seeing the present challenges and opportunities.
- To highlight areas of good practice and flag up common failings and concerns.
- To outline the strategic process and show how it can help businesses grow and be successful.
- To outline some of the key legal and taxation issues that arise around technology businesses.
- To explain the basis for the accounting treatment of technology related items.

And across all of these to do it in a practical and user-friendly format.

The guide is not intended to have all the answers. Indeed, as in all businesses, the solutions that each technology business needs to look for will vary depending on the business, its aims, ambitions and market place.

This is particularly true with regard to the legal, patent and taxation aspects of the book. A guide of this type can only ever provide the highest level overview of what are, by their nature, often highly complex, dynamic and often seemingly illogical rules, regulations and practices.

♦ **Readers should therefore take professional advice on all issues relating to taxation and legal matters so that the advice received is tailored to their specific situation.**

The authors have aimed to include sources of information and help to build on the information in the guide. Sensible use of these sources should allow readers to tailor the answers into solutions for their own business.

Further, the guide is aimed at helping readers prepare and understand the information and advice they will receive from those sources.

Again, there are areas that this guide is not intended to cover. These include certain day to day operational matters such as:

- Personnel management techniques and certain areas of employment law.
- Negotiation techniques and styles.
- Management styles and business ethics.
- Office and other facility design and related property law issues.
- Environmental issues (beyond basic legal points) and good environmental practice.
- The detail of targeting, initiating, negotiating and running acquisitions, disposals, mergers and the requirements of being a stock exchange listed company.
- Social responsibility for businesses and sustainability issues.

Capturing the current state

1.6 Technology businesses operate in a dynamic environment. Rules and regulations are updated, tax regimes modified and accounting standards revised. The regulators and legislators react to public opinion and the development of concepts, ideas and products that were not envisaged when the last set of rules were drawn up.

At other times changes relate to commercial concerns or developments made by other regulators. In the UK the changes can come from the EU, for example.

Even as this first edition was being drafted company law reform is under consideration and the rules over insolvency are already being revised. The US patent office is reconsidering certain areas of patent law and has already strengthened its view on what constitutes utility with regard to granting patents on genetic discoveries.

This guide is, therefore, representative of the status of regulation and knowledge in the third quarter of 2001.

♦ **This makes taking professional advice on the technical aspects of the business and how best to make decisions relating to tax, IP and other legal aspects all the more important.**

Overall structure of the book

1.7 Following this section the book is divided into three main sections:

I Lifecycle

1.8 This section looks at the different stages that businesses go through as they develop. Using an eight stage growth model the chapters examine the activities, challenges and common difficulties faced by technology businesses.

II Forming Your Strategy

1.9 Strategy is made up of a series of elements. Focusing on the activities and challenges highlighted in the *Lifecycle* section the chapters create links to the elements of strategic thinking needed.

III Technical Considerations

1.10 The *Technical Considerations* chapters are designed to act as a reference archive on specific issues around:

- Practical issues such as legal points, the patent process, sources of funds, valuation issues, project management and quality and accreditation.
- Taxation issues and practical points.
- Accounting issues and the standard layouts of accounts.

Chapter structure

1.11 As this book is intended to act as both a guide and a reference the objectives of each chapter are set out at the beginning.

Each chapter in the *Lifecycle* section of the book also sets out the main expected activities across a range of eight business functions:

- Intellectual Property and Knowledge Management
- People
- Market Knowledge
- Channels to Market
- Offerings
- Operations
- Infrastructure
- Funding

This model is generic both by nature and by design. Without abstracting the issues to a fairly high level it is difficult to generate a framework that allows useful insight for businesses as wide ranging as tracking technologies and drug development. There will often be no clear doors to be opened to move from one stage to the next and businesses may not be aware that they have moved. However, the basic model and the summaries of expected activities at each stage are designed so that businesses should be able to identify with reasonable accuracy where they currently are. As might be expected, there will be occasions when a business will feel that in certain areas they are in, say, the Development stage, whilst in others they are in the first Expansion phase. This is quite natural and shows that they are on the borderline between the two.

Perhaps more importantly it should allow businesses to identify the challenges that they will face in the next stages and help them prepare for them.

The chapters in the *Forming Your Strategy* section are designed to help structure the thought processes around building a strategy for the long term and then drilling down from that firstly to a business plan that guides decisions and then to business and revenue models that allow the validation of the plan through the creation of financial projections. They aim to draw together the different aspects that need consideration from the commercial to taxation and from the integration of e-business techniques to the strategy of brands.

The *Technical Considerations* chapters are overviews of areas that impact the business planning process. They have been pulled out so that they can be more easily referred to and do not break up the flow of the earlier chapters.

Boxed items

1.12 Throughout the chapters there are parts of the text in boxes. These are either:

DEFINITIONS

Explanations or definitions of *terms* used in the preceding text. The term being defined is italicised.

---

or:

EXAMPLES

Worked examples or illustrative examples to help illuminate the surrounding text.

Lifecycle

I

Overview of the Lifecycle

2

OBJECTIVES

- To provide an overview of the lifecycle.
- To introduce the stages of development and related activities.
- To introduce the concepts of growth stages, exit points, and exit routes.

The Sigma model

2.1   The lifecycle of a business can be viewed in a number of ways. For the purposes of this book we have split the life of a business up into different phases that reflect the evolution of the activities and focus of technology businesses over time.

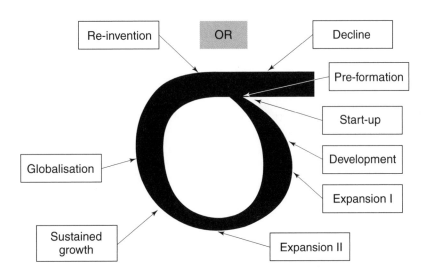

Figure 2.1 sets these phases out in the form of the Greek letter Sigma.

The eight stages have the following characteristics and profiles:

Pre-formation

2.2
- The basis of the business is a concept or idea or it is technology that is, at most, developed to proof of principle stage.
- The management team is unlikely to be complete.
- Business plans are technology focused and may not include a fully developed commercialisation plan.
- The legal structures of a company or other entity have not been set up.
- Intellectual property is likely to be know-how or a very broad initial patent submission.
- Funding is largely ad hoc and from friends and family.

Start-up

2.3
- Proof of principle has been achieved and the initial product(s) are being developed.
- Some market research/testing has taken place.
- A commercialisation plan is beginning to be developed.
- Holes in the team have been identified and are starting to be addressed.
- A company or other legal structure has been set up.
- A patent strategy is starting to develop alongside a view of the commercialisation route.
- Initial partnership contacts are being made.
- Further friends and family sourced funding and starting to progress to business angels and early stage venture capital.

Development

2.4
- Development of the initial offering is well advanced and further products or applications are being started.
- Clearly defined target markets have been identified and structures for sales are being developed.
- The business is beginning to move from being technology led to being sales led.
- The patent/intellectual property portfolio is growing as the breadth of coverage is expanded and a patent strategy developing.
- Partnerships are starting to be created and formalised.
- Funding may require sums available only from venture capital sources.

Expansion I – pre-flotation

2.5
- This stage sees businesses aiming to gain critical mass.

- Can be very sales focused or, in certain subsectors such as biotechnology, focused on broadening out the technology platform and the number of products in trials.
- Management team is completed.
- Internal systems and controls are developed to aid monitoring of cash and Key Performance Indicators (KPIs).
- Patent strategy is formalised and the patent wall continues to be built and the security of the IP checked.
- A pre-IPO funding round may be undertaken to aid the development or allow for bolt-on acquisitions that bring technology, critical mass, geographic range or remove competitors.

Expansion II – flotation

2.6
- Flotation is the start of the large scale growth stages.
- The management team needs new skills such as investor relations.
- Performance against budgets and/or milestones is a key focus.
- Securing intellectual property is both offensive and defensive at this stage.
- Internal systems and controls have to manage both the growth and the Corporate Governance issues of a publicly traded entity.
- The cash raised has to be monitored and the return evaluated.
- Opportunities to use the shares as currency arise to grow the group.

Sustained growth

2.7
- Focus is on KPIs and growing the technology and customer pipeline.
- Focus is often still in the local territory.
- Public reporting takes place at least half yearly so the short and longer terms have to be balanced.
- New management skills may be needed to manage the growth.
- Access to funds may be limited while the business proves its worth to investors but borrowings may become an option.

Globalisation

2.8
- In order to sustain the growth the business pushes out into new territories.
- New skills here include identifying potential acquisition targets and negotiating large-scale deals.
- Management needs to see the big picture and take hard choices.
- Systems and controls move onto a different level and the structure of the business may well be more complex.
- Access to new funding sources (such as through the bond markets or stock markets in other countries) become options.
- Managing the growth and scale is key, so the strategy may be refined and often needs paring down to avoid the risks of unstructured spread.

Re-invention

2.9
- Products and technologies have natural lifecycles as the business needs of customers progress.
- The business therefore moves and develops to mirror or lead the anticipated needs of the customers.
- Often this stage is heralded by changes in management, re-focusing of the activities and strategic acquisitions and disposals of entire activities.
- New activities are developed to replace those being wound down or spun out and these new businesses begin the cycle again.
- If the re-invention does not occur or is started too late then the business can enter the *Decline* stage where sales fall and the viability of the business diminishes so that in an extreme case stakeholders are likely to look to realise their investment by winding up the business.

Exit points and exit routes

2.10 Not all investors look to stay with a business throughout this lifecycle. Their requirements for differing rates of return and their need to realise cash or simply their investment constitution (for example in a venture fund or Venture Capital Trust) mean that they may look to sell out along the way.

There are a series of potential exit points through the process which are set out in Figure 2.10:

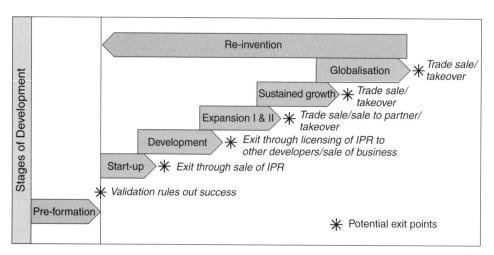

Figure 2.10 – Exit points

Source: PKF

Exit routes

2.11 Figure 2.10 also sets out some of the different exit routes that arise. The key routes and their definitions being:

- A trade sale – the sale of the whole of the business to a third party for cash or an interest in that third party.

- The licensing out of the technology/IP to a third party who will develop and sell the product. Here the business may receive both cash up front and a share of the future sales generated by the third party through a royalty arrangement.
- Takeover – the purchase of a publicly traded business by another large entity such that the activities of the business become subsumed in the operations of the purchaser.

In the following chapters each of these stages and the exit routes are considered in more detail.

Expected Activities

3

OBJECTIVES

- To give an overview of the 8 Functional Areas.
- To introduce the concept of challenges.
- To explain The 3 Challenges.

The 8 Functional Areas – an overview

3.1 Throughout this book, the activities of technology businesses are classified into 8 Functional Areas:

Intellectual Property and Knowledge Management
People
Market Knowledge
Channels to Market
Offerings
Operations
Infrastructure
Funding

This is very much a horizontal slicing of the business. In some ways the Functional Areas match up with the concept of business processes.

> **DEFINITION**
>
> *Business processes* are the systems and controls in place that regulate the running of certain strands of a business.
>
> A business process is generally put in place to manage one of the key business drivers such as Generating Revenue. Hence, business processes are pervasive across the departments of a business as they draw on the activities of a number of departments along the way.
>
> The business process for Generating Revenue, for example, will involve activities within the Marketing department and the Sales department but could also draw in:
>
> - Product Development (*developing the right solution for customers*);
> - Quality;
> - Distributor Channel Management (*if sales are generated through a distributor network*);
> - Project Management;
> - Manufacturing;
> - Purchasing (*to ensure Manufacturing has the materials or bought in product it needs to fulfill the order on time and to ensure that the pricing of the product is generating adequate margin*); and
> - Distribution.

In other ways the 8 Functional Areas are hybrids having some alignment with more traditional departmental structures.

Their objective is not, however, to allow an extensive and complex analysis of business activity (as business process analysis does for example). Rather they provide a generic classification framework for the activities and thought processes that happen in any technology business to one extent or another and hence they have been selected to provide consistency across a range of differing businesses.

Businesses are active in each of the 8 Functional Areas to some extent at each stage of their development. At the start of each chapter of the *Lifecycle* section of this guide there is a generic summary of the types of activity that technology businesses tend to be involved in during that stage.

Intellectual Property and Knowledge Management (IP/KM)

3.2 The building of intellectual property (IP) from which technology is developed and the protection of that intellectual property is at the core of technology businesses. This functional area deals with how all the knowledge within the intellectual property, the know-how within the people and other operational and cultural information is made available and tapped into by those that need it within the organisation and by its customers.

It also addresses the need to protect certain pieces of IP either by gaining legal protection through patents, design rights, database rights, copyright, etc or by strategically keeping the knowledge private (sometimes referred to as trade secrets) within the business. The decision as to what is formally protected and what is treated as a trade secret should be driven by an agreed IP strategy. The practicalities of IP protection are addressed in more detail in Chapters 22 and 23 and IP strategy is covered in Chapter 19.

People

3.3   Having the right people doing the right jobs is one of the most important roles of management. Recruiting, retaining, motivating and positioning the right people in the right place within the organisation is therefore a key area of any business as is the need, on occasion, to lose people who are not adding to the business.

In addition to addressing these items this functional area also covers the skills needed by the business as it grows and the training and people development that go hand in hand with those needs.

Market Knowledge (MK)

3.4   This functional area is sometimes referred to as strategic marketing. It combines the gathering of information on the market and customer needs/wants and the communication of those needs internally with the communication of benefits and features of the technology to customers and targets.

Strategic marketing is about far more than producing sales literature or setting up meetings with customers. In many technology companies the marketing department acts as the balance to the technology development activities. Technologists are often motivated more by the development of technology than by pure commercial success. There is therefore a danger that development times get extended and the final offering becomes either overly cumbersome or over specified for the needs of customers. One of the roles of strategic marketing is to ensure that the initial specification of the offering meets the needs of the customer while staying within their budget and that the development plan is aligned with that specification.

Often the relationship between the sales and marketing activity, the development department, and the customer can look like the diagram below. The potential danger here is that the developers will, quite naturally, get messages from the purchaser and particularly the users about all the things they would like to have in a perfect world – including all the features and functionality they are not willing to pay for. In this situation it is easy for the development department to be diverted from the specification that the purchaser is willing to pay for onto adding in the extras that the users might possibly find interesting but the purchaser will not pay for.

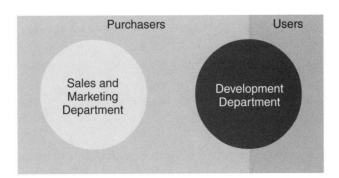

The model below is one way around the issue. Here the marketing activity is truly strategic. It acts as the interface between the customer and the development department. In this scenario the Strategic Marketing activity can include far more than just sales and marketing people. It will also often include technical personnel (perhaps on secondment from development) to help in drawing up the initial specifications with the customer. It may also include the post-sales support team. The idea is that the development team is allowed to get on with development and is not distracted by other issues.

Channels to Market (C2M)

3.5 In order to generate revenues businesses have to be able to get to their customers. Channels to Market addresses the options for reaching the markets as well as the active management of the chosen options.

Depending on the business model adopted, this activity may be a business development role – as when revenues are achieved mainly through licensing intellectual property – or it can involve distribution and sales teams. Account or channel management (the term used for the activity of controlling and supporting distributors) will also fall into this area. Supported by the Market Knowledge activity, C2M will be the final driver of revenue generation, interacting with customer and sales channels, identifying opportunities for sales and opening the door for others or winning the order themselves.

Door opening is important in that in a technical sale there is often a dual-layer relationship needed to make the sale:

- The sales team interact with the customer's purchasing team.

But neither party here necessarily has the technology knowledge to show that the proposed solution is the right one. So the second layer is:

- Technical sales to technical user.

Offerings

3.6 Technology comes in different forms and in different formats. This functional area looks at the development and delivery of the business's products and services as well as the nature of the offering itself. By necessity some of the activities in this area, such as next generation offering development will run ahead of the rest of the organisation.

From what has been said before, there is a clear link into this activity from the Market Knowledge activity. MK collects the market needs and wants and prioritises them. Along with the Offerings activity this prioritised market facing information is collated into a roadmap of product development which is fed into the development teams to be turned into offerings.

Operations

3.7   Technology businesses deliver offerings to their customers. At some point in the process those offerings are developed, refined and, in certain cases, physically produced. The operations area encompasses these development and manufacturing processes and can include other linked elements of the business such as product support.

Operations is the engine house of the business. Without an efficiently run and well monitored operations activity, businesses will lose out either financially or to competitors. Hence, the operational activity will also encompass some elements of the management reporting function as well as areas such as Quality control.

Infrastructure

3.8   Business activities need supporting structures. The infrastructure functional area includes consideration of elements such as:

- Premises
- Utilities (light, heat and power, water, etc)
- Administration
- Finance and management information
- IT and communications
- Strategic planning

Funding

3.9   All of these functional areas take cash. Over time the offerings should generate more than enough cash to pay for the other activities – if they don't then the business doesn't survive! However, at certain stages in its growth a business needs cash up front to develop either its infrastructure or its IP or its offerings or a combination of these. This up front cash may have been self-generated by past activities or it may need to be sought from external financing agencies. The funding activity also includes the monitoring and managing of existing cash as well as the seeking of new funds from outside.

Challenges

3.10 PepsiCo's philosophy is that there is no such thing as a problem or an issue: there are only opportunities. This can be viewed as a truism and is, certainly, a good mindset for any business. As one listed company chairman is wont to say 'winners win' whereas businesses that see only problems tend to be negative in their internal and external dealings.

However, this can seem like an unduly optimistic view. It may, therefore, be more acceptable to the British psyche to think in terms of challenges.

DEFINITION

Challenges are events that have to be faced positively, positively managed and out of which the business will grow in strength in some way.

In running a business decisions have to be made every day and challenges can arise in all of the 8 Functional Areas.

Examples of everyday challenges in the 8 Functional Areas include:

- Deciding whether to patent a discovery (*IP/KM*).
- A key employee being off sick (*People*).
- Competitor announcements (*MK*).
- Supporting an overseas distributor in a sale tender (*C2M*).
- Launching a new offering (*Offerings*).
- A tight delivery timetable for a key customer (*Operations*).
- VAT or PAYE visits (*Infrastructure*).
- Balancing foreign currency bank accounts against projected requirements (*Funding*).

Challenges are not things to avoid or run away from. They are the lifeblood of business and, according to many entrepreneurs, challenges are the excitement that keeps people in business.

However, challenges must be faced and addressed against a background that is more complicated than simply the day to day activities of the business.

The 3 Challenges

3.11 Alongside the challenges of day to day activities across the 8 Functional Areas businesses face the necessity of fitting the 8 Functional Activities into the strictures of:

- The general legal and regulatory environment.
- Tax efficient structures and tax legislation around the world.
- A strategy that is acceptable to shareholders and stakeholders.

DEFINITION

A *stakeholder* is someone (a person or an entity) that has a vested interest in the successful running of the business. So stakeholders include:

- Employees
- Suppliers and suppliers of suppliers
- Customers
- End users
- Government (for employment and tax policy reasons)
- Advisors
- Potential as well as present shareholders

These three additional potential constraints on the business need to be faced and are referred to in this book as The 3 Challenges.

Each chapter within this *Lifecycle* section highlights the key elements that need attention in each of the *3 Challenges* alongside the *Expected Activities* in each of the 8 Functional Areas.

Layout

3.12 In order to draw the Expected Activities and the 3 Challenges together each chapter includes a diagrammatic summary on the following lines:

The 8 Functional Areas and The 3 Challenges	Expected Activities and Challenges
Intellectual Property and Knowledge Management	
People	
Market Knowledge	
Channels to Market	
Offerings	
Operations	
Infrastructure	
Funding	
Legals	
Taxation	
Strategy	

SUMMARY

3.13 Every business is different in the way it is set up. The Expected Activities are high level constructs designed to help set out in the following chapters the challenges that technology businesses face as they grow. Within real businesses the activities may well overlap and elements included in one activity in the descriptions above may fall within a different activity in practice. The positioning of after-sales support is one area that can appear in a number of areas – in the descriptions above it is noted that after-sales support can sit in Operations or Market Knowledge. The positioning will depend on the nature of the business and the way that the business is structured internally.

This internal structuring relates to both the business model adopted and the philosophy of the business. The important thing is not where individual departments or activities lie but that they are included and that their interactions with the rest of the business make logical sense.

The structure has to aid the achievement of the businesses goals. Any structure where it appears that one activity is either isolated or hindering others (development can hinder sales if it is focused on producing offerings that the market does not want, for example) needs to be re-assessed and adjusted to bring the business back together.

The interactions between the activities are comprehensive: a diagram attempting to link them together starts by doing just that, linking each one to every other one. It would then go on to attempt to pair up and show the flows of information and value through the system. Having attempted just such graphics in the past (and having found that they end up being totally unintelligible) the authors have concluded that the simple strip basis works best, showing the support structure directly and indicating that each activity is dependant on the others for success.

Pre-formation

4

The 8 Functional Areas and The 3 Challenges	Expected Activities and Challenges in the Pre-formation phase
Intellectual Property and Knowledge Management	Technology/concepts being developed and proven at least to proof of principle stage. Prior art checks, concepts being tested and patent advice being sought.
People	Generally only the founder(s) with support from family and friends. Can be a larger team if a spin-out. The business plan needs to consider where the rest of the team will come from and what skills they need to bring with them.
Market Knowledge	Basic market verification being undertaken: needs, alternative solutions and competitors, pricing, market size, market location, etc. Based on this analysis the business plan needs to include the consideration of the channels to market that are most appropriate for the type of offering and the objectives of the business.
Channels to Market	
Offerings	The business plan needs to consider the nature of the product offering and hence the revenue model for the business.
Operations	Very limited. Often just carried on in the founders' homes/garages or borrowed lab/development space. At the same time as the technology is being developed a business plan needs to be created that sets out the strategy and anticipated development of the technology and the business.
Infrastructure	
Funding	Relatively small-scale funding requirements raised from friends and family or through grant awarding bodies.
Legals	Avoiding falling foul of existing employment contracts, considering the strength of existing patents/products and potentially setting up the legal entity that will undertake the business.
Taxation	Limited at this stage unless there are already employees and costs are being incurred. Otherwise consideration of pre-formation costs needs to be undertaken.
Strategy	The big questions need to be answered: What is the business? What will it do? Who are its customers? Why will they buy from the business? What will it be known for? How will it do? Who will run it? How will it make money? What is its lifespan and can it be regenerated?

OBJECTIVES

- To look at the business pre-formation.
- To highlight the key questions and areas of focus.
- To consider the thought processes.
- To consider possible sources of help.

Looking at the business

4.1   At this very first stage there is no *business* as such. What does exist is a concept and a determination to see the technology being developed get to market or, alternatively, to find a solution to a problem that can be brought to market.

Generally based around a very small team, and often really just one person, there may be more energy than direction at this point. The important activities are therefore focused on channelling the energy and ensuring that the vision is not too blinkered by either the excitement of discovery or the self-induced belief that the idea must have a massive market.

Balancing technology and the market

4.2   The main area of effort therefore has to be put into finding a balance between proving the technology, or at least the principle behind it, and seeking evidence that there is a market that is willing to pay for it once developed.

It is very tempting to rush ahead, form a company, start talking to potential funders and look at recruiting a team to push the project on. Likewise, substantial amounts of money can be sunk into research and development to push the idea forward. Without the balance of market validation, however, the funding will not be forthcoming and the money spent on development may prove to have been wasted.

Some time taken at this stage to verify the market potential of the technology will be time well spent. This does not necessarily need to be a long and expensive market research project but it should provide more than the gut feeling that is probably the only market research undertaken to date. Sadly, the world is littered with examples of ideas developed because 'people must want to buy this'. Just because you think your potential offering would be good to have does not mean that other people will.

The difficulty here is with intellectual property. In order to gain patent protection later you have to be careful not to talk to people about your discovery directly – if you make a discovery public first then you will run into problems with patenting it later. So, to undertake the market validation you will either have to find suitable information from, say, the Internet that supports your view or else be careful in discussing it with others.

Worse still, by discussing it with people you may end up passing over the intellectual property and risk someone else patenting it.

On the technology front itself, it is worth considering whether there are ways of gaining outside verification of discoveries. Again, beware the patent protection position, but there are ways of doing this under non-compete/non-disclosure agreements that should not impact the patent position later.

♦ **This is an area where advice from a specialist IP lawyer or a patent agent could be invaluable.**

Strategy

4.3 Having proved both the principle of the technology and the market opportunity the next steps are to start building the strategy. At this stage the strategy may be fairly rudimentary but it should act as the cornerstone of the fuller strategy that will start to be needed in the *Start-up* phase.

There are some basic questions to ask here:

- What are we going to be selling?
- To whom?
- What IP protection do we need/can we get?

These are the first steps towards a business model. It is vital that the answers to these questions are realistic. Chapter 14 on business models points out that not every business needs to be able to take the process from discovery right through to market. In particular, areas such as manufacturing need very careful thought.

Setting up and equipping manufacturing facilities is expensive both in terms of cash and time. Without a proven product and market it is unlikely that investors will be willing to put up the funds for manufacturing to be done in-house.

It is interesting to note that James Dyson first licensed his vacuum cleaner technology to a Japanese company (the resulting G-Force vacuum cleaners sold for $2,000 each!) and used the licence fees to set up his UK operations and design and build the DC01. Likewise, new small-scale car manufacturers, such as the reborn Jensen Motors, tend to gauge public opinion by launching their first cars with mock-ups or prototypes and using the orders gained as the basis for raising funds to build factories.

While talking to the IP lawyer or patent agent it is worthwhile starting discussions about the IP protection strategy. Knowing what to protect and what to keep as a trade secret is very important. It is important that your advisor knows what you are trying to achieve and which elements of the intellectual property really are key to the technology. You can talk openly with these advisors as they work under strict rules of client confidentiality.

It is possible to adopt a defensive strategy built around IP. This works by progressing the patent route and building as good a patent wall as possible and then sitting back and waiting for others to breach the patents. This may not seem a very attractive approach for an inventor but it is one route that can be considered. The downside is that there is a cost in defending a legally protected position and the funds to protect the rights have to be available.

Legal entity

4.4 Now is also the time to think about what, if any, legal entity should be formed for the business. Chapter 24 gives an overview of the options and the differences between the types of legal entity available. However, there is no need to rush into forming an entity until the rest of the balancing act mentioned earlier is completed.

Sources of help, guidance and information

4.5 As mentioned already meetings with IP lawyers and/or patent agents are generally very useful at this stage. Other sources include:

- The Internet and market research organisations for market information.
- The Business Link network run by the Government's Small Business Service.
- Firms of accountants and lawyers, who are generally only too happy to help businesses with real potential.
- High street banks, who often have business start-up teams.
- Local Chambers of Commerce.
- For younger entrepreneurs the Prince's Trust runs a mentoring scheme with experienced business people helping younger businesses get off the ground.
- Contacts and friends who are successful in business already.

The important thing when selecting advisors is to pick ones who not only understand technology businesses, and preferably have some insight into your business opportunity and the technology, but are also people you feel you can get on with and can work with.

When you have selected advisors listen to them and consider their views. If you do not agree with them say why – they may have missed something but then again, so may you.

Start-up   5

The 8 Functional Areas and The 3 Challenges	Expected Activities and Challenges in the Start-up phase
Intellectual Property and Knowledge Management	Protecting the initial products (where appropriate) and developing an IP strategy. Documenting the technology and the IP both for protection purposes and for internal use. Simple systems in place – probably just pen and paper or, at most, a basic computer database.
People	The skill sets needed for this stage and the development stage have been identified and the team is either in place or the mechanism for completing the team is known and costed.
Market Knowledge	Market research and market testing have taken place. The customer-required functionality or the market opportunity for the technology has been identified (depending on the offering).
Channels to Market	The proposed channel to market has been identified, matching the nature, size and location of the market and the business's plan to access the market. Initial structures are being developed to meet the strategy for getting to the market.
Offerings	The format of the initial offering(s) is agreed and specifications/functionality/stage of development have been set internally to act as a milestone for issuing version 1.
Operations	Still relatively small-scale and limited. Actual scale will depend on the business model and the funding available.
Infrastructure	Ad hoc but beginning to formalise. Towards the end of the phase, with funds available, first premises may be taken on and office staff developed. Systems and controls around finance and administration need to be set up to meet the legal requirements of the entity.
Funding	Still largely funded by friends and family/grants but starting to need funds beyond the means of these sources. Initial contacts may well be made with business angels and early stage venture capital houses.
Legals	Company formation and the associated transfer of the business and IP into the company need careful consideration as do, potentially, first employee contracts and property matters. IP protection will need attention as may advances from current IP owners who believe the business may be infringing their patents/IP.
Taxation	Likely to be loss making so loss protection is important. Employee tax issues and potentially VAT as well become a day-to-day focus. If any IP has been transferred in the treatment needs thought. Personal tax positions for founders need consideration as do mechanisms for attracting and retaining staff.
Strategy	The answers to the big questions need refining to match the findings of the development and market knowledge activities. In addition, as other funders are approached, the strategy may need to be developed to meet their requirements for investment. Likely to become more action and milestone based.

OBJECTIVES

- To look at starting up the business.
- To highlight the key questions and areas of focus.
- To consider the thought processes.
- To consider possible sources of help.

Looking at the business

5.1 For the first time there is a real business to look at. Having been through the pre-formation stage there may well be a legal entity set up and initial cash from friends and family to kick-start the journey that may end up with a global enterprise.

Funding is one of the key areas of focus for this stage. It is unlikely that, for most technology companies, friends and family funding will be adequate to keep the business running for any length of time. There are exceptions, such as certain software businesses, but even then if resources are to be deployed full-time on the business it is likely that additional funds will be required.

Grant funding may be available to assist in development, but even this will only pay for a proportion of the costs. In addition, grant funding is generally retrospective – the business has to pay the bills and then claim the correct proportion back from the grant provider. It is worth discussing the availability of grants with your advisors as there are specific technology related grants such as SMART awards.

Strategy

5.2 Moving onto the next level in funding terms means looking to business angels or seed-capital providers from the venture capital sector. This means developing a business plan, which, in turn means having the strategy thought through and captured.

Chapters 12 to 15 set out the process of going from idea to strategy to business plan and financial projections.

The technology

5.3 Work also needs to continue on developing the technology. Having got through proof of principle the momentum needs to be maintained – another reason why funding may be the major focus at this stage. Development needs to be progressed along a path that heads towards the specification that has been captured for version 1, the first version that will be launched commercially.

At the same time the IP strategy will have been fleshed out and it will both be being actioned in terms of existing IP and will also be driving research in areas where the need for a protectable piece of IP has been identified. The idea here is that all the bricks in the IP protection wall are important. So, there may be elements of the offering where adding further IP protection adds to the overall value of the IP.

The Five Bar Gate approach to IP protection shows how this process works:

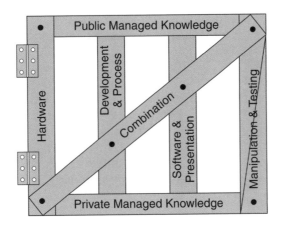

Figure 5.3 – the Five Bar Gate of IP protection

Source: PKF

Each of the vertical elements and the crosspiece are areas where formal protection may be available and they link into the top bar of public managed knowledge. The bottom of the gate, the starting point, is private managed knowledge – the trade secrets that stay within the business and are not formally protected. The purpose of the IP strategy is to understand where any one piece of IP fits into the model and therefore what protection, if any, should be sought for it.

Back office

5.4   With start-up comes the need for a certain amount of administration to meet legal and tax requirements. In order to meet these requirements the business infrastructure starts to take place. For certain elements, such as bookkeeping, VAT returns and other accounting matters it may be possible to involve a local accountant on a part time basis. In other areas, such as general administration, some resource will be needed.

As funds become available the business may enter its first dedicated premises. Up to this point the business will have been run from studies, bedrooms, garages and sheds. This has become a tradition to the point that the then newly appointed CEO Carleton Fiorina used the garage where Hewlett and Packard first worked as the backdrop for an advertising campaign intended to signify the rebirth of Hewlett-Packard.

Its first premises are a significant milestone for a business. However, as with everything else along the path of growth, taking on premises should not be rushed. There will be a natural point where they are needed, usually sign-posted by:

- The business taking over the domestic space to an unacceptable degree.
- The need for somewhere to meet clients in a businesslike atmosphere.
- The need for specialist equipment or research facilities (such as clean rooms or wet laboratory space).

When the need for premises does arise the choice is still important. At this early stage it is realistic to believe that the business may need to move as it grows unless it is going to spend significant amounts on specialist fitting out of the building. Hence, for most businesses, the first premises are reasonably small and are viewed as a short-term home. This approach should also help to keep costs down to the minimum.

Keeping costs down is always important but never more so than at this stage where the business is having to prove itself on relatively limited funds. Thus, in the same way that the overall size of the building is important so is the location. Picking a brand new building in the smartest part of town may feel as if the business has arrived but the costs are likely to be prohibitive. Besides which, investors want as much of their money as possible to go into the development and selling activities. Nice premises may be very pleasant for the staff but they do not bring revenues and profitability any nearer.

Some businesses show real creativity at this stage seeking out and making use of unlikely premises. One start-up biotech company converted an old asphalt factory into wet-lab space and reused the offices at a significant saving to having new premises or renting existing laboratory space. Other technology businesses have been based in barns or even converted high street shops.

The team

5.5 With funding comes the opportunity to build the team. Again, the focus needs to be kept on the development area. The other members of the team that should be put in place are the advisers. The basic team members in the advisory area will include:

- IP adviser (IP lawyer or patent agent)
- Commercial lawyers
- Accountants
- Bankers

They will all be able to provide you with advice and help you avoid some of the pitfalls.

Other sources of help, guidance and information

5.6 As mentioned in the last chapter both the Business Links and the local Chambers of Commerce can be valuable sources of help and information for growing businesses alongside the more traditional advisers.

Development   **6**

The 8 Functional Areas and The 3 Challenges	Expected Activities and Challenges in the Development phase
Intellectual Property and Knowledge Management	The IP protection strategy should be in place and research and development work outputs being treated accordingly. As the number of people grows the need for more accessible knowledge-management tools increases. The pipeline of offerings either based on the initial or newly created IP is being grown to support future revenues.
People	As the business moves from a technology focus to a commercial focus new skill sets (particularly in the channel to market area) are needed. New technologies and offerings being developed may also need new skills. At this stage a head of finance is often brought in full-time to manage the spend and cash positions.
Market Knowledge	Markets are clearly defined and the structure of the offering package matched to them. Constant surveillance is undertaken to ensure that the offerings continue to match requirements and maintain the Unique Selling Point advantages identified earlier.
Channels to Market	Structures to deliver the offering to the market are in place and actively seeking to generate sales and feedback into the Market Knowledge area.
Offerings	A range of offerings (or a range of applications for the offering) are developed with supporting documentation and structures as needed. The pipeline is being developed in conjunction with the IP/KM area to underpin future revenues.
Operations	Scaling up as the pipeline of offerings and customers develops.
Infrastructure	Premises likely to be in place and back-office departments are being developed to support the day-to-day running of the business and maintain the books, records and returns needed. Quality may well become a new focus at this stage with ISO or other accreditation being sought.
Funding	Likely to have moved on to a point where funding may be in the venture capital arena but, if the offerings are cash generative, will also be coming from revenue already being generated. Development lead times and the nature of the offering will determine this.
Legals	IP protection and the related strategy need to be monitored and updated. Strategic network agreements (either on the C2M or IP/KM sides) may be needed as will terms of trade and other contractual matters. People-related legal activities are also likely to increase.
Taxation	Maximising allowable R&D expenditure and ensuring that the strategic network agreements do not crystallise gains can give rise to tax versus legal tensions.
Strategy	Managing the growth and ensuring that customer feedback is validated before the strategy is flexed is key. Also important is the change in emphasis to commercial focus. While not allowing the IP development to proceed without controls, the creative nature of the business should not be entirely sacrificed to the generation of revenue.

OBJECTIVES

- To look at the business in the development phase.
- To highlight the key questions and areas of focus.
- To consider the thought processes.
- To consider possible sources of help.

Looking at the business

6.1 This is the stage at which the business has to move from being driven by the research and development to being a truly commercial organisation.

What does this mean and which areas of the business are affected by the change?

6.2 The change is really one of mindset as much as anything. Up to this point the business will have been largely focused on:

- Developing the technology.
- Proving it works.
- Protecting it.
- Building prototypes or example offerings.
- Demonstrating them to customers and getting feedback.
- Gathering ideas as to the potential uses of the technology.

At this stage the focus needs to change to actually getting the offering out to the market and generating real revenues from it. It is time for version 1 and all that goes with it. In summary, the mindset becomes one of being market focused, motivated by generating sales and profits not simply improving the technology.

The challenge of version 1

6.3 Getting version 1 out can be a real challenge. There are many reasons for this – from the perfectionist nature of people through to the challenge of marketing an offering for the first time. But facing the challenge and addressing the issues is vital for the continued life of the business. Sadly, few businesses can spend their entire time doing development work. Even those that do also have to ensure that customers can take the development work and turn it into offerings if they are to survive.

There is a natural tendency for people to want version 1 to be perfect in every respect. The danger here is that while 85% may be more than adequate for the market, the remaining 15% can take a very long time. One listed company CTO refers to this last 15% as being 'fiddler's paradise'. By this he means the period when the developers claim that with 'just a few more weeks' they will be able to deliver that illusive something from the product which, in all probability, the customer will never notice. Indeed, his rule of thumb is that, when the developers tell you that the product is 85% of the way there, it is time to get out version 1.

The important thing to remember is that version 1 *does* have to be tested and reliable. What it does *not* have to be is everything that everyone will ever want. Indeed, from a marketing viewpoint, the perfect all-encompassing solution is a real problem – it is all you can ever sell. Hence, for marketing and profile it is better to hold back some things – then you can add these to later versions to keep the company's name in front of customers.

This has lead to some software companies actually charging customers for beta copies of software and using them to find bugs which are then addressed in version 1 when it is formally launched. Even then, some commentators have suggested that software houses do not mind bugs in version 1 as it allows them to issue upgrade packs, which are charged for, and, in due course, entire revisions of the software marketed as specifically addressing the known problems in the previous version.

Marketing version 1 can be a challenge for a company where the team is basically technology focused. In this case it is worth looking for assistance from marketing professionals with experience and expertise in the technology arena. It is important, when selecting someone to work with, that you are happy that they understand the scale of the marketing budget available and what you are trying to achieve. It is easy to spend a lot of marketing money very quickly and it needs to be focused on the real target market. For example, big public events look very impressive and TV coverage even better – but, for most technology companies, the public is not the target market. Hence, whilst the events may boost name recognition they will do very little to generate real revenues.

Analysing the events that companies do sponsor indicates that most public events are sponsored by brands which have the public squarely as a target market such as:

- White goods manufacturers.
- Cigarette manufacturers.
- Domestic telecoms providers.
- Manufacturers of PCs designed for home use.
- Food and beverage manufacturers.

Version 1 may well need sales collateral – the brochures and other sales literature that the sales team need to ease the sale process – and your marketing activities need to take this into account.

Post launch

6.4 After the launch of version 1 close monitoring of the market will be required to measure the impact and feedback from the market. This feedback needs to communicated to the development area to ensure that the positive points are built on and the negative points are addressed in both version 1.1 and in any following offerings.

At the same time, follow on offerings and/or other technology developments will be taking place. The lessons learned with version 1 need to be incorporated into the plans and project management for these new offerings.

The feedback from version 1 will also help in confirming the opportunity for the range of targets for future offerings. No matter how well planned, it is likely that the initial offering can be refined to better meet the target market requirements.

This process is seen in all areas from electronics through to drug design, where formulation and even minor changes to the base compound may be required as trials progress, in order to optimise the performance of the drug in patients.

Accreditation

6.5   At this point accreditation may start to become important. Certainly, a number of potential purchasers may not be able to buy if the business is not accredited. Chapter 29 looks at accreditation processes and what accreditation means to businesses.

Management reporting

6.6   With potentially considerable sums being spent within the business and sales beginning to be generated, internal controls and management reporting become more important. These systems for ensuring that overspends are at best avoided or at least highlighted early are important – funding is unlikely to be limitless. The directors, for legal reasons if nothing else, the investors and the bank will want to know how the business is progressing.

For this reason it is generally by this stage that a dedicated in-house finance capability is built up. The head of finance role will include creating and implementing controls around the business and building meaningful reporting systems. These systems have to be efficient and capable of providing useful information to management reasonably quickly. All too often accounting and management information systems provide reports upwards of a month after the event – these are of little use to management.

More than that, often finance departments provide data rather than information. The difference is simple – data is just numbers while information provides useful input to the actions needed to correct situations that have arisen. As a result it is important that the business creates its own Key Performance Indicators (or KPIs). KPIs are true business measures and not just financial ratios. If management uses some particular facet of everyday activity to determine how development is progressing then that facet is a KPI that should be captured and reported.

Examples include:

* Numbers of boards passing through the factory (for an electronics business).
* Hours worked in the software department.
* The percentage of failures in quality.
* The number of chemical combinations produced in a combinatorial chemistry business.

What is important is that the KPI provides an insight for management to both take action when needed and not take action when not needed.

In a similar way, many businesses produce monthly management accounts that are simply that: sets of numbers. This can border on being data rather than information. It becomes much more useful if it is discussed with the departments and interpreted in an accompanying commentary. In this way the financial results, which due to accounting practice may not reflect what the business feels is happening, can be explained and used as a tool for directing the business.

Sources of help, guidance and information

6.7 With the in-house team building and a management structure being created, a lot of the help and guidance will be available internally. When information is needed from outside, or if situations are faced where advice would be useful, then the external team comes into play.

Most good advisers will have seen analogous situations and will be able to provide practical advice on that basis. They will probably also have seen many more different businesses than the founders and so can bring the experience of working with those businesses to help the in-house team.

Expansion I – Pre-IPO

7

The 8 Functional Areas and The 3 Challenges	Expected Activities and Challenges in the pre-IPO phase (Expansion I)
Intellectual Property and Knowledge Management	This is a stage of consolidation on the IP front with positions tidied up ahead of the flotation process. Some new work or in-licensing may be needed to complete the commercial position. Rechecking of the patent positions of others can also be undertaken as part of the preparation process.
People	If not already in place an FD is often added to the team. A pre-IPO funding round may bring non-executive directors on board and, if not, they are sought ahead of float. This may also be the time when founders reconsider their own longer term involvement in the business and external CEOs and COOs are often brought in to manage post-float.
Market Knowledge	The aim is critical mass, so marketing becomes sector/niche focused. The objective is to be able to illustrate the strength in the business's chosen markets. Hence, strategic decisions may be made to focus on some markets to the detriment of others – for example, forgoing turnover for profit.
Channels to Market	Marketing becomes strategic. Channel management will focus on building sustainable, profitable sales pipelines that underpin the ongoing business and hence the value at float. Processes to allow better performance prediction also need to be developed for the post-float period where this knowledge becomes a key to managing the share price.
Offerings	The offerings are clearly defined and focused on the target sales sectors. The pipeline is well developed and projected launches are tied into the newsflow plan around the float and after. Again, systems need to be developed to aid the prediction of future development timetables and costs to help manage the profitability post-float.
Operations	Preparation is under way for the post-float growth stage. Plans are developed to make best use of the funds to be raised on any pre-IPO round and at float. Systems and controls around the operations are enhanced in line with those being developed elsewhere in the business.
Infrastructure	Infrastructure should shrink as a proportion of the business in this stage as the revenue and profit generation elements receive most focus. The introduction of new reporting systems and Key Performance Indicators heralds the involvement of non-executive directors and the focus on investor relations that will come post-float.
Funding	New funding at this stage is designed to enhance the float value or complete the picture for the float by allowing bolt-on acquisitions (diversification acquisitions are generally avoided at this stage). The new funding and any acquisitions must be able to deliver value to the business quickly to make the expense worthwhile.
Legals	General tidying up will be needed ahead of the float. In addition, a pre-IPO funding round and any acquisitions of technology or businesses will need to be thought through, documented and will take management focus off the day-to-day business. The day-to-day relationship with the lawyers may now move from CEO to Company Secretary/FD.
Taxation	There are tax questions to ask about any funding round and any acquisition. In addition, this is the point at which the group structure needs to be reviewed ahead of the float. In turn this is a good spur to review share schemes and other incentives to help tie in key employees.
Strategy	The key is keeping focused on running the business. As noted the strategy may call for certain 'obvious' opportunities to be left aside to avoid queering the pitch for the float. The strategy may be reviewed by incoming executives and should include a decision on who is the project manager for the float. Revenue and profit are foci.

OBJECTIVES

- To look at the business in the pre-IPO stage.
- To highlight the key questions and areas of focus.
- To consider the thought processes.
- To consider possible sources of help.

Looking at the business

7.1 The business is likely to look very different from the way it did on day one. With revenues being generated either directly or through partnerships it is time to review and tidy up structures and other arrangements put in place earlier on. At the same time, it is important to build on the public relations front to increase the visibility of the business ahead of a float.

DEFINITIONS

A *flotation* is the process of gaining admission for the company's shares to one of the public markets. These markets or stock exchanges provide a mechanism for investors to buy and sell shares in the company as and when they wish. Often a fund-raising is undertaken at the same time as the float by offering shares to the public and institutions.

A flotation is sometimes referred to as an *Initial Public Offering* or *IPO*. This is an American term that strictly refers to the fund raising activity but has come to be adopted as a term for the flotation itself.

In reality it does not matter whether the aim is to float, to sell out by trade sale or just to continue the business as a stand alone private entity. There will come a stage at which the business needs to be given the commercial equivalent of an MOT. Regardless of the route to be followed, the process of preparing and re-evaluating is important to the continued health of the business.

Which is not to say that it is time for navel gazing – in fact, quite the opposite, as targeted sales wins are as much a key part of the process as programmed offering launches and continued IP strengthening. It is often best to appoint someone to undertake the review as if it were a stand alone internal project.

The team

7.2 The person appointed to undertake the review may be a newcomer to the business. This is because this is the stage at which the existing management need to consider their own long term roles in the business. Being CEO or COO of a larger and growing business, and particularly one that may have publicly traded shares, is a very different challenge from running a small and rapidly expanding private company.

By looking at the challenges in the next few chapters founders may be able to tell whether they will be the right people to take on the job. It is worth noting that very few people have the skills to be both a successful founder and a successful long-term manager of a business. Indeed, some people recognise that they have skills in one or other area and focus on that. There are now a number of high profile individuals who have been founders of a number of businesses – often referred to as serial entrepreneurs. These individuals or teams recognise that what they are good at is taking the idea, putting a team together, and driving the early stage development. What happens then is that either the business gets too large for them to manage directly, or they simply get bored once the revenues come in and the business is on an even keel. Their great skill is, firstly, knowing when this is and, secondly, that they need to get out and bring in new blood to take the business forward.

If you have professional investors they will generally be happy to talk to you about this. Going to them to talk it through is quite natural and is not a sign of weakness. If you go to your investors with the pros and cons and with a clear view of the road you would prefer to take then they are more likely to be open and honest back.

The other people you can talk to are your advisers. By now they should know you and understand the way you work reasonably well. If they do, and if they really have experience of working with management teams at the next levels, then they will be able to help you with the decision.

Tidying up

7.3   The float process will involve a significant amount of due diligence.

> **DEFINITION**
>
> *Due diligence* is investigation of the business undertaken to ensure that there are no difficulties or lurking issues that could arise and cause difficulties in the future. Due diligence is a normal activity and is not designed to be adversarial. In fact, in this case, it is actually there to help protect directors, founders and shareholders from future problems.

The process will involve all the company's agreements and contracts being reviewed – the employment agreements; the terms of trade; compliance with VAT, PAYE/NIC, corporation and other taxes; health and safety; pensions (including compliance with the stakeholder pensions regulations); and any other areas where there could be an exposure to fines, penalties or just negative publicity. If any issues are uncovered, and most businesses have some things that could have been done better, they can be addressed and corrected.

This housekeeping exercise will put the company in good stead no matter what it decides to do in the future.

M&A activity

7.4 As part of the review process, consideration should be given to the strategic plan and whether there are areas within it that could be achieved more quickly or more cheaply by buying rather than building organically. Examples of opportunities in this area include:

- Acquiring a technology or IP to overcome a problem rather than developing an alternative in-house.
- Acquiring a business or IP in order to gain critical mass or to help meeting the criteria for a float such as those for Chapters 20 and 25 of the Listing Rules*.
- Acquiring a business to avoid IP litigation which can be time- and money-consuming even if your IP protection is strong.
- Making a vertical acquisition in order to regain margin currently being 'given away' to distributors, manufacturers or others.
- Buying in a sales team.
- Disposing of technology, IP or a business activity that is not core to the future strategy of the company as a whole.

* *The Listing Rules are the rules set out by the UK Listing Authority that apply to companies wishing to have their shares traded on the Full List of the London Stock Exchange.*

All of this is referred to as M&A (short for Mergers and Acquisitions) activity.

M&A activity should not be rushed into at any stage. The proposed transaction has to fit clearly into the strategic and business plans. Too often businesses rush into superficially attractive acquisitions only to regret them later.

The M&A process is covered in more detail in Chapter 9, *Sustained growth*, but it is important to discuss the activity here from the point of view of timing.

There may be very good reasons for undertaking M&A activity at this stage and, with adequate due diligence on the target and strong shareholder support, it may well assist in jumping the business forward. The timing can be more difficult, however. Acquisitions just before a float can make potential investors nervous. The acquisition needs to be integrated and given time to show that it is delivering if investors are to be comfortable that it really adds value to the business as a whole. Hence, acquisitions need to be timed carefully. Alternatively, acquisitions can be timed for the period after float and become part of the strategic plan and the planned flow of news used to continue the growth in value of the business.

As ever there are exceptions and the one obvious exception is where two or more businesses are being consolidated in order to be floated. For preference, each of the businesses should have a decent record of development, management should likewise have a good track record, and there should be a cogent and persuasive reason for the combination. In these cases potential investors can be shown that they will benefit almost straight away from the combined entity and the associated savings of putting the businesses together. Sometimes the combined entity is only actually formed at the time of the float itself. However, these occasions are the exception and not the rule.

Funding

7.5 As part of the growth process and very often around any acquisitions, there may be a need for additional funds either to make purchases or to provide working capital for the business to support the growth. Hence, a round of funding is often undertaken at this stage. Indeed, some investors focus on investing in just such pre-IPO rounds.

Their objectives in coming in at this stage include:

- Reduced risk over investing at earlier stages.
- Opportunity for significant capital growth – companies often double in value from a year pre-float to the float date.
- Shorter investment periods – they have reduced the length of time they have to wait before they can realise their investments by not coming in earlier.

PR and building the story

7.6 Public Relations (PR for short) activity is very important ahead of a float and, indeed, as part of growing the business. PR is about more than just telling everyone how wonderful the business is – good PR is targeted at building the positive reputation of the business and thereby helping to ease both the fund raising and the sales generation processes.

There are three main types of PR that a company can utilise:

- *Trade PR* – aimed at the trade press and target buyers; this uses the specialist publications or journals that exist in almost all sectors as a mechanism for getting the story over. Attendances at trade fairs and exhibitions together with speaking at conferences can help to build and secure the image being projected.
- *General media* – this focuses on any angles that may be of interest to the mainstream press. Particular areas of interest could be around technologies that improve everyday life, solve a common problem, or touch a sensitive spot in the nation's conscience (or at least the press's view of the nation's conscience), such as the environment or health matters. Great care has to be taken not to over-hype the technology at this stage as perceived delays to launch can become a negative influence for the business.
- *Financial PR* – Financial PR houses specialise in communicating strategy and business stories to analysts and investors. Financial PR is a specialist area and most stories have both a trade and a financial aspect to them that may differ in subtle but important ways. For example, a significant sale may be of interest to the trade press because of who the customer is or because it is the first sale of the product. To the Financial PR team the importance is probably the size of the sale and the impact on earnings against expectations. The capture of a blue chip customer is also important as it underpins the revenue potential of the offering.

Both trade and financial PR will be important after the float and so getting used to both at this stage can be very useful.

The PR programme needs to have a strategy attached to it.

DEFINITIONS

This PR plan setting out the nature and timing of the individual events that will drive PR activity is often referred to as *newsflow* and controlling it *newsflow management.*

Newsflow management is one of the most important skills and activities for a company with publicly traded shares. In fact, by the time that the company is going through the final float process, described in more detail in the next chapter, the newsflow plan should be in place and active. Newsflow management may include managing items such as the timing of sales announcements or even the timing of the launch of offerings.

For example, while it may seem like good economy to launch two or three offerings at the same time and even on the same day in a mass launch, this has to be weighed against the fact that it will only generate one set of PR opportunities.

By measuring share price movements and the volumes of shares bought and sold in companies on AIM, research by PKF identified a relationship between management of liquidity in a company's shares and the newsflow of the business. This did not come as a surprise as investors are not privy to the everyday events within businesses and so rely on announcements to make decisions regarding their shareholdings. If companies stay quiet for too long investors can become nervous and assume the worst, sending share prices down as they look to sell out. However, the research also suggested that companies that communicate regularly and openly with their investors are more likely to be supported in hard times than those that habitually announce only what is absolutely required.

It may seem early to be thinking about Financial PR but the important thing is to build the Financial PR activities into the normal everyday PR activities of the business. Learning what constitutes a Financial PR story, and what would need to be announced if the company had floated, is a key area of internal expertise. Often companies practise for quite a long period before float, drafting Financial PR releases alongside trade announcements.

Sources of help, guidance and information

7.7   The range of sources of help expands at this stage. If new management has been brought in to help the transition it will have the founders to use as a resource. As well as any full-time executives it is likely that, through the pre-IPO funding round or otherwise, the company will have identified non-executive directors to help the board.

The Companies Act does not recognise any difference between executive and non-executive directors and so non-executive directors have to be selected with care. They have to be able to bring value to the Board, either through specialist knowledge or general or specific market experience. Non-executives may seem at first to be an imposition on the day-to-day running of the business – another set of people who need to have actions explained to them. However, they are there to help the board in its decision-making and can often stop the executive directors from being carried away with enthusiasm.

One professional non-executive director says that there are only five things a non-exec needs to say:

- Why?
- When?
- How much?
- Well done

and

- Not good enough,

and one of these gets used much more often than the first four! Whilst this is a slight exaggeration it does underline the non-executive's role as a voice of reason within the business. Because of the importance of the non-executive directors, particularly after a float, it is very important to ensure that the non-execs selected can work with the executive directors, and vice versa.

Alongside the internal resources the external team should now include lawyers and accountants with experience of moving the business forward through a float. As well as these advisers there may well be PR and a Financial PR house and, once a float route has been selected, an advisor for the float in the form of a Corporate Finance and/or Broking house.

Expansion II – Flotation

8

The 8 Functional Areas and The 3 Challenges	Expected Activities and Challenges in the Flotation phase (Expansion II)
Intellectual Property and Knowledge Management	Keep hitting the development milestones will be the call from management. The patent position has to be strong and keeping up with the roadmap set before potential merchant banks. Buying in IP may be part of the float story but either way a defensive review is called for.
People	Someone is running the float and the rest should focus on running the business. If not done in the previous phase the founders need to re-assess their roles and any new skills needed (investor relations and public company experience for example) brought in. Share schemes and tie-ins should be high on the list for key individuals.
Market Knowledge	Market conditions can make or break a float so they need to be checked and rechecked. Building up the story ahead of the float takes time and effort and the newsflow needs to start before the marketing of the share issue.
Channels to Market	Should be tied down and stable for the float – disruption in this area can easily blow the float. Revenues need to come in when forecast.
Offerings	A relatively stable period for the offerings to underpin the share issue. Launches in line with the newsflow plan and often not as significant as those due in the quarter or half year after float. Everything is focused on the announcements in the quarters either side of float and how they fit with the longer term roadmap.
Operations	Again, focused on stability alongside the offerings. Ready for take off on Day 1 post-float.
Infrastructure	Time spent on a tidy up and review in the pre-IPO phase should be paying dividends. Often the FD is the project manager for the float. If so, everything under finance and admin has to run smoothly while they focus on the float itself.
Funding	The pre-IPO round has provided adequate funds to cover this period plus some contingency for market conditions to turn against the business. However, in case this happens, the funds have to be carefully managed just as they will be post-float. Alongside the float, banking arrangements need to be reviewed to cope with the significant deposits.
Legals	The float generates significant amounts of legal work – due diligence before and agreements around the float itself. Hence, the pre-IPO clear-up is vital to a smooth float.
Taxation	A tax efficient structure should now be in place but the ends of that structuring may stretch into this phase.
Strategy	The strategy has to look through the float – it is the start not the end of the process. Hence, strategic growth flowing through to revenues and profits/cash generation should be on the plans. Whatever goes into the prospectus and is in the analysts' reports is what the directors have to deliver once the excitement of the float itself is over.

OBJECTIVES

- To look at the business during the flotation process.
- To highlight the key activities during a flotation.
- To highlight the key questions and areas of focus.
- To consider the thought processes.
- To consider possible sources of help.

Market options

8.1 In the UK there are a number of different stock markets that companies can consider for a flotation. The major domestic markets used by technology companies are:

- The Official List regulated by the Financial Services Authority and traded on a platform provided by the London Stock Exchange.
- The Alternative Investment Market (or AIM for short) also run by the London Stock Exchange.
- OFEX, a market for trading unlisted and unquoted securities operated by J P Jenkins Limited and other members of the S J & S plc group.

In Europe there are a number of national markets for early stage companies, some of them members of the EuroNM grouping. In addition, there is an international European market that was launched as Easdaq and is now known as Nasdaq Europe. This exchange is now majority owned by Nasdaq Stock Market Inc, the company that also runs the US based markets that specialise in technology businesses.

Indeed, some UK companies have floated on the original Nasdaq markets in the US.

Choice of market

8.2 The choice of market is dependent on a number of factors including:

- The age and size of the company both in terms of financial performance and opportunity.
- The nature of the business and the potential investor base, including the tax advantages they may be looking for.
- The level of ongoing regulation that the company wants to have.
- The proportion of the shares that will be available to the market after the float.
- The location of the company's operations, customers and potential investors.
- The amount of money being raised now and that might need to be raised in future.

Market regulation

8.3 Each market has its own set of rules and regulations. The strength of these rules, which cover both the entry requirements and ongoing obligations, is matched to the level of risk of an investment on the market.

OFEX

8.4 OFEX is the least heavily regulated of the UK markets, although there are both entry and ongoing obligations particularly around reporting financial results and significant events. The market was launched in 1995 and took on the mantle of the unlisted matched bargain facility that the London Stock Exchange used to provide under rule 4.2.

OFEX also includes more earlier stage businesses and it is possible to obtain an OFEX facility at a very early stage. However, OFEX is by no means a technology-centric market and it has a wide range of companies on it from retailers to football clubs. A number of businesses such as BioFocus and Telecom *plus* have used OFEX as a stepping stone onto the London Stock Exchange markets.

AIM

8.5 AIM was launched in 1995 replacing the old Unlisted Securities Market and the other junior markets that the London Stock Exchange ran. AIM has proved to be a popular market with technology companies – 20% of the 587 companies on the market at the end of July 2001 were in technology-related sectors.

AIM is technically a trading facility as the shares admitted are, technically, not listed and are not quoted. This is important for a number of reasons including the tax treatment of the shares. Unlisted and unquoted shares have the potential to carry significant tax advantages under the Enterprise Initiative Scheme and the Venture Capital Trust Scheme.

AIM is more heavily regulated than OFEX with some of the regulatory activity delegated to the company's Nominated Advisor (known as the NomAd). The NomAd is responsible to the Exchange for the good behaviour of the company across a range of areas. Unlike either the Official List or OFEX companies (other than start-ups – those companies without a three-year trading history) companies on AIM have to have someone in this advisory/overseeing role at all times. In the same way, AIM companies have to have at least one Broker who is willing to match buyers and sellers of their shares.

There are shareholder protection rules regarding certain very large transactions, such as very large acquisitions, that require shareholder approval. Generally the regulation is relatively light – so long as the company keeps the market and shareholders informed of significant events, the business is allowed to run without undue reference to the market. However, given the importance of communicating with the market, most companies choose to maintain a dialogue with shareholders and potential shareholders anyway.

AIM has been a very useful support to the growth of companies since its launch and, while not necessarily as technology-friendly as the US Nasdaq markets, it has shown itself to be a good home for technology businesses. A number of technology companies such as K S Biomedix and Alizyme have moved up from an initial listing on AIM to the Official List.

Official List

8.6 The Official List is the most regulated of the UK based exchanges. The exchange is regulated by the UK Listing Authority, part of the Financial Services Authority, and is operated by the London Stock Exchange. The rules for entry and ongoing obligations are set out in the Listing Rules, a publication that runs to 27 chapters.

The major areas of regulation on the exchange relate to entry to the Official List and the exchange itself and to transactions that the company may enter into after float. Whenever a transaction is contemplated, the company needs to use a Sponsor to act as intermediary with the UK Listing Authority over compliance with the rules. A Sponsor is generally a Corporate Finance house or the Corporate Finance arm of one of the major Merchant Banks. The rules over transactions include safeguards for shareholders such as the need for shareholder approval for transactions over certain sizes (proportionate to the size of the business) and/or those which could dilute their holdings.

Reporting requirements relating to developments and events within the business are significant and can, on occasions, seem to run contrary to commercial good sense. However, the objective of the rules is to ensure that investors have the best possible knowledge before entering into sales or purchases of shares.

The Listing Rules include two chapters relating specifically to scientific research based companies – mainly chemical, pharmaceutical and other biotech companies (Chapter 20) – and innovative high growth companies, aimed at allowing suitable companies access to the markets before they are three years old (Chapter 25). These special chapters set out rules which assist these companies in gaining a listing. This is necessary as the basic rules for companies wishing to gain a listing can exclude technology-related businesses simply because of either a short trading history or a record which does not show significant revenues. The chapters do, however, set out additional requirements for these companies both at entry and afterwards.

The London Stock Exchange runs techMARK as a market within a market. techMARK companies are all part of the Official List but share the attribute of 'a commitment to technological innovation'. This sub-market of technology businesses now includes 240 companies. Most of these companies fall into one of the following industry sectors:

- Computer hardware
- Semiconductors
- Telecoms equipment
- Computer services
- The Internet
- Software

A number are also biotech or pharmaceutical companies.

Choice of market

8.7 The choice of market is very important and great care should be taken to select the correct one to meet the needs and ambitions of the business. Early advice should be sought from advisors on which option is the best match to these objectives.

Looking at the business

8.8 Lots of people will be looking at the business during the float process. Whichever market is selected for the float, the process runs in three broad strands:

Strategy and Newsflow
Due diligence
Raising the money

Strategy and Newsflow

8.9 The Strategy and Newsflow strand is the continuation of the process started in the pre-IPO phase relating to acquisitions, any strategic or business re-alignments, and ongoing PR activities. In addition, a post-float strategic acquisition plan may be developed to allow the business to take advantage of its new currency – its traded shares, which can be used as a substitute for cash – so as to build critical mass or the technology portfolio more rapidly.

The plan may well involve targeted sales wins or other PR activities; hitting the milestones for these is very important. Likewise, continuing to hit internal milestones on technology development is key to the smooth running of the float.

Due diligence

8.10 The due diligence is, in part, a re-run of the investigative work that should have been undertaken as part of the tidying up exercise. However it will be extended to cover:

- Commercial due diligence – looking at the market opportunity, competitors and alternative solutions.
- Technical due diligence – looking at the technology itself to ensure that it has a sound basis and the capacity to be used for the offerings.
- IP due diligence – to look at the strength of the IP position and also other pieces of IP that have been registered to highlight any potential issues, conflicts or parties who might attempt to take an opportunistic chance to challenge the company's position.
- Financial due diligence – looking at the financial track record, the current position and the systems and controls in place. Assessing the reasonableness of the accounting policies and reviewing the compliance with tax law. The financial due diligence also tends to cover the history and development of the business.
- Legal due diligence – covering the other legal agreements in place.

Alongside this there will be:

- An exercise to support the statements made by directors in the fund-raising or admission documents relating to the adequacy of working capital (often leading to a report of significant length).
- A review of the group structure and the potential need to put a new PLC on the top.

- A review of directors' service contracts and other key employees' contracts.
- A review of share option schemes and other incentive packages.
- An exercise to verify the accuracy of statements made in the fund-raising or admission documents.

Documents used to raise money are regulated under the Financial Services Act 1986, soon to be replaced by the Financial Services and Markets Act 2000, and the Public Offering of Security Regulations 1995. These rules, together with the rules of the individual exchanges and the Listing Rules, set out the requirements for the contents of the fund-raising or admission documents.

Given that these documents are largely produced to provide investors or potential investors with information about the businesses that they may decide to invest in, the accuracy and reasonableness of the contact of the document is of great importance. The directors take on significant personal liability when they issue the documents and therefore, from both points of view, spending time to check the veracity of the statements made on the history, future, and market places of the business is time well spent.

Raising the money

8.11 This process is relatively compressed but relies heavily on the output of the previous two strands. It involves:

- The creation of the fund-raising or admission document.
- The creation of a potential investor profile.
- The identification of potential investors meeting that profile and setting up meetings with them or identifying the access route to inform them of the float which can be through a mailing out of the fund-raising document.
- The creation of a presentation and the delivery of the presentation to the potential investors.
- Follow up and signing up of the investors.

All but the last of these will involve significant input and time from the management team. Indeed, it is the management team who will generally give the presentations and answer potential investors questions.

It is worth considering that a significant proportion of this activity has to go on in parallel with the due diligence activity.

Running the float

8.12 Not only does the *Raising the money* strand run alongside the due diligence, it runs alongside the business itself. Going through a float is a major undertaking and requires significant investments of time and effort. In that sense, it is not unlike any other major internal project and, just as with developing the technology, it requires project management and a dedicated team.

The best and smoothest floats occur when one member of the top management team is given both responsibility for the float and authority to make all but the most major decisions relating to it. This person should have a small and trusted staff to help them pull together all the information and background data that will be needed during the process.

There will be occasions when other members of top management have to be involved, such as when the due diligence is focused on certain areas including the history of the business or the technology. However, by making the float an internal project, the other members of the team are released to ensure that the fundamental job of running the business is not forgotten.

Where no one person takes responsibility for the float process, and everyone tries to be involved, there is a great danger that management will concentrate on the float and take their combined eye off the ball with regard to the business. This can lead to real difficulties being encountered after the float as the business may have slipped and it may not be easy to get it back on track – a sure-fire way to see the share price slide.

Sources of help, guidance and information

8.13   The team will by now have expanded to include:

- Executive directors and top management.
- Non-executive directors.
- Current investors, including potentially venture capital houses.
- Lawyers, accountants and patent agents.
- Corporate finance house as corporate advisor (OFEX), NomAd (AIM) or Sponsor (Official List) and associated brokers.
- Technical due diligence specialists.

Together this team should provide advice on most areas that will be faced. Additional knowledge can be gained from the exchanges and the UK Listing Authority, either directly or through their publications and websites, and from people who have been through the process themselves with other businesses.

♦ **It is vital that significant thought is undertaken prior to starting on a float. It is easy for a growing business to be either pushed into a float by investors who are keen to see their investment rise in value or for the directors to be seduced by the money that is on offer. The combined pre-IPO and float activities should be prepared for and spread over a period of around a year to give time to get things right. It is possible to do a float in two to three months but most AIM and Official List floats take closer to six months to get from the final decision to float to hitting the market.**

♦ **Advice should therefore be taken from a number of quarters before the button is pressed and the float process, with all its attendant disruption and cost, is started.**

Sustained Growth

9

The 8 Functional Areas and The 3 Challenges	Expected Activities and Challenges in the Sustained Growth phase
Intellectual Property and Knowledge Management	IP is about renewal and extension in this phase – renewal as the earlier offerings peak in their lifecycle and extension to extend the life of the protection and use of the offering. KM is now focused on reducing this development cycle and the associated costs. IP protection should by now be truly international in focus.
People	People needs are around driving the revenue/profit position and managing the growth. In addition, investor relations skills may need to be enhanced.
Market Knowledge	Building on critical mass to generate significant market positions is a focus. MK can also become defensive, linking up with the IP protection activities to ensure that competitors cannot easily outflank the business.
Channels to Market	Performance reviews are regular occurrences as is a re-evaluation of outsourced arrangements such as distributorship arrangements. With public paper to use as currency, some formerly outsourced activities may be brought in-house. KPIs on customer pipeline should become as important as KPIs on sales themselves.
Offerings	The renewal and extension activities in IP should be focused on flowing new ideas through to the offerings – new ideas that mirror customer requirements. Likewise, feedback on the offerings should be focused on value added additions to the range and considering the value in in-house information or other potential revenue generators.
Operations	These need to expand to maintain the revenues. The question of whether or not to invest ahead of the curve will arise – hence the focus in earlier stages on predictive systems. With growth may come new multi-location issues that will need to be managed in line with announced programmes.
Infrastructure	Should expand only so far as is needed to support the operations and the requirements of the strategic plan – for example, if the plan calls for an aggressive acquisition programme (for example as a consolidator) then an M&A department may be set up. Again, alongside multi-location growth may come the need for internal audit teams and not just in finance.
Funding	While further equity injections may be needed (in line with the expectations set at float) bank debt may now become an option for some businesses. In addition, having quoted shares allows the company's paper to be used as currency in certain transactions. Multi-currency and deposit/investment management systems may be needed.
Legals	General ongoing legal work (contracts, employees, etc) will arise and acquisitions or restructuring of arrangements (such as those around outsourced activities being brought in-house) will generate work.
Taxation	Structuring plans developed earlier should be followed through and regularly reviewed in the light of changes in legislation and Government policy announced and expected.
Strategy	While still forward looking the strategy becomes a three part exercise – delivering the short-term (this half/year) result, while the medium term (next 3–5 years) and the longer term will focus on the same big questions that arose back at the *Pre-formation* phase.

OBJECTIVES

- To look at the business as it grows after flotation.
- To highlight the key questions and areas of focus.
- To consider the thought processes.
- To consider possible sources of help.

Looking at the business

9.1   Far from being able to draw breath after the effort and exertion of the float it is at this stage that most people recognise the truth of the advice they will have received during the float process: the float is not an end point – in fact it is only the start.

After the float, the management has to move the business forward to deliver on the promises and opportunities that were set out in the float documents. That is another reason why so much care needs to be taken over the production of the float documents – whatever is in there has to be delivered if the company is to maintain the support of its investors.

In the main this will be about building on critical mass to generate the return that shareholders are expecting, either through profits or through increases in the share price. This focus will go right across the business from IP to operations. The important aspect is to manage the growth.

Don't get carried away

9.2   A float often brings with it significant new cash from investors. This is not a treasure chest and any spending should be targeted on fulfilling the objectives set out in the float documents – after all, that is what investors expected it to be used for. There is always a danger that opportunities will arise and, with the cash in the bank, it will be easy to spend.

The message has to be: controlled expansion. Controlled expansion really implies two things:

- The expansion itself is controlled and managed and undertaken at the company's pace.
- The new extensions to the business are controlled to ensure that, once in the group, they are delivering what was expected.

Decisions have to be made in advance about areas such as capacity requirements and geographic reach. It is these decisions, made in the cold light of day, that should drive the expansion plans. All too often, companies that have recently floated are tempted into buying up opportunities that come their way because they are there. In these cases the strategy is often bent to fit the acquisitions rather than the acquisitions bolting on and enhancing the strategy.

In the long term, no matter how attractive the opportunity appears to be, it is better to walk away from something that does not fit rather than take it on, try to change it, and expend too much time and money in doing so.

The M&A process

9.3 There is, however, a role for targeted M&A. The strategy supporting this will have been developed over the last two growth phases and will not only have identified the profile of the businesses that would be of interest but may also have identified specific targets as well.

The important point here is that the M&A activity is targeted; it is not a question of running with whatever is put forward. It is very important that the brief drawn up should be as comprehensive and tightly defined as possible, so that advisors know what to be on the look out for and also that the directors know what is and is not going to be of real interest.

Once a target is identified, and negotiations have progressed to a stage where it is clear that the target's owners would be interested in a bid, it is time to get into due diligence. This is not unlike the process that is undertaken during the float and is likely to focus just as much on the future potential as on past history. However, rather than the scope of the work being set by the Corporate Adviser/NomAd/Sponsor it will be set by the directors, often in collaboration with the advisers. If the transaction is likely to be significant enough to require shareholder approval, the process may well end up looking like the full-blown float process in order to meet reporting requirements.

In addition, depending on the nature of the target company, it may be necessary to consider the Takeover Code which deals with transactions involving the purchase of quoted and certain large businesses. Your advisers should be able to help you with this aspect if it applies. Deals which need clearance through the Takeover Code process can often be much longer drawn out and are always more public than those that fall outside its scope.

The results of the due diligence should be used in negotiations. Hence, negotiations on pricing and terms should be left open, at least until the due diligence is well under way.

As for a float, the main due diligence is often undertaken by accountants and lawyers reporting to the directors. The directors themselves may well get involved in the process and, indeed, may well do an initial investigation of the target business before the advisers are let loose on it.

Either way, it is well worthwhile briefing advisers at an early stage and keeping them up to date so that, when needed, they are up to speed and the process does not have to be slowed down while they catch up.

Lawyers, corporate finance or audit specialists and tax advisers are particularly important when it gets to structuring the deal itself, as they can explain the implications of things such as:

- Using shares, cash or loan notes to pay for the acquisition.
- The use of deferred consideration and contingent consideration (further payments depending on performance).
- The implications for the accounts of the different structures on offer.

This last point is important, given the focus on earnings that comes with being a public company. The best deal in the world may not look that way to investors if the way it has to be accounted for ruins the profits or the balance sheet.

Internally the output of the process should include a detailed integration plan as well as a revised set of enlarged group projections.

The problems with integration

9.4 It is an oft quoted statistic that up to 70% of mergers or acquisitions fail to deliver the levels of benefit that were expected or put forward to shareholders at the outset. The reasons for this are numerous but generally they revolve around:

- Failure to understand the complexity of the business being acquired.
- Underestimating the time it will take to put the businesses together.
- Leaving the target's management to bring the business into the group without adequate support and guidance on group aims and culture.
- Overestimating the costs that can be taken out by combining the businesses and underestimating the cost of reducing headcounts and property holdings.

It is therefore vital that the integration plan is questioned, challenged, and tested before it is put into action. In addition, being overly optimistic about the benefits of the acquisition, particularly in the short term, is likely to lead to disappointment for management and shareholders alike.

A number of areas need to be covered outside of the pseudo-political questions such as involving the target management in the running of the enlarged group. These include:

- The new parent must have control over the acquired entity.
- This will generally involve parachuting a top management team member into the management of the acquired business – not usually as CEO but in a position where they have influence and can bring the group culture with them. They may not stay permanently, but they should be there long enough to help the business integrate into the group.
- Ensuring that the management information, IP/KM, and other systems are compatible or instigating a process to roll out the preferred solution across the enlarged business.
- Making the newly acquired business feel part of the group through activities ranging from involvement in meetings (video-links now make this easier) through to secondments or transfers of staff into other areas of the group.

The plan must include actions around each of these areas as well as focusing on the activities within the enlarged group operations where cost improvements have been identified.

As with a float, this is a large scale project which requires dedicated resource to see through to the logical conclusion. Project management is an active process throughout any acquisition and subsequent integration.

Globalisation

10

The 8 Functional Areas and The 3 Challenges	Expected Activities and Challenges in the Globalisation phase
Intellectual Property and Knowledge Management	New IP may be needed to cover global markets. Likewise, as the business becomes multi-national the KM systems need to expand to address this.
People	The spread of operations often leads to country or divisional structures with their attendant management. Again, the start of this phase is a time to re-assess whether top management has the skill sets to run a global business – some people are happy with the scale of global businesses, others thrive on smaller geographic units.
Market Knowledge	Now needs to cover all the intended markets fully. Marketing will now be working strategically with the M&A department to identify potential growth enhancing acquisitions and also, potential disposals that are no longer core to the group.
Channels to Market	The strategy review that started in the *Sustained Growth* phase should have taken account of the global ambitions of the business. This now needs to be put into practice in as cost efficient a way as possible.
Offerings	The range of offerings needs to match the geographic as well as target sector customer needs. While often less frequent new offering launches are much more significant now than before and need multi-national co-ordination both for the launch(es) and ongoing support. Alongside MK, bolt-on offering opportunities should be considered.
Operations	Multi-location often becomes multi-national in this phase. Co-ordination between centres both for day-to-day matters and for communicating strategy and policy needs to be enhanced to cope with this.
Infrastructure	Can easily expand out of proportion to the growth in the business. It is easy to be convinced that the infrastructure in the home territory needs to be reproduced in every country. Getting the balance right, communicating the policy and practice while recognising local practice takes listening skills. Get it wrong and the creativity suffers.
Funding	A range of new options can be available from large scale re-financing of debts to bonds to dual stock market listings. These can be attractive but should only be considered if they are really needed for the business. Some schemes appear to generate more issues than they provide solutions and value to the business. Currency needs thought.
Legals	Cross-border deals bring in additional legal issues – what works in the UK may not work elsewhere and vice versa. Legal cultures differ as much as national cultures so flexibility may well be needed to get the optimal deal done.
Taxation	Likewise, cross-border activities introduce multiple tax regimes. Getting the planning right is a combination of the right advice and having the right starting point – hence the need for a review back at the *Flotation* phase.
Strategy	Is now global in scope and dealing with the global issues. It also has to address the key issue for shareholders: where is the continuing growth going to come from? Managing the growth to date will have helped here but sustaining it will take harder concentration on maximising what the group is best at.

OBJECTIVES

- To look at the business during the globalisation phase.
- To highlight the key questions and areas of focus.
- To consider the thought processes.
- To consider possible sources of help.

Looking at the business

10.1 As the expansion of the *Sustained Growth* phase continues it naturally extends into a global programme. Some businesses get here very early through alliances and mergers that bring technologies together. Others progress a long way in their home territory before branching out into other countries or continents.

At this stage the focus of the business has moved onto control:

- Control over IP, wherever it is used.
- Control of earnings and profits.
- Control of the individual performance of activities within the group.
- Control of market shares in the different territories.
- Control over license arrangements and alliances.
- Control over the management of often substantial cash funds.

However, disproportionate growth in infrastructure can come with this focus on control. The controls required do not necessarily have to lead to a substantial increase in the number of administrative heads. In situations where unwanted takeover bids are received it is often interesting to see how much cost businesses find they can take out of the administrative area.

Defensive or offensive?

10.2 The emphasis on control can seem like a very defensive posture and, indeed, for many companies it turns into just that. For others the controls are there to help drive forward continued growth. For these companies the controls are part of the culture – as such they do not restrain the culture. Everyone benefits if the jobs are done right and the controls are there to help that happen.

The challenge in this phase is to maintain the excitement that underpinned the founding of the business and not to let bureaucracy stifle the creative element that is present in any technology business.

Strategy

10.3 The strategy needs to be maintained alongside the control element of the business. As part of this, once operations become multi-national, a number of structural questions arise that need to be considered. They include:

- From a tax viewpoint, are the right activities in the right jurisdictions?
- Are there other economic or political reasons for moving operations from their current locations?

- Are there natural centres of excellence in certain activities that should be strengthened or used to centralise the activity?
- Has the natural centre of activity moved and does this have implications for the location of any head office and the location of the stock exchange listing?
- Are there elements of the group that are not really core to the strategy that could be spun out or sold off?
- Is the funding structure optimised for the structure of the group?

The first item and the last two items may require specialist advice. Tax structuring is a complex exercise, involving not only setting up the best structure but also working out whether it is possible to change from the current structure to the optimal position – without incurring such substantial tax penalties along the way that it is not economical to do it.

Identifying non-core activities can be difficult in that there was, presumably, something about them that was germane to the strategy when they were set up or acquired. There may be examples of non-core elements of a business that were acquired along with an activity that is core. The difficulty here is ensuring that any business that can be sold is complete enough to be attractive to potential purchasers, or is capable of standing alone if it is to be spun out or floated off.

Restructuring the funding, which by this stage may involve a mixture of debt and equity, possibly in multiple currencies, is again a complex activity. The level of analysis and modelling involved can be substantial, as can the costs of changing.

Communication

10.4 The business will be managing a global portfolio of IP and a matching portfolio of offerings. To do this effectively, communication systems within the group must be able to cope with multi-national, multi-location activities. These activities may include:

- Multi-country development projects with teams built up from the group's operations around the world.
- Support for offerings sold in a number of different territories.
- Access to KM systems that provide information matched to the reader's market.
- Access to systems that explain the differences between versions of the offerings where they vary from country to country for technical or legal reasons.
- Manufacturing or other processes that are spread across different locations or even countries (this is not unusual in the pharmaceutical industry where processing of intermediates may take place in a different country from the final formulation and packing).

The relative cost of these communications systems can reduce as the scale of operations grows; businesses should seek out and investigate deals that have the potential to provide enhanced capabilities at reduced costs.

Sources of help, guidance and information

10.5   Most areas of help will be available internally. However, some areas, particularly those relating to disposal analysis and funding structures, may need external input from the team of advisors.

Marketing a business for sale is also a task often delegated to advisors so that management can stay focused on running the business.

This last point is a recurring theme throughout the lifecycle. There is really nothing more important than running the business. Buying and selling companies, raising money, floating, building an international group and all the excitement that goes with those activities is fine but, in the end, investors expect businesses to deliver. Deliver on their promises; deliver a return on their investment; and deliver on the belief that has been put in the business.

Management teams that forget this tend to run out of steam at some point – that point is often when the building stage has to slow down and the businesses have to be made to work to generate the returns. History suggests that these two activities need different skills and, therefore, may need different people to head them up. Not only that but, when those changes do occur, it is often the case that some of the building has to be unwound in order to get back to the real core business.

It is not easy to see how to avoid this overrun of momentum but, in part, it can be monitored through a process of continuous re-invention.

Re-invention

11

OBJECTIVES

- To consider the concept of re-invention.
- To set out a process of continuous re-invention.
- To highlight the alternative of decline.

Re-invention

11.1 Re-invention is a fact of life in business. Commercial life, just like any other, moves on. Fashions change, needs change and technology either drives that change or changes with it. For some businesses, such as the PC industry, the change is extremely rapid with individual PC models having a lifecycle of around 3 to 4 months and new microprocessor families being launched every 18 months to 2 years.

Not all of the technology sector sees such rapid growth but it is certainly true that new ideas and new technologies are continually being work on, developed and launched. This means that existing IP is constantly in danger of being overtaken and the companies that produced it are in danger of going the same way.

Indeed, when they are first set up businesses may well tacitly flag this up. Business plans often include statements along the lines of 'the directors estimate that the company has a six month lead over competitors'. All well and good, but the six month lead has to be maintained – otherwise a six months ahead now will become six months behind in a year's time.

The risk of losing direction

11.2 Alongside the changes in the market as a business grows there is an ongoing risk that the business itself may lose its way. This tends to happen for one of three reasons:

- Success leading to feeling comfortable.
- Focusing on the wrong areas.
- Too many options being available.

Feeling comfortable

11.3 Comfort comes with success. Up to a point is it a good thing – nervousness can lead to people trying too hard to be successful. But it is easy for a business to slide into a state where it comes to believe that winning is easy and gradually reduces the effort that it puts into driving forwards. A number of indicators point towards too much comfort in an organisation – these range from too much hype in the PR to exhibition stands with more hospitality than product.

In his famous humorous book *Parkinson's Law*, C. Northcote Parkinson points to perfect head office buildings as another worrying indicator. While the book has comic intent it does have an uncanny knack of highlighting reality and this is one good example. The point it makes is that any business that has enough time to design, commission and move into the perfect offices cannot be focusing all its efforts on the business of business.

A related danger is that of feeling that all the business's goals have been met. Often, when management teams have achieved what they set out to achieve, they find it difficult to set new targets and new challenges to keep the business motivated and focused. The history of commerce is littered with companies that have lost their way through success.

There is a fine balance between risking this situation arising and the opposite – changing strategic direction too often and never approaching achievement of the target. The real goal is to stay just ahead of the curve to show that the aims have been achieved but at the same time refocus everyone's eyes on a further horizon. The goals do have to have been reached, or at least they have to be reached early on the path to the new objectives. The Stalinist approach of announcing the success of the last five-year plan at the start of the next one, no matter what the real position, fools no-one. Both staff and customers see the accounts and the staff can see what is happening around them.

A variant on this approach is the concept of focusing the internal mission statement or strap line on a specific goal or objective. Having focused minds on that one area for a period the statement or strap line can be re-worked to focus on another area. Again, there have to be real signs of positive movement towards the objective, before the focus is redirected, if staff are not to become cynical about the programme.

Focusing on the wrong area

11.4 This is losing your way by picking and sticking rigidly to a position or an area of activity when the evidence suggests that other activities would be more beneficial. A number of technology companies show either the ability to end up in these blind alleys or, for the successful ones, the ability to spot the wall or the competitors closing in and change direction.

Sony was in danger of running into this problem with the Betamax video cassette system. It offered the potential of better performance than VHS but did not get adopted as the standard. Sony stuck with the standard for some time and watched as VHS became the standard and won the race. In time Sony realised that it had to move and eventually it accepted the inevitable, pulled Betamax, and embraced the competing technology.

Strong CEOs or CTOs with very personal likes and dislikes can often be at the core of this problem. Sometimes their problem can simply be seeing the right idea too early, at a stage when the technology and the market are not yet ready. The Apple Newton can be seen in this light. John Sculley had taken over the role of CTO as well as CEO in Apple by 1990 and seems to have made championing the Newton PDA platform his personal mission. Unfortunately, the Newton technology was not stable enough and the project failed. In the meantime, Apple's share of the personal computing market had plummeted and it took the best part of a decade for the damage to be repaired.

Too many options

11.5 The opposite of the 'focus at all costs' problem; having too many options can lead to management paralysis. Surrounded by a group with a portfolio of offerings for different sectors, and a raft of new ideas coming forward, management becomes either incapable of making decisions as to which paths to follow or totally inconsistent in its decisions. With top management unable to pick a route for the business, middle management has two choices:

- Keep ploughing on with the new developments, no matter what, so that top management's decision is made for them; or
- Play safe and keep doing what they've done before.

Top management can end up mistaking mere action for strategic planning. Subsidiaries are bought and sold regularly and the direction of the group seems to change annually with the latest fashion. Even if there is no flow of transactions, some management teams fall into a pattern of swapping and changing the strategy to fit whatever technology is coming through development. This is a sign of poor investment decisions earlier on – it is easier to spread the cash thinly on as wide a range of projects as possible than to have to decide which to back and which to drop.

There is a way out of this position, but it is the commercial equivalent to an austerity budget: look at what you have and make now the decisions that should have been made earlier. Sometimes only new eyes can do this but some investors have failed to allow those new eyes sufficient time to deal with the problems. International research undertaken by Drake Beam Morin showed that in mid 2001 nearly half of CEOs had been in post less than three years with two thirds of companies having had a new CEO in the last five years.

Identifying what is going on is difficult enough in big organisations. Trying to decide what to do with that activity is harder still. There are really three options for every project identified:

- Back it
- Kill it
- Sell it

None of these is an easy option. Backing one thing almost certainly means killing something else; both are risky options. Selling it can be even higher risk – if someone else makes it work then you made the wrong decision, even if you got a good price at the time *and* picked right elsewhere.

Some CEOs go for a halfway house. They look to identify groups of similar projects and put them together in a unit that can, hopefully, be spun out and financed with third party funds. These spin-outs have often been popular with investors as they show a renewed focus in the original business while giving them an interest in the new business unit. This interest can arise either directly – shares can be passed through to existing shareholders as part of the spin out – or indirectly if the new unit remains part-owned by the original business. Either way, the danger for the CEO can be that the new unit is more successful than the original business.

Continuous re-invention

11.6 Any process of continuous re-invention starts with a process of continuous internal and external monitoring: measuring the marketplace, keeping up with technology developments, assessing the future and the status of existing offerings. *If this sounds like the Market Knowledge activity, it should – that is what it is rooted in.* Without this continuous monitoring, management risks being lulled into a false sense of security.

The next element is a light hand on the tiller. Knee-jerk type reactions to the results of the monitoring are likely to over-correct and risk damaging valid projects. What is needed may simply be a re-assessment of the life of the current offerings and a revision of the timetables on new offering development. It may mean changing the priorities in development – to move one project on faster than originally expected – or it may mean dropping some items to refocus efforts on work that now carries a higher priority.

If the monitoring results suggest something truly fundamental to the business then the strategy should be checked to see that it is still sound and the business plan re-evaluated to ensure that it is still robust. If, after close scrutiny, both need polishing then polish them. If they need more, then assess what is needed and why; consider how it can be implemented without destroying the business. Feedback that suggests the fundamental strategy of the business is flawed needs very careful consideration to avoid implosion.

Often the market monitoring is really feeding back that the business has wandered away from its strategy. That, despite the smooth movements, the craft has moved too far off course.

In these circumstances the answer can be to re-invent the business as itself, to go back to what the business was originally about and to where its strengths lie. That is what Steve Jobs set about doing with Apple on his return to the business. He took it back to providing computers that are easy to use and, as the fashion has moved on, recaptured Apple's sense of style not only in the on-screen graphics but in the design of the computers themselves. Apple has continued to adopt technologies early – firewire and wireless networking being just two recent examples – but has not suffered for it.

The advance of technology

11.7 One area that requires constant attention is the technology itself. Technology evolves and new ideas appear regularly. As with the rest of the monitoring process the information gathering process needs to feed an assessment phase before actions are taken.

The difficulty is that the assessment phase needs to include objective assessment of the new technologies. This can be a challenge to in-house teams with their own technology and, potentially, their own projects on the line. However, developing a mechanism is vital in the long term. Some businesses do this by splitting the role of CTO into two:

- *Internal development manager* – charged with taking technology to market.
- *New technology assessor* – charged with finding, internally or from other sources, the next generation of technology to refresh and refill the intellectual property pipeline.

If this approach is taken, the two roles need to be separate so that the new technology assessor has the decision on which technologies to back and the internal development manager runs the development. Too much overlap of responsibilities and '*Not Invented Here*' syndrome can become entrenched.

So long as lifecycles are understood then there is no reason why a company cannot, in effect, develop technology that competes with its own existing offerings. The idea here is that, in due course, the newer technology can be launched when the older one reaches the downward curve of its useful commercial life. In this way, the growth in revenues can be maintained as one technology supplements, and eventually replaces, the previous one.

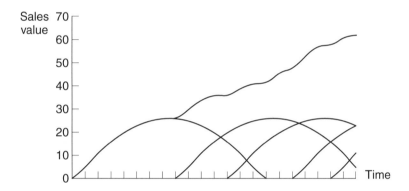

Figure 11.7 – technology launches timed to maintain revenue growth. The top line is total period revenues, the curves below are sales per period over the economic life of the technology. For the purposes of this graph, each technology is assumed to have the same sales profile and the same economic life.

Adapt: Adopt: Advance

11.8 Alongside this mechanism there needs to be a process to address the event of alternative technologies attacking the business's market space.

When this occurs the business has three options:

Adapt

11.9 Improve the existing offering either by price or technological development so that it matches the functionality or price of the new competitor. The objective is to match the newcomer's strengths but utilise the longer track record of the existing technology to leverage sales.

But this may not be possible

11.10   If the existing technology has reached its limits – for example there are physical limits to how small the elements can be on a silicon based integrated circuit – then there are only two options left.

Adopt

11.11   The first is to *adopt* the new technology. This can be done in two ways:

* *By licensing it in and utilising it,* thus building the technology as a standard but delivering something extra that the competitor cannot match, for example in terms of customer service or added value data.
* *By re-engineering or reverse engineering the solution.* This route is more difficult as there may well be patents to be circumvented, or elements of private knowledge held by the competitor that cannot be easily worked out, but it is an option.

Advance

11.12   The final option is to look at what is in research and development, or what ideas are in the minds of the technical team, and search for a new solution that trumps the competitor technology. This crab-wise movement has been seen, for example, in the PC microprocessor market.

Here, Intel's chips have set the standard and the likes of AMD have had initially to use an *adopt* type approach and re-engineer the solutions. AMD has tended to aim for compatibility and comparable data processing speeds but with a lower overall clock speed. So, in the main, Intel has set a standard that AMD has matched. The market has then seen Intel launch a faster product, through innovation in the chip or through faster clock speeds.

Then, in early 2000, AMD surprised the market by beating Intel and launching the first commercial PC microprocessor to run at a clock speed of 1 GHz. Intel has since responded with further advances in technology, both in design and in manufacturing technology in order to regain the leading position.

The bio-information business Incyte Genomics has kept itself ahead of the competition in the same way. As other entities made similar gene sequence database information available to the pharmaceutical and biotech communities, sometimes even for free, Incyte moved further into the detail to maintain its added value position. It now has databases covering sequence, gene expression, and proteomic data along with genetic data on areas such as single nucleotide polymorphisms. It also provides microarray gene chips and gene cloning services.

Focusing on market needs

11.13   This is the underpinning of any re-invention process. Often management focuses on the internal needs of the business first and forgets that re-invention is about maintaining market presence. The direction of the market can be assessed by maintaining the market monitoring. Informed decisions can then be made about the offerings and technology, with the business needs slotting in alongside.

If this sounds like business planning, it should. Business planning is not a once and forever exercise. It needs reviewing and reworking in the light of circumstances.

The alternative

11.14   In the longer term, the alternative to re-invention is decline. No matter how many businesses the group buys and how many markets it enters, if it is not rejuvenating itself then, as the offerings age and the markets move on, it will decline.

Some businesses do this spectacularly quickly, disappearing from view in a very short period of time. Others go into a steadier decline and can last for many years before either being reborn or fading away.

Forming Your Strategy

II

The Strategic Planning Process **12**

OBJECTIVES

- To introduce the strategic and business planning processes.
- To explain the differences between them.
- To introduce the elements of the strategic planning processes.
- To set out the key questions and thinking.
- To highlight the pitfalls.

Overview of strategic and business planning

12.1 Yogi Berra, the celebrated baseball player and homespun philosopher, is quoted as having said:

> 'If you don't know where you're going, you're liable to end up some place else.'

Knowing where you are going is the concept behind strategic and business planning. The two are elements of the same process – a process which has the objective of capturing the aims, intentions, and raison d'être of the business in a form that can be communicated to employees, funders, and other key stakeholders.

Strategic planning is the element that builds up the roadmap that the company intends to follow: it aims to capture the philosophy and outline the deliverables. It includes a number of stages with ever increasing levels of detail and interaction.

Business planning is about encapsulating the strategic plan and condensing it into a series of statements of intent, linked to actions, and supported by a financial model that shows the anticipated outcome and validates the viability of the plan.

Commentators have produced a variety of ways of differentiating strategic and business such as :

Strategic planning	*Business planning*
Capturing the vision	Communicating the action
Cerebral	Practical
Emotionally charged	Hard headed
What and why	How and when
Top down	Bottom up

The key is that there is more to strategic planning than writing the strap line and more to business planning than the financial projections.

DEFINITION

A *strap line* is the very short phrase that is used to encapsulate the vision of the business. Examples include British Airways' strapline: '*We fly to serve*' or Andersen's: '*The greatest place to do great work*' – a recruitment strapline from the mid-1990s.

This chapter focuses on the challenges of strategic planning and the next two on business planning and the related topic of business and revenue models.

Strategic planning

12.2   Strategic planning is a top down process. It starts at the very highest level by asking the Big Questions:

- What is the business for?
- What is it going to do?
- What is going to make it special?
- What does it want to become?

It is worth looking at each of these in turn.

What is the business for?

12.3   This may seem like a very strange question. However, it should not be difficult to answer. Every technology exists to meet a real world need – that is one of the key differences between technology and science. Hence, the answer to this question is likely to be related to the reason for the existence of the technology itself.

It may, however, be more complicated or more subtle than this. Michael E. McGrath in *Product Strategy for High Technology Companies* suggests that Apple's core strategy vision was originally to make computing easy for the masses. That was it. Everything else that Apple did was driven by that central desire.

Other businesses attack this in different ways. Merck & Company, a major pharmaceuticals business, in its Corporate Policy Statement from its 1989 Management Guide stated that 'we are in the business of preserving and improving human life. All of our actions must be measured by our success in achieving this goal.' This is more of an ethical statement but, again, it is a fundamental statement that guides and directs the detail of strategy and helps to act as a touchstone for all decision-making.

All this does not mean that the answer to this question will necessarily be as neat, concise and well formed as the Merck example. Moreover, it may well be that the answer evolves over time and certainly during the strategic planning process.

What is being recognised by researchers and academics like James Collins and Jerry Porras is that, for long lasting and successful businesses, the answer to this question is not a simple 'to make money' nor is it a flippant 'to be the best' or 'to make a difference'. Often the answer looks outside of the business itself – it is focused on the raison d'être for the business's existence from a customer viewpoint rather than purely from a shareholder's viewpoint.

What is it going to do?

12.4   Having got over the hurdle of the first question this second can, at first sight, look equally innocuous. But again, the difficulty can be to come up with a non-flippant and meaningful answer.

The answer is very important as it is the first step to developing the business and revenue models for the company. The answer to this question goes to the heart of the nature of the business, the scale of the operations, the timetable for development and the type of revenues that the offerings will deliver.

Items to consider under this question are:

- What form will the offerings take – ideas and proven concepts, fully developed and in-house produced products or somewhere in between, or a service?
- Where will the offerings be sold?
- What sort of customer are the offerings aimed at?
- What sort of interaction will the business have with the customers and the end users (if different)?

Hence the complexity of the question. In turn, each of these questions can generate further questions and options. At this stage, however, the goal is not to be drawn into the detail but to set out the landscape in which the detail will sit.

All too often technology companies get drawn into the detail of strategic planning too early. This is often simply because the founder has a single end in sight – an end that can be as simple as to get their discovery/invention/insight onto the market. These companies are referred to as being *technology led*. They often thrive initially, only to find life gets a lot harder later on when they are expected to generate real revenues and support themselves.

Diving into the detail of the specification of the technology that the company will develop and sell, its performance and its functions, is not the right answer here. Indeed, if that seems to be the obvious answer to this question then it may well be that the technology is not the basis for a lasting business at all and that other options should be investigated. For example a licensing arrangement or a sale of the concept to a business that can develop it.

Why such a harsh diagnosis? The reason is simple: a sustainable business must be just that: sustainable. That means that the technology at its core is either very broad in application opportunities (as is the case for example for a number of biotech companies) or that it is the first of a set of technologies that will be developed.

In turn, this second option suggests that the technologies will be in some way related such as:

- Addressing different aspects of the same market or customer need.
- Addressing similar market needs but in markets with subtle but significant differences.
- Utilising different platforms available or preferred by different users.

Examples of this abound from the portfolios of products produced by software houses:

- The elements of suites of programmes such as Microsoft Office™, Star Office™ or Corel's graphics products are examples of offerings that address different aspects of the same market/user need.
- Microsoft™ produces both Windows ME™ for PC use and Windows NT Server™ for server use. Both are operating systems but they meet different needs – a standalone or networked PC has different demands on it from a server.
- Lotus Notes™ is produced in versions that can be run on a variety of operating systems such as Windows NT™ or OS/2™.

What is important here, however, is that at their core these different examples all have the same end in sight – to provide users with tools to undertake tasks.

The answer to the question is therefore rather more generic than specific. This is important because single product technology companies, while they do exist, often struggle and rarely grow to any really significant size.

This is an issue that the environmental technology companies have seen all too clearly. Environmental companies, such as those that have developed effluent treatment solutions, have historically often emerged from scientific institutions. The products themselves are the result of dedicated research and exploration on a specific problem by highly focused scientists.

The difficulty is that, even within potential user groups such as the chemical industry, the requirement for the highly specific type of solution that these companies have to offer is limited. And with only one product to sell they struggle to survive let alone thrive.

What is going to make it special?

12.5 To be successful a business has to have something special about it. Me-too businesses need very large markets to be successful and even then too many me-toos will lead to many failing, as in the home computer industry in the 1980s.

> **DEFINITION**
>
> A *me-too business* is one that apes the offerings of another firm, matching, but rarely going beyond the specifications or innovative position of the leading company in the sector. In the early 1980s there were many home computer manufacturers such as Oric, Sinclair, Atari, Dragon, Commodore, Acorn/BBC and Apple. Of these only Apple is still a high profile manufacturer and many of the rest have disappeared without trace – Commodore several times.

Again, this can be a difficult quality to identify but it is vital as it is another primary driver within the business planning process. Examples of business characteristics that can be the basis of the 'something special' include:

- Innovation in the technology, its application or the service.
- Time to market – the speed with which the technology hits the market place.
- Absolute focus on customer needs – ease of use or matched functionality for example.
- Quality and/or range of offerings.
- Environmental or social policies (as exemplified by Ben & Jerry's, the US ice-cream manufacturers).
- Pricing or business case.

Clearly, this can be a difficult area for a pre-formation or start-up business to identify but it comes down to the commercial vision of the founders. If founders find this a difficult, or impossible, question to answer then experience suggests that they will need to either look for someone with commercial experience to come into the team to add that vision, or re-consider whether the technology is really going to lead to a sustainable business.

The second option does not mean that there is no value in the technology or even that a company should not be formed to develop it. Rather it implies that any such company is likely to be relatively short-lived and will need to have a clear exit through licensing the technology or looking for a trade buyer once the technology is sufficiently developed.

In turn, this rather implies that what makes the business special is the technology itself – there could be a feedback loop here to help the founders re-consider the question.

What does it want to become?

12.6 For some, the ultimate vision question: the answer will shape the development plans and, therefore, the business itself.

This question can be split down into a series of sub-questions to help focus the strategic thought process. These sub-questions include:

- What will it be known for?
- Where will it fit in the value and food chains?
- Where is its target market (local, regional, national or global and how can it be accessed)?
- What, if any, is the exit route and when will it come?

What will it be known for?

12.7   There is, to some extent, a link to the previous question: *What will make it special?* Here, however, the emphasis is on the image that the business will present to the outside world of competitors, customers, funders and other stakeholders. A first step on the road to creating the brand (see Chapter 20), the answer to this question will resonate throughout the branding process.

As set out in Chapter 20, this is not simply about creating a glossy and superficial picture of the business. It is about the creed that the business will live by and therefore the values that underpin the decision making processes within the business itself.

It can therefore be the case that the answer to this question is subtly different from the answer to *What will make it special?* For example, a company might wish to be known for its leading, or even bleeding, edge research while what makes it special may actually be the time to market capabilities it has that give customers what they want earlier. Or it could be that the what is special is a technique that provides high quality at lower cost, where the company's image is built around quality alone, so that the business benefits from the enhanced margin.

Where will it fit in the value and food chains?

12.8   The concept of a value chain is that the stages of development through which an offering goes before it is sold to its end user increase the value of the underlying technology itself.

This can be illustrated through a highly generalised development process:

Stage	Functionality	Utility to end user	Relative value
Concept	Non-existent	Fascinating but of no use to me yet	Minimal
Proof of principle	Basic	Can I use it yet?	
Development mule	Growing	Can't it do this as well?	
Beta version	90% settled	I like this but these bits need work	
Completed unit	99% in place	Meets my needs in this area	
Integrated into total system	Greater than the sum of the parts	Meets my needs for this activity	Maximised

Technologies often need to move between organisations to progress from one stage to the next. Different skills come into play at each stage and few companies are big enough to have the full set in place to move technology through the whole process unaided. Examples of those that do have the full set would form a list of some of the world's largest businesses, such as the biggest pharmaceuticals companies, and even here they are looking outside to biotech companies for the early stages of the development cycle.

The food chain is really a financial equivalent of the value chain. The position of the business depends on factors such as:

- The relative increase in value generated by the stage of development.
- The number of other parties that the business is ultimately dependent on for revenues.
- The strength of the intellectual property position.
- The size of the ultimate end user market by value and the cost of producing and marketing the offering to it.
- The overall return achievable from the offering.

This realisation can lead to a natural reaction that the business should be fully integrated.

DEFINITION

A *fully integrated business* is one which owns and controls the entire process from conception through to the end market. Pharmaceuticals companies have traditionally been examples of this with their ownership of discovery, drug development, clinical trials, regulatory approval knowledge, manufacturing, distribution and sales and marketing functions.

However, as noted earlier, even the largest businesses like the pharmaceuticals companies are moving to models where parts of their value chains are 'outsourced' to other companies.

The reason for this is a combination of a need for skills focus, an emphasis on the most value adding parts of the process and the ability to de-risk the development of offerings.

A very high level analysis of the activities within the drug development area of the pharmaceutical industry shows the reasoning behind the outsourcing. Figure 12.8 overleaf is a representation of the stages that drug development goes through from initial research and discovery through to sustained sales growth.

The process is a good one for analysis as, on average, it takes 7 to 10 years to get from the lab bench discovery to regulatory approval and product launch.

Further, the process is highly regulated with clinical trials, those involving testing the new drug on animals and then humans, controlled by government or EU approved agencies such as the Medicines Control Agency (MCA) in the UK or the Food and Drug Administration (FDA) in the US.

Drugs go through a series of tests, which start well before the clinical trials process, to ensure that they are not overly toxic, are generally safe and appear to have the expected effect on the condition they are going to be used to treat. The results from this battery of tests are reviewed by the regulator before approval is given for clinical trials to begin.

The clinical trials process is designed to ensure that the drug is as efficacious as expected, or at least adequately efficacious to make the side effects worth risking. They also cover areas such as the minimum dosages required for the drug to be effective and the format in which the drug is delivered – options including orally, by injection, by patch or by nasal spray. During the clinical trials process side effects are also picked up and dosages, formats, and even subtle changes to the basic drug itself may be made, with appropriate approvals, in order to try and optimise the trade off between side effects and efficacy.

The clinical trials come in three broad phases (known as Phase I, Phase II and Phase III) which move from extended safety testing through to large scale trials in disease sufferers, usually benchmarked against either existing drugs for

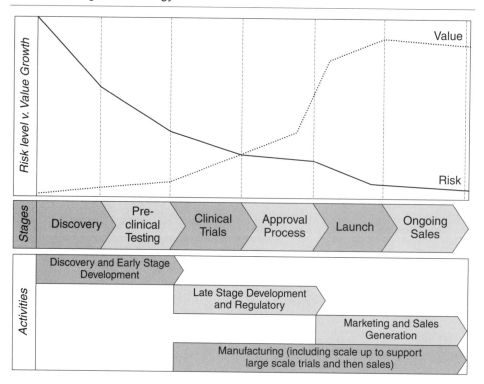

Figure 12.8 – High level overview of the drug development process, activities and risk and value growth profiles

Source: PKF

the same condition or a control group receiving a placebo. Within each phase there are a series of sub-phases that build up the data on the drug and its effects. Approval from the regulator is required to move from one phase to the next.

Another aspect of the trials process is that the manufacturing method has to be finalised. The details of the composition of the drug as it will be sold have to be set and controlled at an immensely detailed level and small changes in the process can alter the composition significantly enough for regulators to consider the output to be a different product. Indeed, arguments about the chemical identicalness of certain generic drugs have hinged on minute amounts of substances that may have been active elements of the drug or may just have been a passive element of the bulker used to make capsules big enough to handle.

All of the information obtained from the discovery stage, the development stages, and the pre-clinical and clinical trials is then presented to the regulators who consider whether the drug should be approved for sale in their regulated territory. The information delivered generally runs to van loads and the review process can take 10 to 25 months.

Once regulatory approval is gained, which includes approval not only for the specific use of the drug but also for the claims that can be made for it in use, the marketing machine goes into action. Some work will have been done already to pave the way for the drug through the clinical trials and certainly during the period of regulatory approval. The marketing includes training of the sales force about the new drug, its uses, and the allowable claims. It will also include information on targeting the sales and developing sales materials needed.

Two more statistics alongside the 7 to 10 year average timescale are vitally important in understanding the scale of the risks involved in this process:

* It costs on average $450 million to get a drug to launch.
* Only around 5% of all drugs in pre-clinical trials make it to the market.

Historically drug companies have undertaken the full range of activities in-house, and many still do. However, the risk profile shows that the very early stages are where the risk is highest and the stages through clinical trials and approval to launch are where the value growth is biggest. Hence, a risk/value trade off suggests that pharmaceutical companies should try to avoid the discovery and early stage development phases of the drug development process.

This would lead to a concentration on *Late Stage Development* and *Regulatory, Marketing and Sales Generation* and *Manufacturing*. However, analysis of the value generation shows that the capital intensity of running manufacturing (particularly under the strict regulatory framework of Good Manufacturing Practice, or GMP, imposed on pharmaceutical production sites) means that the return on investment is relatively lower in manufacturing than in the other two activities.

The development of new types of drug based on biological substances rather than chemical bases, so-called biopharmaceuticals or biologicals, places a further capital requirement on manufacturing facilities as the techniques used to process these drugs can be significantly different from traditional chemical entities.

The result of this analysis is that a number of the major drug companies have spun off their manufacturing or have at least reduced it significantly. In-house facilities may not have the critical mass to be adequately profitable but an out-sourced facility, which can trade with more than one drug company, has the opportunity to build that critical mass and generate an adequate return for its shareholders.

In the same way, biotech companies have taken over elements of the *Discovery* and *Early Stage Development* activities. It has been estimated that 30% of the pharmaceutical industry's research and development budget is available for in-licensing of technology/drug candidates.

By going down this route the pharmaceutical companies make two major gains:

* Someone else (the investors in the biotech companies) is taking on the highest risk element of the process; and
* They do not risk spending time and money developing a compound or biological that turns out to be of use outside their specific areas of disease focus; they only need to look at candidates with early stage results indicating a good likelihood of utility in a disease area of focus.

The trade off here is that the pharmaceutical company has to pay often size-able access fees, development milestone payments and ongoing royalties on sales to the biotech companies. But overall the calculation suggests that this still works out cheaper for the pharmaceutical company than running its own discovery activities.

This leaves the pharmaceutical companies to do what they do best and most profitably: later stage development and management of the clinical trials process (although the trials themselves are these days often outsourced to specialist

Clinical Trials Houses) and the marketing and sales generation. Sales generation fits in through the concept of critical mass. With sizeable portfolios of drugs and teams or sales programmes focused on specific disease areas the return on the investment in a sales organisation is higher the larger the portfolio.

Where is its target market?

12.9 Another beguilingly simple question: this will again drive the size and complexity of the organisation. A whole range of factors need to be taken into account when considering the target market.

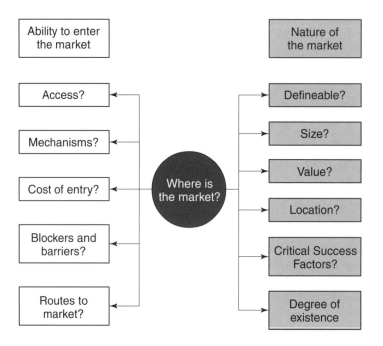

Figure 12.9 – factors to consider on 'Where is the market?'

Source: PKF

The nature of technology means that more factors need to be considered than might be the case with other industry sectors. An example of this is the acceptability of the technology itself and therefore the degree of existence of the market for the technology.

Technology can be analysed by the degree of development and, therefore, the degree of risk involved from a user's perspective in adopting the technology now rather than waiting for it to become proven and accepted by others. The risks involved include:

- The risk that the technology will not stand up to scaling up to industrial use.
- The risk that adopting the technology will destabilise existing systems.
- The risk of adopting the wrong technology for the application.
- The risk of adopting a technology that is overtaken or not generally adopted (sometimes called *the Betamax risk*).
- The risk of over-investing – in effect, the risk of paying too much for the technology by helping to pay for its development but then seeing competitors benefit from it at a lower price.

- The risk of technology seduction – that is investing in technology because it is new rather than because it is needed.

These risks lead to a pathway of acceptability down which technologies pass:

Stage	*Characteristics*
Bleeding Edge	Barely escaped from the lab. Largely unproven, certainly in commercial use, little understood by developers and not at all by almost all end users. Often difficult to set up and use. Getting value out of the technology is more trouble than most users will put up with. Carries with it the implication of instability and likelihood of damaging surrounding systems or development programmes if not very carefully controlled. Proponents often seen as very technical – 'a techie's delight'.
Cutting Edge	Starting to be talked about; the technology is being demonstrated and is creating interest. Developers can see uses for it and are suggesting enhancements that will make it useful to them. It is gaining advocates and starting to appear in magazines and, potentially, giving rise to jargon that users want to understand.
Leading Edge	The technology is now in commercial form and showing that it is a major step forward from the status quo. Real applications or useable formats are available and reference users are starting to adopt it – albeit perhaps on a trial or free use basis. It has moved from the lab into the real world.
Proven	The reference users have embraced the technology. Those who did not invest at the leading edge stage have gained enough comfort from those reference users, or at least the reporting of the reference applications in the trade press, that they are looking seriously at the technology – for the next time they need to change.
Accepted	When customers need the functionality the technology is automatically on the list of potentials. The track record is such that customers can invest in the technology with a low level of fear about the risks involved. They and the technology business are in a mutual comfort zone.
Old Hat	Newer technologies have arrived that provide greater benefits. These newcomers have reached at least the leading edge if not the proven stage, eroding and then overtaking the lead that the technology once held. Some users will still adopt the technology either through investment in surrounding systems or through comfort but the viability of the technology is now limited.

What, if any, is the exit route and when will it come?

12.10   Chapter 2, *Overview of the lifecycle,* looks at the different types and potential timings of an exit from the business.

The only thought to add is that there need not be a formal exit unless that is what the founders are looking for personally, or it is driven by investor requirements. There are plenty of business models that generate an adequate enough return for shareholders that an exit by sale or float just is not necessary. Indeed, the vast majority of companies are not publicly traded and most are not sold throughout their lifetime.

There are some points to consider here, however:

- Technology companies can often need significant sums of money for development.
- The providers of that cash, if professional investors or funds, are looking to generate a return – for example, venture capitalists are, in general, looking to realise the return after a 3–5 year period.
- In that time it is unlikely that most companies will generate enough profits and cash to meet the required return so some, if not all, of the increase in value must be in capital growth – the growth in the value of the business as a whole.
- To realise that capital growth, and recycle the return, investors will look to sell at some point.
- Hence, a trade sale or float is on the cards as the mechanism for realising the return.

However, if the founders' funds can cover the cost of development then there is no reason why the business cannot stay as a private undertaking in the founders' hands. The only issue arises here at the point at which the founders wish to retire from the business. The key, as with most things in business life, is succession planning – an issue somewhat outside the general scope of this book.

Capturing the strategic thinking

12.11   Even though only an overview, this chapter should imply that there is a lot of thinking and heartache, and a significant amount of research needed, to come up with a strategic plan.

There is no one right way to capture this thinking and research. The mechanism used will be very personal to the people and the business. The important message is that, as the strategy will direct the day-to-day activities and decision-making in the business, it needs to be in a form that can be referred to and can be accessed by the decision makers.

A range of techniques are available including:

Approach	Details
Q&A	The answers to the questions that have been asked are set out in question and answer form. The answers have to be high level enough to allow a reader to apply them to the wide variety of situations they may need to consider.
Black Book	The key tenets of the strategic plan are set out in a single reference work of more or less detail.

(Continued)

Approach	Details
Vision, mission, values	These are a series of statements designed to encapsulate the strategy. • The *Vision* is the highest level and sets out the goals of the business for the long term. • The *Mission* adds a level of specificity around markets, quality, position in the value chain, etc. • The *Values* are the tenets by which the business will operate both internally and externally.
Goals and objectives	Not dissimilar to the vision, mission, values approach this sets out the goals (the less concrete elements) and the objectives (measurable targets) for the business generally spread over a time period that show the desired long-term future for the business.
Roadmap	A roadmap sets out the way that a business will develop. Often in the form of a timeline, strategic roadmaps can be complex graphical representations of both the external growth of the business and the internal culture that goes with it.

It is not unusual for a combination of these techniques to be used.

Vision and mission statements were a great favourite of the 1980s and 1990s. The difficulty with the almost strap-line like vision statements that came out of that period is that they were either too vague to be of use or too trite to communicate the fundamental beliefs of the business. However, they can be useful as part of the education process of inculcating employees with the strategy and the culture. Having something to latch onto as a reminder of the strategy can be a useful mechanism in this process. Values statements, which can become quite lengthy, are more useful as a reference. They should therefore capture the essence of the approach to projects, customers, staff and shareholders.

Experience suggests, however, that really meaningful vision and mission statements are produced by individuals or very small teams and not in committee.

The best communication tools are often hybrids of vision, mission and values. One example being the Credo that R.W. Johnson, Jnr wrote for Johnson & Johnson in 1943:

Our Credo

WE BELIEVE THAT OUR FIRST RESPONSIBILITY IS TO THE DOCTORS, NURSES, HOSPITALS, MOTHERS, AND ALL OTHERS WHO USE OUR PRODUCTS. OUR PRODUCTS MUST ALWAYS BE OF THE HIGHEST QUALITY. WE MUST CONSTANTLY STRIVE TO REDUCE THE COST OF THESE PRODUCTS. OUR ORDERS MUST BE PROMPTLY AND ACCURATELY FILLED. OUR DEALERS MUST MAKE A FAIR PROFIT.

OUR SECOND RESPONSIBILITY IS TO THOSE WHO WORK WITH US – THE MEN AND WOMEN IN OUR PLANTS AND OFFICES, THEY MUST HAVE A

(Continued)

SENSE OF SECURITY IN THEIR JOBS. WAGES MUST BE FAIR AND ADEQUATE, MANAGEMENT JUST, HOURS REASONABLE, AND WORKING CONDITIONS CLEAN AND ORDERLY. EMPLOYEES SHOULD HAVE AN ORGANIZED SYSTEM FOR SUGGESTIONS AND COMPLAINTS. SUPERVISORS AND DEPARTMENT HEADS MUST BE QUALIFIED AND FAIR-MINDED. THERE MUST BE OPPORTUNITY FOR ADVANCEMENTS – FOR THOSE QUALIFIED AND EACH PERSON MUST BE CONSIDERED AN INDIVIDUAL STANDING ON HIS OWN DIGNITY AND MERIT.

OUR THIRD RESPONSIBILITY IS TO OUR MANAGEMENT. OUR EXECUTIVES MUST BE PERSONS OF TALENT, EDUCATION, EXPERIENCE, AND ABILITY. THEY MUST BE PERSONS OF COMMON SENSE AND FULL UNDERSTANDING.

OUR FOURTH RESPONSIBILITY IS TO THE COMMUNITIES IN WHICH WE LIVE. WE MUST BE A GOOD CITIZEN – SUPPORT GOOD WORKS AND CHARITY, AND BEAR OUR FAIR SHARE OF TAXES. WE MUST MAINTAIN IN GOOD ORDER THE PROPERTY WE ARE PRIVILEGED TO USE. WE MUST PARTICIPATE IN PROMOTION OF CIVIC IMPROVEMENT, HEALTH, EDUCATION AND GOOD GOVERNMENT, AND ACQUAINT THE COMMUNITY WITH OUR ACTIVITIES.

OUR FIFTH AND LAST RESPONSIBILITY IS TO OUR STOCKHOLDERS. BUSINESS MUST MAKE A SOUND PROFIT. RESERVES MUST BE CREATED, RESEARCH MUST BE CARRIED ON, ADVENTUROUS PROGRAMS DEVELOPED, AND MISTAKES PAID FOR. ADVERSE TIMES MUST BE PROVIDED FOR, ADEQUATE TAXES PAID, NEW MACHINES PURCHASED, NEW PLANTS BUILT, NEW PRODUCTS LAUNCHED, AND NEW SALES PLANS DEVELOPED. WE MUST EXPERIMENT WITH NEW IDEAS. WHEN THESE THINGS HAVE BEEN DONE THE STOCKHOLDER SHOULD RECEIVE A FAIR RETURN. WE ARE DETERMINED WITH THE HELP OF GOD'S GRACE, TO FULFILL THESE OBLIGATIONS TO THE BEST OF OUR ABILITY.

This one page set of statements captures the essence of the business and communicates it in a way that makes reference to it as a benchmark for decision making. This has to be the objective of any mechanism for capturing strategy.

SUMMARY

12.12 This chapter has set out the thought process for the strategic planning stage of the process. The outputs from this stage have profound implications for everything that follows. The vision, aims and ambitions captured at this stage need to be turned into a plan of actions that can be implemented.

How the thought process is captured is a very personal matter and different entrepreneurs and founder teams will approach that aspect in different ways. What is important is that it is captured in a way that is useful for the founders and the management as a reference for future decisions. That is why there are so many questions and aspects to consider at this stage – strategy is much more than just the high level concepts and the nice and pretty words; it is the creed that the business will live by.

The other important point to make is that strategies do need to be reviewed and revisited. They should be referred to regularly and, if conditions change or the business plan falters, should be re-assessed. However, once happy with the strategy it should not be lightly tampered with – it is easier to update the business plan than the strategy because changing the strategy means changing the very character of the business.

Business Planning **13**

OBJECTIVES

- To introduce the business planning process.
- To consider the elements of a business plan.
- To introduce the concept of business and revenue models.
- To introduce the role of financial projections.

Business planning

13.1   Business planning picks up where the strategic planning process concludes. As defined in the last chapter *'Business planning is about encapsulating the strategic plan and condensing it into a series of statements of intent, linked to actions and supported by a financial model that shows the anticipated outcome and validates the viability of the plan.'*

This means that a business plan is action based. However, as business plans are often used for internal communication and as the basis for attracting investors they regularly include brief summaries of the strategy as part of their framework.

Indeed, for communication purposes a business plan can often act as the link from the more conceptual strategic plan to the everyday operational level plans that department heads use to direct activities.

Background considerations

13.2   It is important to understand the reader's criteria when drawing up the document. Research with technology venture capitalists has shown that there are four key elements that they are looking for in a technology business they are considering backing:

- Management.
- Market opportunity.
- Intellectual property strength.
- Sustainability of the idea.

The business plan therefore needs to draw out the salient points in each of these areas.

Management

13.3   Venture capitalists and other funders often point out that, at the early stages of a business, what they are backing is management. The management team will make or break the company even more than the strength of the technology itself. Management not only controls the spending on the research and development and the commercialisation of the offering it also performs the primary review of progress in the R&D area.

This means that management has to be objective in its assessment of issues and hurdles that arise during development. More than that, management has to be willing to take tough decisions if the development plan seems to be heading in the wrong direction.

This last point can arise for two quite different reasons:

- A fundamental or key assumption about the technology proves to be incorrect or a key hurdle cannot be overcome (for example, certain pharmaceutical products are easy to produce at lab scale qualities but prove immensely difficult to scale up to industrial production levels needed to support sales); or
- A developmental nicety has distracted the development team down what is a very interesting path from a technical viewpoint but which provides no extra commercial benefits to the user. A regular complaint amongst CEOs of software houses is the ability of software engineers to overrun the budget due to adding in features that *'seemed interesting'*, even though they were not included in the functional specification approved for the product.

In both of these scenarios, decisions need to be made early and actions taken to correct the position. This implies both that management has to be able to stand back from the excitement of development and that some form of fall back position has been considered to address the contingency requirements of an issue.

Strong managements face these challenges as part of the day-to-day running of the business. Weak managements expect everything to work well, ignore the signs that progress is not occurring, and then take panicked decisions, often when it is really too late.

An oft-repeated mantra of funders is that good management can take a mediocre idea and make it successful but weak management will fail even if it has the best ideas to work with.

Market opportunity

13.4   This is very similar to the *Where is its target market?* thinking discussed in the *Strategic Planning* chapter.

There is, therefore, more to this than simply the size of the market for the sector or even the size of the addressable market for the offering. Other factors including the ability to enter the market, the size and nature of competitors, and the costs of supporting sales come into play here.

These and other related issues will be considered later in more detail.

Intellectual property strength

13.5   As set out in Chapter 22, intellectual property comes in different forms. The importance to the business plan of being able to analyse the strength of the intellectual property is threefold:

- It is a measure of a key barrier to entry for potential competitors.
- It is an indicator of how quickly other technologies can be developed that could match or exceed the benefits of the business's technology.
- It is an indication of the likelihood of an intellectual property-based attack on the business by a competitor.

Barriers to entry and development timescales for competitors are vital elements in the value of a business. Business plan ideas, particularly in the software and internet arenas, often include statements such as: '*this technology gives us a 6 to 9 month lead on any potential competitors*'. The question that follows is simple: what does the business have to do to maintain that lead? The implication of the statement is that in 12 months time the business will be 3 to 6 months *behind* the competition if nothing is done.

   Intellectual property can therefore be a cornerstone in answering the question and providing comfort that the business has a real future and will not just be overtaken by those who can adapt or learn from the mistakes that are made along the way.

It is, however, important to be realistic about the strength of the intellectual property the business owns. A reminder of the relative strengths of intellectual property (represented by the value they add to a business) is given in Figure 13.5 below:

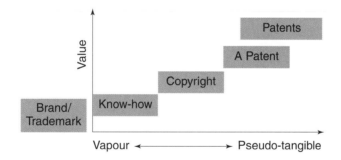

Figure 13.5 – relative strengths of intellectual property

Source: PKF

Even at the highest value position, a realistic evaluation of the strength of patents needs to be made. Patents can be challenged and have been found to be unenforceable on a number of grounds. Of particular relevance, and a very important balancing act when drawing up a patent claim, is the breadth of the patent. A claim that is too broad is unlikely to be sustainable. Hence, while a patent may seem to be an all-encompassing claim that would rule out all competitors it may be challenged on the ground of being too vague to be useful.

Sustainability of the idea

13.6 The point about being ahead of the game now but potentially behind the game in the future is the key to this element. It is unrealistic, even with the best patent wall, to imagine that the offerings will not be challenged by competitors at some point. The competitors may simply take a different approach. This is a particular risk in areas like biotechnology where a series of different approaches can be taken to, say, the treatment of cancers. The fact that a company has a strong current offering does not mean that they will necessarily maintain that position going forward.

Hence, in order to feel that the risk of failure or falling behind is not too great, investors and staff will be interested in what the business is going to do to sustain itself in the longer term. To address this, it is important that the plan sets out a longer term framework for the business showing how it will regenerate itself over time to continue to generate revenues and opportunities.

Structure of a business plan

13.7 No two business plans are ever the same as the business plan has to reflect the underlying business and its strategic intent. However, there are some guidelines as to the scope and expectations of readers of business plans – particularly those plans designed for potential funders.

The first and most obvious is that the plan should be documented. It would be truly exceptional for a funder to provide cash to a business without some form of plan both to show what the money is going to be used for and to enable the investor to monitor the performance against their expectations.

Beyond that, the structure of the document is flexible.

However, experience suggests that for a technology company the plan needs to cover areas such as:

- History and status of the technology.
- Intellectual property position.
- Market opportunity.
- Offerings and marketing approach.
- Technology development plan.
- Business model being adopted.
- Management.
- Strengths, Weaknesses, Opportunities, Threats analysis.
- Financial projections.
- Proposed business structures and current status.
- Controls and reporting.
- Funding approach and associated disclaimers.

In addition, it is normal to have an Executive Summary. The roll of the Executive Summary is two-fold:

- it pulls the key information together, avoiding the problem of information overload for readers and ensuring that the main points are clearly communicated; and
- it acts as the outline briefing for a potential investor – it therefore has to be attractive and include the key hooks that are likely to attract their attention.

This last point may seem flippant but it is actually very important. Venture capital houses that specialise in technology investments tend to run with relatively small teams. They also receive significant numbers of business plans – some of the most high profile can receive hundreds a week – varying in quality and style from two or three pages of very high level concept to volumes of intricate data analysis and technological background. They need to have a mechanism for sifting this volume of information and this tends to be through the Executive Summary.

An example outline, for a biotechnology company, is included at the end of this chapter for further guidance. This outline is generic but provides practical guidance on the style and format that could be used to prepare a plan for submission to funders.

Contents of an Executive Summary

13.8   As with all parts of the plan there can be no set format for the Executive Summary. However, it would not be unusual to see section headings along the following lines:

- Introduction and overview.
- Unique Selling Points of the technology/service.
- Overview of the technology.
- Intellectual property.
- High level R&D plan.
- Commercialisation plan. $\}$ clearly setting out the Critical Success Factors
- Management team.
- Finance requirements.

The Executive Summary is also a selling document – either internally to the team or externally to funders. It therefore needs to make clear where the value lies in the business and how it will be realised.

Each of the sections needs to be compact and concise – generally two or three paragraphs in length – simply to keep the Executive Summary down to a reasonable length. Using the font size and character spacing of this book the target length for an Executive Summary is 4 to 5 sides of A4 and certainly no longer than 6.

This means that, in places, simple diagrammatic representations may be needed to pull points together more succinctly than is possible with words.

The most challenging aspect may well be summarising the technology. To do this it is necessary to focus heavily on what the technology does and less heavily on the basic science involved. Given that the potential reader is likely to be either a member of staff or a specialist venture capital investor, a good basic understanding of the science behind the technology can generally be assumed.

It is also important to recognise the difference between the Unique Selling Points (USPs) and the Critical Success Factors (CSFs) and to understand the role that each plays in the Executive Summary:

DEFINITIONS

Unique Selling Points are the key benefits that a technology provides to its user. They are the reasons why the users/customers will pay for the company's offerings.

Critical Success Factors are the key steps that the business has to achieve in order to deliver both the USPs to customers and the financial returns to backers.

Another important distinction arises here: the difference between benefits and features.

DEFINITIONS

Benefits are the factors inherent in the technology that deliver value to users. Examples include:

- Ease of use.
- Solution to a specific user problem.
- Time/cost reduction.
- Ability to enhance the user's offering to customers.

Features, by contrast, are facts about the detail, presentation or application of the technology itself.

For example, a Graphical User Interface (referred to as a 'GUI') is a *feature* of a software programme. Ease of use through the provision of an intuitive front end (the GUI) is a *benefit* to the user.

It is important to realise the difference between the two. It is a well known saying in sales and marketing that customers buy benefits not features. The difficulty is that, for the initial technology developers, the features may be the driving force for the technology project. However, it is vital to stand back and evaluate the benefits to users. A technology can have a myriad of features but without any benefits it is likely to struggle to be commercially successful.

Examples of this last condition abound in the technology arena and are often referred to as *ideas looking for a market*.

Detailed sections

13.9 The more detailed sections that follow the Executive Summary expand on the key points and include further relevant background information to allow the reader to gain a better rounded picture of the plan.

The individual nature of each plan will come through most obviously in these sections. Rather than attempt to second guess the contents or make the guidelines too specific, it is probably more useful to look at these sections from the point of view of a checklist. The types of questions that need to be answered in each section are set out below. However, certain of the sections need further explanation and these are discussed in more detail after the checklist itself.

Checklist for the business plan sections

History and status of the technology

13.10

- Where did the technology come from?
- What was it designed to do?
- What stage is development currently at and what level of functionality has been achieved?
- Who has funded the development to date?

Intellectual property position

13.11

- What form does the intellectual property take?
- What protection is in place for the intellectual property?
- What is the strategy for protecting intellectual property that will be developed (see Chapter 19 for a discussion of intellectual property strategy)?
- What searches have been done on competing intellectual property and competing technologies?
- Who has undertaken the intellectual property protection work?
- What systems or techniques will be used to provide knowledge management systems and what is the knowledge management philosophy of the business?

Market opportunity

13.12

- See comments below.

Offerings and marketing approach

13.13

- Overview of the offerings including their key benefits and key features.
- Link into the technology development plan.

Technology development plan

13.14

- Set out the roadmap for developing the technology.
- Link this into the offerings benefits and features sets outlined above.
- Highlight the resources needed to undertake the work.
- What elements are key to the success of the development?
- What are seen as being the major development hurdles to be overcome?
- How does the plan build on the existing intellectual property?

Business model being adopted

13.15

- See the section on *Business Models* below.

Management

13.16

- What is the management structure (see below for comments on structures)?
- What is management's track record prior to founding/joining the business?
- What experience do the members have of commercialising technology?
- What holes are there in the team and how will they be addressed?
- It is worth setting out both roles and responsibilities and a management structure chart to show how the interactions work.

Strengths, Weaknesses, Opportunities, Threats analysis

13.17

- This summarises the key elements of the business, generally through bullet points.
- It needs to be realistic and balanced in its views of current status and plus and minus point.
- Care needs to be taken that strengths and opportunities, weaknesses and threats are not confused (strengths and weaknesses tend to be internal whereas opportunities and threats are external is one general rule that may help here).

Financial projections

13.18

- See the section on *Financial projections* below.

Proposed business structures and current status

13.19
- What legal form will the business take (company, partnership, etc)?
- It may be necessary to explain why that form has been chosen.
- Has the entity been formed yet?
- Have the legal and tax requirements been met (see Chapter 24)?

Controls and reporting

13.20

- What controls will there be on spending (in effect, over the R&D activities)?
- How will financial and business activities be reported and how often?
- What information will be available to investors/employees beyond the statutory accounts?

Funding approach and associated disclaimers

13.21

- What approach is being proposed to funding (form and stages, for example)?
- If the document is to be used for funding purposes then advisors should be consulted over the need for disclaimers, etc to ensure that the rules of the Financial Services Act, soon to be replaced by the Financial Services and Markets Act, and the Public Offering of Securities Regulations are not breached.

Market opportunity

13.22   There are a number of important points to be made regarding the way in which the information on the scale of the market opportunity is communicated. It is always tempting to put forward the largest numbers first and, in the technology area, this temptation can be all the greater due to the number of reports available on specific sectors.

However, the important figures are not the overall global turnover figures for the sector but the actual addressable market that the technology is aimed at. It is extremely rare that a single piece of technology will be able to address a global market valued at billions of dollars – the drug development sector is perhaps the big exception here. It is much more likely that the market will be first a UK one, then European and then, potentially, the US and the rest of the world. Each of these markets may be tens or potentially a few hundred millions of dollars in size.

Hence, being realistic about the figures provides some comfort to investors that the basis of both the revenue estimates and, by implication, other key areas of the plan are not based on fantasy numbers. It may therefore be more useful to start at the bottom with the addressable market and then move up to show that the addressable market is realistic by reference to published reports' estimates of the total market. Even then, the methodology used by some research firms to make their estimates suggests a degree of overstatement. Where a sales process includes a series of transactions with the value of the product building up along the chain, it can be very difficult to avoid effective double counting.

EXAMPLE

A extracts a mineral, Z, and sells it to B at £100 per tonne. B refines the Z and sells it at £150 per tonne to C who processes it (without adding anything further) into its useable form as Zee, and then sells the Zee to D, a distributor, for £250 per tonne. D sells to a retailer at the equivalent of £350 per tonne and once the retailer's margin is included the end cost of Zee to a user comes out at £400 per tonne.

If 1 million tonnes are extracted, processed and sold to end users in the year this equates to a market value of £400 million. However, if the estimate is based by capturing the total value of transactions in the Z/Zee sector then the market estimate will be £1.25 billion – a significant overstatement of the real market value.

The moral of the story is to be careful with large scale market estimates and show that the business stacks up without them.

Management structures

13.23   A complete business plan needs to include an overview of the roles and responsibilities of the management team. This recognises that there is a mix of skills and experience needed in a successful business. The plan should set out the initial roles and map out any changes that are expected.

Where holes in the skills or experience mix needed are identified, as is often the case, the plan should include the actions that will be undertaken to fill the positions as well as a recognition of the need to do so.

Titles do not make positions but it is worth understanding what readers are likely to expect from someone fulfilling a named role. This is made more complex by the different styles of management title available.

The range runs from the traditional UK titles to US stylings and beyond into new economy and experimental business roles such as *Chief Software Architect* (Bill Gates' title at Microsoft), *Chief Visioning Officer*, and *Fount of All Knowledge* (a title adopted by the head of IP and knowledge management at one experimental technology business).

UK titles

13.24   The UK titles are rather like the positions in a UK Government cabinet. They are relatively rigid in the areas of responsibility and suggestive of an internal hierarchy. Some of the more normal terms used in this title set include:

Title	Role
Chairman	Head of State role. Can be more active than a normal non-executive position with input into the strategic planning process. Often a role filled by a founder or an experienced entrepreneur. There are occasional Executive Chairman but this tends to be on occasions when either the roles of Chairman and Chief Executive are not split or alternatively in a transitional phase as a new Chief Executive is being taught the ropes.
Managing Director (MD)	The Prime Ministerial role. Collects the consensus from the rest of the team and then distils it into strategy and actions. Traditionally the role involved managing the business in every respect but has tended to become a more strategic position over time. On rare occasions there are joint MDs. However, it is generally the case that, as with joint managers at football clubs, this is a difficult arrangement to sustain for the long term.

(Continued)

Title	Role
Finance Director (FD)	The equivalent to the Chancellor of the Exchequer. The FD is responsible to the Managing Director for both the finances and the financial results of the company. Often also given the portfolios for administration and in-house IT systems.
Operations Director	The Home Secretary role charged with ensuring that everything in the business runs smoothly. This role is becoming more widely recognised and important in technology companies. Outside of the technology sector the Operations Director role can be effectively that of head of manufacturing.
Engineering Director/ Science Director	A role that is a hybrid of the Environment and the Science portfolios in a UK cabinet. Responsibilities cover both the identification and development of technologies and offerings.
Sales and Marketing Director	The equivalent of the Foreign Secretary, the Sales and Marketing Director is responsible for generating sales and also for building the image of the business in the marketplace. In a technology business this role can be extremely challenging as the selling aspect can be very technical and the sales themselves may be non-traditional, as in the licensing area.

US titles

13.25 Corporate positions in the US reflect the different legal structures in place. For example, it is possible for the person responsible for strategy and tactical development not even to be a director of the corporation.

The titles therefore are more general in nature and less suggestive of a formalised hierarchy than the UK equivalents. Normal terms include:

Title	Role
Chief Executive Officer (CEO)	Responsible for strategic planning and for strategic communication of the plan. Often also the external face of the business to the financial community and to customers.
Chief Operating Officer (COO)	Takes the strategic vision and turns it into the day-to-day action plans for the business. Often largely responsible for the running of the business operationally across all departments.
Chief Financial Officer (CFO)	Not unlike the UK equivalent but tends to be seen as more of an information provider and support role for the business.

(Continued)

Title	Role
Chief Technology/Scientific Officer (CTO or CSO)	The CTO/CSO is responsible for the development of the technology within the business. They work closely with the Sales and Marketing area (particularly Strategic Product Development) to ensure that the technology being developed supports what users are asking for.
President (or Vice President) of Sales and Marketing	The sales and marketing role tends to cross over into the technology development area as the specifications for technology development may well come from this department. Such Strategic Product Development sees the development resource as either shared with the CTO/CSO or it may even have its own development resource that sits alongside the research departments, taking the technology and building the applications on it.
Chief Knowledge Officer	A term becoming more widely used to denote the person responsible for capturing, protecting, and disseminating the intellectual property of the business. The role is both internally and externally focused as, alongside managing internal knowledge access, the Chief Knowledge Officer may be responsible for the IP strategy, interacting with patent agents or other IP professionals and for monitoring for breaches of IPR.
President of Business Development	This is a term that is often used for businesses with a revenue model built on licensing. Biotech companies will often sport people in this role (or the UK equivalent the Business Development Director). The role involves identifying and negotiating licence positions with strategic or tactical partners. Close involvement with the CTO/CSO and the Chief Knowledge officer is required as is the ability to work with lawyers on deals.

The important point to remember is that the title itself is not important. What is important is the role being fulfilled and that the full range of skills is available within the business.

Business models

13.26   The concept of a business model is that the way a business operates, and particularly the way that it sees itself in relation to other players in its market, can be classified into broad types. These types are important because they carry with them implied information about the nature and scale of costs, the customers and the risk levels.

The technology business model chain can be thought of as having the idea at one end and the customer at the other. In between there are a series of subtly but significantly different areas of emphasis that a business can have.

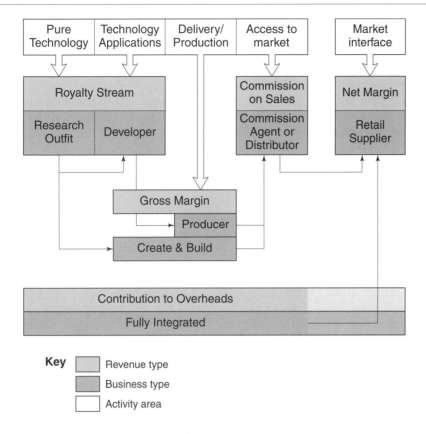

Figure 13.26 – the spectrum of technology business models

Source: PKF

The different models and the related revenue types are considered in more detail in the next chapter.

Financial projections

13.27   The business model is a key element in the process of drawing up the financial projections. The projections are part of the testing process for the business plan as well as an illustration of its financial effect.

The role of the projections is twofold:

- to set out the anticipated near term financial results of the business; and
- to provide an illustration of the potential for the longer term

The difference here is significant. The short term is manageable and controllable, at least to some degree, and, certainly whilst the technology is being developed, variances from the projected levels of expenditure should be easy to spot and explain.

The longer term is uncertain. The financial outcome will depend on earlier technology development results, the adoption of the technology and the ease of developing a business case that attracts customers.

Indeed, the difference is highlighted in formal accounting terminology by referring to a short period of projected financial results as forecasts but anything much over a 6-month period as projections. The difference here is partly semantic but it is important because the further out the projections go the more they are likely to deviate from what actually occurs.

Projections are therefore just that: projections. They are management's estimates of what might happen in the business. Projections differ significantly from budgets in that whilst budgets are expected to be achieved or beaten, projections are purely illustrative of the outcome given a certain set of assumptions about the future of the business.

The process of drawing up the projections from the business plan is set out in more detail in Chapter 15.

SUMMARY

13.28   Time spent on the business plan is time well spent. The business plan itself differs from the strategic plan in being far more action focused. Some business plans border on the military from the action view point. While this may be an extreme position the words often attributed to General Patten can act as a useful guide: *'A plan without actions is just paper!'*

Some business plans concentrate on the outline of what has to be achieved and are then supported by more detailed and rolling action plans.

Either way, the business plan document itself must be reasonably compact and readable. It will form the basis of the day-to-day management of the business. It must therefore be clear and understandable. This is particularly important where the document is also used as the basis for agreeing funding from a third party such as a venture capital house. Here, management will be measured against the actions and performance criteria set out in the business plan.

This can lead to a difficult juggling act for the management team: should the plan be watered down to the easily achievable to avoid missing key targets but risking devaluing the business now and making it less attractive to investors, or should it be aggressive but higher risk?

The answer depends on a combination of management's view of the likely risk levels and the investors' view of an acceptable level of risk versus their expected level of return. This is a case by case judgement and is one of the areas where good advice from professionals who are used to discussing investment opportunities with funders can be invaluable.

The other important point is that the business plan will be reviewed and revised more frequently than the strategic plan on which it is based. The basic guideline is that the plan should be followed and the results monitored until it is clear that the plan is not going to deliver. At this stage the plan should be revisited, solutions proposed and the plan formally flexed and re-adopted in its new form. This is not a sign of weakness (unless the plan has to be flexed too often) but rather a sign that management is in control and is willing to propose corrective action when required.

See the 'Appendix – Outline Structure for a Business Plan' over the next few pages.

Appendix

13.29

OUTLINE STRUCTURE FOR A BUSINESS PLAN – BIOTECH COMPANY USED AS THE EXAMPLE BUSINESS

Contents

1   Introduction

2   Executive Summary

3   SWOT analysis

4   Technology

5   Patent Position

6   Market Opportunities

7   Research and Development Plan

8   Business Model

9   Management Team

10   Critical Success Factors

11   Finance and Other Areas

12   Other Sections and Appendices

1. Introduction

This section should include the requisite disclaimers and other investor protection information required by EU and local laws.

Generally, the advisers can provide standard wording for this section depending on:

• Legal requirements.
• Target audience for the plan.
• Purpose of the plan (information or fund-raising for example).

While legalistic the information in this section is vital both for the company and the directors/management to ensure that they are not exposed to claims from investors or others.

2. Executive Summary

This section should summarise the key points about the business. The following structure could be used as a guide and should run to preferably four, or potentially five, pages:

Introduction to the business

Two paragraphs (maximum) setting out the focus area of the business including:

- Diagnostic/therapeutic/database/medical device or other focus.
- Key disease focus.
- Background of the technology.
- Business model (service to pure R&D to fully integrated).

Unique Selling Points

A maximum of 6 key bullet points explaining:

- Why the business's approach is unique.
- Why the products are needed.
- Where the value lies in the business.
- Scope of opportunity for the technology – range of potential products from a platform or range of potential partners/customers for a product.
- Any other key points that underline the value in the business.

Technology

A brief overview (2–3 paragraphs) of the underlying technology used in the business. You should assume good general knowledge of:

- Previous public company technologies.
- Bio-chemistry/small molecule/monoclonal or poly-clonal antibodies.
- Genetics/Genomics/Proteomics.
- Drug development process.

Any areas involving newly emerging technologies need explanations aimed at less technically knowledgeable readers. In general, think about communicating your findings to a first- or second-year undergraduate in a related subject.

Intellectual property

The source of the technology and terms of acquisition should be set out briefly.

Patent position and strategy for developing a patent wall or other intellectual property protection strategy should also be set out clearly. If not already evolved, some of the funds being raised should be earmarked for patent work.

Research/Development Plan

This section (3–4 paragraphs or better 2 paragraphs and a graphic) should set out the pipeline of candidates, their current stage of development and a timeline to potential market launch.

Potential investors will understand the standard development processes and the key regulatory authorities – if they don't they shouldn't meet the criteria to be investors!

Where there is a range of possible applications for a platform technology, this section should confirm the priority applications by including only those in the graphic. Other opportunities should be listed, maybe in a table, but it should be made clear exactly where the effort is expected to lie in the first instance.

Commercialisation plan/Business model

This section should set out clearly, either in words or graphics, what the business strategy is with regard to commercialising the research and how it intends to generate revenues.

Where partnering is highlighted as a potential revenue source market research should be adequate to provide a list of target Big Pharma or other players who make up a potential partner population.

Potential investors will understand the timescales so these should be set out with reasonable prudence.

This section should also set out, for the lead candidates, information on the potential markets. In the summary the information should be limited to 2–3 lines per product.

Management team

The key here is to ensure that the roles and the backgrounds of the individuals are made clear. Investors invest in management as much as anything in early stage technology businesses. Hence, it is vital to show a balanced team of science, development/partnering, finance and commercial experience.

If this balance is not in place it is necessary to explain how it will be achieved – for example by stating that part of the required funds are targeted on bringing in people. In a technology company it is worth acknowledging that stock options will be needed to help tie in new team members.

Finance requirements

This section should set out a high level overview of the finance plan. It should include some details on staffing levels by area and build up an overview of the cash spend.

It should also set out the cash requirements and the expected level of cash burn (ie the time between fundings). It is unlikely that investors will provide more than 18 months to 2 years of cash. At early stages of development it may be only 12 months with milestones for further tranches.

Unless already well developed it is not generally wise to include deals with third parties in projected revenues for the early years. Given the size of such deals they can significantly skew the funding requirement and at least if they are excluded then the funding should be adequate if they do not arise.

3. SWOT analysis

This section should set out as bullet points the:

- Strengths of the business, business model and technology.
- The weaknesses.
- The opportunities.
- The threats.

It has to be realistic at each level. There may well be 5 or 6 bullets per section and they are likely to be evenly balanced – many more strengths and opportunities than weaknesses or threats looks odd and unlikely.

4. Technology

The first full section should focus on the technology. This section needs to expand on the Executive Summary.

Key areas to be covered include:

- History of the technology (who developed it, who paid for the development, how it was acquired/spun out and why).
- Explanation of the basic mode of action of the disease and other features so that the reader can understand the basics of the technology.
- Broad overview of the range of potential applications for the technology.
- Explanations as to the reasoning behind the initial areas chosen.

In all these areas do not be afraid to use simple diagrams to explain modes of action, interactions, etc. Giving a clear explanation of the technology and its potential is key to getting buy-in from investors. Investors rarely invest in single product companies – they look for a portfolio of products or applications of technology to help spread the increased risk involved in investing in leading edge research.

However, you should try to keep this section, as with all of them, down to 4 to 5 pages if at all possible.

5. Patent Position

Patents are a key asset in a technology business. They are the security that the investors look for to underpin the funds they are putting at risk with management.

Hence, this section needs to set out clearly the current patent position, any known issues or prior art that could impact the position and the directors views on the company's overall patent position.

It may be useful to have a patent attorney review the position and write a paper, in place of this section, which could appear as an appendix.

The other area that needs to be covered is patent strategy – how patents and other intellectual property protection mechanisms will be used to build a stronger position for the company. Comments on opportunities to extend patent life should also be considered if they are likely to be both successful and give rise to significant extensions.

This may be a technically challenging section for the team to write. However, someone on the team has to have responsibility for the patent portfolio and if the task proves difficult then professional expert advice should be sought to help.

6. Market Opportunities

This section can be relatively brief for an early stage business but may be quite long for more developed companies.

The key here is to provide supported evidence for the size of the target markets for the products/candidates.

Each target area should be addressed in turn showing clearly both the size of the market, the route to that market and any competing products already on sale or known to be in development elsewhere. Where competitors are in place some analysis of their strengths and weaknesses together with a realistic assessment of their competitive position, particularly in relation to comparative technologies.

This section effectively kicks off the two to follow which build on the market size reasoning to illustrate the R&D plans and the business model for the company.

Beware of enormous totals in reports. The most accepted sources are organisations like the WHO or the UN who do not stand to gain from inflated figures.

7. Research and Development Plan

This section should set out in detail the R&D plan of the business. This needs to be a project plan based approach tying development activities into the related developmental milestones (eg toxicology testing or pharmacodynamics modelling) Again, graphical models or tabular layouts may be useful to give a clear view of:

- Lead candidates and targets in order of priority.
- Their status in development.
- The plans for them and likely introduction into trials or other verification processes.
- The development methodology being used.
- The regulatory framework under which the development is taking place, including the specific FDA/EMEA product type references which set the criteria.
- The expected end points and required measures.
- Commentary on why the technology is being applied first to these areas, including items such as the potential market size and existing competitor products (or those known to be in other peoples' pipelines).
- Commentary on complementary development (eg diagnostics to sit with therapeutics as a managed healthcare package or vice versa) and plans for that or partnering/outsourcing of it.

The section should then go on to tie the R&D effort into two further areas:

- Premises and equipment requirements.
- Staffing requirements.

Again, the section should set out a plan for building the team and acquiring the requisite premises with a timeline that ties into the R&D plans above. Take care to take account of lead times to recruit and get in the key people.

8. Business Model

This section should set out the business model for the company. The key here is to identify the revenue streams and their likely timings.

Key areas for consideration here include:

- The range of activities that the company will undertake itself.
- The range of activities it will outsource.
- The stage at which projects will be partnered (if at all) and the likely range of partners.
- The need for co-development on complimentary products (eg a diagnostic for an area with no therapeutic is only theoretically useful – together the value is significant).

Following on from this is an analysis of both the revenue streams (contracts with milestones and royalties, service fees, or actual product sales income for example) and the related cost base of the business. For example, if the model says that the company will manufacture but not sell its products (eg a number of diagnostic test kits which are made by one company but sold through the sales force of a partner) then the related costs include not only the manufacturing equipment but trained staff capable of maintaining a cGMP or equivalent facility.

Again, if a sales team is envisaged, a good analysis of the cost/benefit is needed to show why this is the correct route over a partnered approach. Particularly for early stage businesses it can be very difficult to show how the sales team will be kept busy with only one product and a relatively small target market.

This section is absolutely key to the investor. It tells them what the dynamics of the business will be, what results to expect and therefore what the risk profile is.

9. Management Team

Investors say time and again that the main thing they invest in in an early stage business is management. Hence, getting across to the reader the strength of the team and the quality of the team is vital.

This section should therefore set out in more detail:

- The proposed management structure down to the sizes of R&D or other teams.
- The basic number of people and the growth in numbers should be included in a graph or some other clear illustration.
- The roles of the key management and staff members should be set out – around a paragraph or two per role.
- Timelines for recruitment.
- Proposed salary and benefits packages by key role including share options or other tie-in mechanisms.

A complete team should be included in the structure including finance, admin and areas such as manufacturing experience even if they will not be there on day one. Again, it is worth setting out a timeline.

Do not forget to include non-executives and possibly an advisory board if they are in the plan.

As with all the other sections, the scale of operations should be made clear together with the financial implications of the structure.

10. Critical Success Factors

This section pulls the plans together by setting out in a single page the key actions needed for the business to be successful.

The emphasis here is on actions not concepts. Hence, the technology itself is unlikely to feature. The focus will be on areas such as:

- Monitoring the R&D activities.
- Monitoring and managing the approvals/regulatory process.
- Driving and then monitoring the patent position.
- Building the team in line with the plan as flexed for actual developments.
- Building partnerships and doing licensing or other deals.
- Getting the structures right (both internal and financial) to support all the other activities.

11. Finance and Other Areas

Cashflow projections

This section should pull together the revenue streams and the costs. It should set out the key assumptions on which the financial model is built and should explain why the directors feel that the assumptions are reasonable.

It should include a summary of the projections and from them show the level and timing of funding needed. All of this should be pulled together in a simple table in the text with the detailed projections left for an appendix.

For an early stage company the first three years should be monthly projections with a further two years done quarterly or half yearly. Do not include any fund-raisings at this stage. This helps to show the real cash need both in size and time.

(See Chapter 15 for comments on the periods and detail levels)

Structures

The structure of the business from a financial viewpoint should also be set out together with the aims of the structure from tax and other financial perspectives.

Control

Details of the financial control function should be set out, including responsibilities inside the business. High level comments on the types of controls needed should also be included. Examples include:

- Budgeting procedures on projects.
- Approval processes for costs and authority levels.
- Monitoring processes and key indicators for reporting to management.
- Cash management and payment authorisations.
- Finance involvement in partnering and licensing deals.
- Comments on the size and nature of accounting and other systems needed.

Reporting

The contents of the management reporting pack and the frequency of production should also be included. The emphasis here should be on reporting not only financial statistics but also R&D, licensing and other activities so that the Board gets a clear overview of developments in each period.

The timing of the publication of annual and any half yearly reporting should also be included.

Administrative activities

The section should also cover other areas such as personnel and IT. These should be explained and the size of the staff requirements here and in finance set out clearly.

12. Other Sections and Appendices

Other sections

Other sections may be needed depending on the activities.

For example, if a manufacturing operation is envisaged then there should be a section on that area setting out operational plans, premises and equipment requirements, staffing, regulation, etc. Likewise, the decision to have an in-house sales force would lead to the need for an outline sales and marketing plan for each of the products.

There are no hard and fast rules for what needs to be in a stand-alone section. However, if there is likely to be a director or a manager assigned to an area it should probably have its own section.

When creating these sections focus on the need for action plans rather than theory. Set out clearly what has to be done for the company to be successful and how that will be done.

Appendices

Basic appendices would include:

- Academic references on the technology and applications.
- Details of any existing agreements (eg for the purchase of the intellectual property, previous funding rounds, etc).
- More detailed competitor analysis and additional market information.
- Detailed financial models.

Others could include a third party review of the patent position/strategy or a third party expert's report on the technology and markets.

Business and Revenue Models **14**

OBJECTIVES

- To consider different business models and expand on the business model concept.
- To illustrate the revenue model approach.
- To show how these two areas and the rest of the business plan link into the financial projections.

Business models

14.1 In the previous chapter the concept of business models was introduced. These shorthand overviews are useful to capture the key elements of ways that businesses work and also, from the business planner's point of view, to act as a framework for testing the validity of the business concept and also the completeness of the financial projections.

However, they are, by their very nature, limited as they attempt to split the spectrum of models up into chunks for ease of analysis. In reality a business may use a hybrid approach or, at the very least, straddle the boundary between two neighbouring models. This is likely to occur unless the spectrum is salami sliced into an unreasonably large number of models. Hence, the models described below are, to some extent, caricatures of businesses – exaggerating the differences between the contrasting approaches – in order to show the variety of models available. It should not be assumed that these are the only models or that the apparent gaps between the models do not contain further options that merge factors from the two models either side.

Overview of the spectrum

14.2 The following overview diagram was introduced in the last chapter:

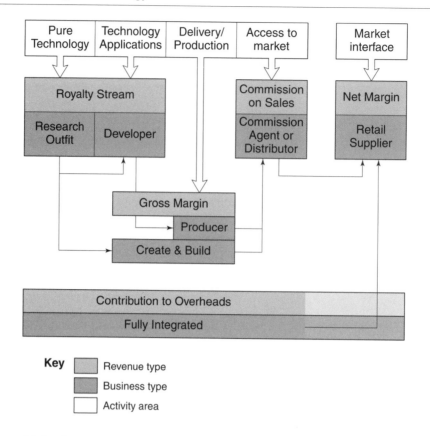

Figure 14.2 – the spectrum of business models

Source: PKF

It is worth looking at certain of the characteristics of each in turn. The key characteristics to consider being:

- The type of activity the business specialises in.
- The revenue type that this gives rise to and how it is comprised.
- How the revenue is generated.
- The cost base and make-up that the model dictates.
- Where the value is added.

In the case of these models the term 'revenue' is used somewhat broadly to mean the variable margin before fixed overheads. The different levels as applied to a standard profit and loss account being struck after:

	Royalty stream	Commission on sales	Net margin	Gross margin	Contribution to overheads
Turnover	✔	✔	✔	✔	✔
Cost of goods sold			✔		
Cost of materials				✔	✔
Cost of production labour				✔	✔
Production overheads				✔	✔
Warehousing costs			✔		✔
Distribution costs					✔
Sales costs			✔		✔

Research outfit

Activity

14.3 A research outfit specialises in discovery. That is, it does basic research and early stage development generating IPR as its major output.

Revenue type

14.4 Royalty stream comprising access fees (for access to the technology) potentially milestone payments during development and royalty income based on the sales of the end product.

Revenue generation

14.5 IPR licences granted to one or more licensees per technology.

Cost base

14.6 Largely around the research activities so costs include:

- Research staff
- Lab or research technicians   } a fixed cost because the salaries would have to be paid whether discoveries are made or not
- Laboratory costs
- Intellectual property protection
- Cost of mistakes/blind alleys

Other normal support costs including finance and general administrative support.

Where the value is added

14.7 In the creation of the IPR. The protection of the intellectual property means that the concepts and technology can only be commercially utilised by licensees.

Developer

Activity

14.8 Takes the relatively raw discovery and refines the technology in terms of:

- Use or usability.
- Production processes for quality, yield and quantity.
- Specificity or purity.
- Stability.
- Interface developments.
- User interaction.
- Regulatory approval (eg for drug development).

Revenue type

14.9 Royalty stream comprising access fees (for access to the technology) and royalty income based on the sales of the end product.

Revenue generation

14.10 On licensing of the technology and associated processes and data.

Cost base

14.11 The cost base includes:

- In-licensing fees for the base technology and associated royalties.
- Development staff.
- Laboratory and scale-up facilities and production engineering staff.
- Prototype/demonstration equipment costs.
- Regulatory approval costs.
- Clinical trials costs (for pharmaceutical or medical devices products).
- Cost of mistakes/blind alleys.
- Out-licensing costs including in-house business development team.

Other normal support costs including finance and general administrative support.

Where the value is added

14.12 By making the technology useable in offerings, ironing out the problems and packaging the technology and usage data.

Create & Build

Activities

14.13 The process tends to start part way through the discovery phase with a very early stage idea or even a problem that needs a solution. The business takes the idea through to a commercial solution with all the attendant testing and data building, but does not undertake the distribution and retail sales exercises, and may outsource any final bulk manufacture.

Revenue type

14.14 Gross margin as the business has product or services to sell – even when outsourcing a manufacturing element, the business maintains control over the sale into the distribution network. Alternatively, may charge a fee for work done and a royalty based on sales of an end product or costs saved.

Revenue generation

14.15 Sales into the distribution channels or service provision to companies closer to the final user. Examples of the service provision route include analysis businesses, proteomics and genome sequence analysis or cloning services.

Cost base

14.16

- Early stage in-licensing costs.
- Development costs.
- Production engineering costs.
- Scale-up facilities.
- Quality management.
- Equipment costs.
- Cost of mistakes/blind alleys.
- Out-licensing costs including in-house business development team.

Other normal support costs including finance and general administrative support.

Where the value is added

14.17 Through the provision of a complete solution to the user or into the distribution channel.

Producer

Activity

14.18 Takes the developed technology and produces it in a form that is easily saleable to end users. Most prevalent in the hardware and product areas of the technology sector but producers can be involved in other areas; for example, by being integrators of existing systems or by drawing technologies together in convergent areas such as telematics.

Revenue type

14.19 Gross margin as they have solid product to sell. Can be value added margin – the profit for knowing how to undertake manufacture or process the product.

Revenue generation

14.20 Either by direct sale to retailers or through distribution channels.

Cost base

14.21

- Capital equipment.
- Processing costs.
- Industrial stage scale-up capability and engineering skills.
- Incentivised sales force.
- Quality management.
- Stock holding costs.

Other normal support costs including finance and general administrative support.

Where the value is added

14.22 The knowledge of how to produce in quantity or to order.

Commission Agent or Distributor

Activity

14.23   Acting as the channel to the end reseller and feeding back into the development chain the needs and requirements of the end users.

Revenue type

14.24   Commission on sales. It is worth noting that often distributors' revenues appear to be sales of product. However, given that they add no value directly to the product their revenue is actually the margin that they make on the products, which is akin to commission.

Revenue generation

14.25   Sales into retailers and development of end markets for the products or services.

Cost base

14.26

- Stock holding costs.
- Distribution costs.
- Retailer credit.
- Marketing and retailer management costs.

Other normal support costs including finance and general administrative support.

Where the value is added

14.27   The contacts with the retailers combined with knowledge of the markets and how to access them.

Retail supplier

Activity

14.28   Sales to end users.

Revenue type

14.29   Net margin (ie after sales costs)

Cost base

14.30

- Premises costs.
- Stock holding and systems costs.
- Point of sale marketing.
- Potentially, customer credit.

Other normal support costs including finance and general administrative support.

Where the value is added

14.31   Knowledge of the market and by being the access point to the end users.

Fully integrated

Activities

14.32   Across the board from discovery to distributor or even retailer. Often fully integrated businesses stop short of actually owning shops. However, the growth of the Internet has allowed companies a new route to market for products so that businesses which traditionally did not sell direct are now starting to. Examples in this last category include hardware manufacturers such as the electronics giants Sony, Samsung and Phillips.

Revenue type

14.33   Contribution to overheads – everything above this level relates to the sales they make hence the revenue line is struck a long way down the profit and loss account.

Revenue generation

14.34   Sales to end users or through retailers.

Cost base

14.35 A combination of all the other business models to date. The only areas that are sometimes avoided are sales premises and the manufacturing related capital costs, if manufacturing is outsourced. In addition, as all the intellectual property related costs are incurred in-house, there are no in-licensing costs incurred.

Where is the value added

14.36 Across the board and through the proportional reduction in the overhead base – functions such as finance and administration, personnel and IT can be centralised thereby reducing the overall costs. In addition, the scale of the activities may allow for deals to be done with suppliers that further reduce the cost base.

Should all businesses aim to be fully integrated?

14.37 The points about the added value and the economies of scale raise the question of why any business should not aim to be fully integrated. The answer is complex and relates to the individual market that the business is operating in.

Reasons for adopting another of the business models include:

- Well developed distribution and retailer networks already in place for similar or complementary products.
- The need for a sales force that would, at least initially, be seriously under-utilised and might not be able to generate sales due to the lack of a portfolio of products or services.
- The cost of setting up manufacturing facilities.
- The inability to generate adequate volumes to justify maintaining an exclusive manufacturing or distribution warehouse network.
- The skill base of the business is in a particular area.
- Funders being unwilling to fund activities outside the skillset of the team.
- The increase in fixed costs to broaden the scope of activities would not be recovered by the additional margin.
- Management's desire to keep the business to a manageable size.

In each of these cases an analysis of the costs versus the revenue streams generated by expanding outside the selected model would, most likely, show little if any return for the investment that would be needed.

A number of technology businesses originally set out with the intention of becoming fully integrated and have ended up changing their model to better fit the sector or skills available. British Biotech is one example of a business which had a stated intention of becoming fully integrated that is now focusing on the pharmaceutical equivalent of *Create & Build*. On the other hand certain businesses have changed their model in the other direction. Examples from the biotech/pharmaceuticals sector include Shire and Elan where acquisitions have spread their activities further down the value chain and, most recently, broadened them out at the development stage.

Revenue models

14.38   The revenue types set out above all have different profiles and the combination of the source of the revenue and the profile of that revenue for a business represents the revenue model. The concept of revenue models is very important when it comes to modelling the revenues in financial projections. In addition, the revenue model highlights the areas of the business that need to be most closely monitored.

In the same way as in medicine all deaths are caused by the heart stopping beating, in business all failures occur due to lack of revenues. It may appear that businesses fail through over spending but in fact over spending is really just cash exiting the business faster than the revenues can be generated to replenish the bank account.

Summary of revenue model characteristics

Revenue model	Revenue source	Revenue profile
Royalty stream	Third party licensee	Initial access fee, often followed by milestone payments related to achievement of functionality based measures. Ongoing revenue arises from charging a percentage of end user sales (the royalty itself). Costs are risk based as there is always the risk of failure either in the initial development stages or during the milestones phase. This is generally financed by risk equity either from investors or, in longer established businesses, from within the business itself – sometimes referred to as *private venture* or PV spend.
Product sales	Distributors or end users	Revenue arises at the point of sale. Hence, costs are incurred before the sale is made (manufacturer or purchaser of the products) and the business must carry this working capital cost. The working capital requirement is increased by the fact that customers are given credit before payments are received.
Service revenues	End users or other intellectual property developers	Revenues arise during the process or, if the service output is productised, at the end of the service. Hence, as for product sales, working capital requirements arise.

(Continued)

Revenue model	Revenue source	Revenue profile
Support/maintenance revenues	End users	A fee is levied on the basis that, if needed, support or maintenance will be provided to the end user. If the quality and reliability of the product is good then the costs should be very low, generating good margins. Indeed, some businesses can charge not only a fixed rate maintenance fee but also for work done when support is required. Generally, support and maintenance revenues are add-ons to the initial product or service sale.
Retainers	End users	A regular fee charged which gives the user the right to a certain amount of the business's time. Over this set level time will be charged for.
Commissions	Producers	Some distributors do not buy stocks from producers but rather act as agents selling on behalf of the producer. On these occasions, as they never own the stock that the end user buys, they earn their income by charging a proportion of the sales value, or a fixed fee per sale.

Linking into the financial projections

Identifying and codifying the revenue model(s) being adopted is a key step in developing the financial projections.

Financial Projections   15

OBJECTIVES

- To provide more detail on the financial projection process.
- To consider the contents of financial projections.
- To explain the difference between projections and budgets.
- To provide a possible methodology for creating financial projections.

Developing financial projections

15.1 Developing a financial model to reflect the business plan is a complex activity. Moreover, the financial projections have to reflect not only the level of expected revenues but also the business and revenue model and the associated cost base. The projections are a vital part of the business planning process as they are a form of mathematical proof of the viability of the business, its offerings and its business and revenue models.

It is important to develop the projections at an adequate level of detail. However, it is very easy to end up going into too much detail, resulting in a model that is both hard to follow and extremely difficult to audit for errors. Finding the middle path is about balancing a positive wish to understand the detail of the figures with the need to retain clarity and usefulness at the high level.

There are a number of software packages available to aid the creation of projections. Some of these are sophisticated and very flexible but some are inflexible and may not be suitable for certain business models. Generally this is because they are designed as simple budgeting tools for traditional businesses rather than because of any fundamental flaws in the software. The alternative is to use a spreadsheet to build up the model from scratch.

Due to the complexities of modelling and the need to ensure that technical items such as VAT and payroll taxes are correctly included, it may be worth discussing with your accountants whether they can assist in building the model. You will, however, need to be closely involved in the process and understand how they have built the model – after all, you will be using it and need to be able to explain it.

Contents of financial projections

15.2 Just as in a set of statutory accounts (see Chapter 32 for information on the content and layout of accounts) there are three main statements that should be included in a set of financial projections:

- Projected profit and loss accounts.
- Projected balance sheets.
- Projected cashflow statements.

It is generally best to follow the standard Companies Act layouts for the profit and loss accounts and the balance sheets and the standard set out in Financial Reporting Standard No 1 (Revised) for the cashflow statement. That way most readers will be able to interpret the projections with a reasonable degree of accuracy.

In addition to these three items there should be:

- Details of the key assumptions made in drawing up the model.
- Details of any key items, such as capital expenditure or share/debt issues.
- Explanations of any unusual items or key points for understanding.

When creating the model there will also be a series of other calculation items such as:

- Depreciation of fixed assets.
- Invoicing generating debtors and turnover and cash collections from debtors.
- Cash payments to creditors.
- VAT calculations and payments.
- Roll-out of any known prepayments (such as rent or rates).
- Staff numbers and payroll costs.

It is generally best to keep these on a separate worksheet, as while they are of limited interest to some readers, investors may wish to check the validity of the basic calculations.

Period to be covered

15.3 One of the most frequently asked questions is what period the projections should cover and in how much detail. The answer is that it will vary from business to business depending on the nature of the activity and the timespan of the research and development in particular. It will also vary depending on the stage of development of the business.

What follows are therefore guidelines rather than rules and the formats suggested should be flexed to meet the requirements of the situation that the business finds itself in.

Initial pre-formation/start-up projections

Quick to market and, potentially, short lifecycle offerings

15.4 With this type of offering it can be very difficult to see out much beyond 18 months to 2 years.

The projections therefore need to cover, say, a 2-year period by month.

It is worth noting that the projections probably also need to include a number of follow-on offerings showing that the business is regenerating itself ahead of the initial offerings coming to the end of their lifecycle. It may be that the business does not yet know what the follow-on offerings will be. In this case it can be worth testing the model by extending the projections out for a further period by using the direct cost and revenues from the initial offering as guestimates for the follow-on offerings. When doing this be careful not to simply reproduce the initial costings verbatim as this would not take account of things such as:

- Developers stopping work on the initial offering and moving over onto the next.
- Set up costs for the business that will not necessarily be incurred again – this will include capital asset purchases as well as some one-off costs.
- Sales team building costs that may not need to be incurred again.

Build, test and sell offerings

15.5 These offerings take some time to develop, often one to two years, before they can be introduced to the market. Related to this is the fact that a longer lifecycle of sales is normally needed for these products to generate the level of return needed on the development investment.

For offerings of this type the projections need to go out between three and five years so that they show not only the build and test phases but also the generation of sales adequate to create a real return on the development investment.

If possible it is worth doing the projections by month but, for year 4 onwards, it may be more realistic to do quarterly projections as the level of estimation involved will be high this far out.

Discover, develop, trial and launch offerings

15.6 Some offerings take significant periods of time to develop to market launch. Pharmaceutical products are good examples of this with development and trials taking upwards of seven years. The revenue potential of these offerings is generally extremely large (blockbuster drugs have target revenues well in excess of $1m per day) but a positive outcome of the discover, develop and trial process can be highly uncertain at the outset.

Here investor focus is often not on end launch; the risks related to getting there are too high. Instead they are focused on intermediate milestones such as the phases of drug trials discussed in Chapter 12. Hence, revenues, per se, are not necessarily important to them.

What is important is the rate of spend – or *'cash burn'* as it is known.

> **DEFINITIONS**
>
> *Cash burn* or *burn rate* is a measure of the speed at which cash is used in the business. It is usually measured on the basis of £ per month. A related measure is the *terminal date* which is the date at which, given current cash and the current burn rate, the business will run out of funds. *Drop dead date* is also a term used with regard to cash burn and relates to the point, some time before the terminal date, when the business has to have generated or raised new funds if it is to continue in business.
>
> The drop dead date falls ahead of the terminal date as, under UK law, the directors of a company should not continue to trade the business if they can see that the business will not be able to pay its debts as they fall due. Hence, the drop dead date is effectively the date at which the directors see that the debts incurred to date equal the cash on hand with no expectation of the cash position increasing.

The projections here will therefore focus on the cash burn. Generally, the projections will go out to around five years with at least three years being monthly and the rest quarterly.

As businesses that develop this type of offering tend to run a series of either similar projects using the same technology or projects around finding solutions to a related set of user issues there is another way of drawing up the projections: draw up project by project or programme by programme projections (where a programme is a set of related projects). This approach is often extremely useful to show how resources such as laboratory space, manpower, etc will be utilised over time. There should still, however, be a summation of the project or programme projections both for cashburn by project on an overall business basis and in the form of the standard financial statements mentioned above.

Ongoing projections

15.7   Projections are not a one off exercise. The business needs to monitor and refine the projections on an ongoing basis. This can often be done alongside the budgeting exercise (see later for the differences between projections and budgets).

The refinements will reflect both the developments to date and any changes in the expectations for the future. The ongoing projections may be drawn up for a variety of uses such as:

*   In advance of a further fund-raising round.
*   To assess the impact of new development programmes.
*   To assess the benefits of a merger, acquisition or sale.
*   To review the impact of sub-target performance or delays and issues faced in development or sales.
*   Post-flotation communication with analysts and brokers.

The period and the level of detail required will therefore vary depending on the use. However, in most cases the scope of the projections may well be similar to the initial projections.

Projections versus budgets

15.8 There is often confusion about the difference between projections and budgets. In format the two can be very similar but the underlying intention is different.

	Projection	*Budget*
Time span covered	Often up to 5 years.	12 to 18 months ahead.
Objectives	To set out what the future could be.	To set out the short-term activities in a form that can be measured.
Types	• Base case (the key expectations). • Worst case (usually includes delays or slow sales). • Upside potential (highlights areas that could be introduced or that could give rise to better the expected outcomes).	• Base (the outcome that management is signed up to). • Target (an outcome above the base case used to avoid complacency). • Stretch (an outcome probably just outside what could be achieved and often used as a motivator). • Working capital (can be in two forms either a simple recalculation from the base budget or a form of worst case to ensure that adequate funds are available).
Contents	• Profit and loss account. • Balance sheets. • Cashflow statements. • Assumptions. • Key notes.	• Results, balance sheets and cashflows in the format used for internal reporting. • Key Performance Indicators. • Commentary. • Normally included in the monthly reporting as a comparative.
Intended users and uses	• Top management. • Investors. • For discussion with analysts and brokers for post-float companies.	• Top and middle management teams. • Used as the benchmark for measuring actual performance and progress.
Other features	Once agreed are set.	Likely to be reviewed and revised regularly during their life to reflect changes in position. May even be rolling monthly budgets that always look out a set period of, say, 12 months.

Clearly there should be a link between the projections and at least the first year base budget but, beyond that, the numbers shown in the two may diverge. It is quite usual for target or stretch budgets to be drawn up to motivate departmental performance, showing financial outcomes well ahead of the base budget or the projections.

The difference between a target budget and a stretch budget is really one of how the middle managers manage their departments and what level of challenge they respond to. Some managers like to strive to achieve something that may just be beyond reach – a stretch budget – whilst others prefer to feel that the target is achievable but challenging.

Another key area of difference between projections and budgets is the way that they are drawn up. Often projections are done solely by the top management team who collect basic data from around the business for the projections. Budgeting is a more spread-out exercise with the involvement of middle managers being quite common. Indeed, progressive budgeting techniques include an approach sometimes referred to as departmental self-budgeting.

DEFINITION

Departmental self-budgeting is the concept whereby a central goal is set out by top management. This is, in effect, the business plan with some very high level indications of expected financial outcome such as:

- Overall levels of profitability.
- Cash resources available for investment.
- Launch dates for offerings (equates to the start of revenue generation for that offering).

With this information the individual departments are sent off to draw up their own budgets for the period. These departmental budgets are then submitted centrally and consolidated to ensure that they provide the required outcome.

This approach implies that the departments will talk to each other – for example new product development will discuss the offerings with engineering and sales to ensure that the offering will be delivered to specification and on time with the required sales collateral. By building a series of interacting budgets that have been produced by the departments themselves and not imposed by top management the theory is that the whole of the business will work together, treating each other as internal customers and suppliers. The end result is therefore a business that is functioning much more closely and efficiently as departments *want* to help each other rather than passing problems (particularly problems that could impact their own department's budget) on to other departments.

Departmental self-budgeting is a process that needs to be introduced over time. It takes time for the middle management team to get to grips with the concepts and the need for interaction. Indeed, where the process is deemed to have failed it is probably either because the middle management could not move to a team-based culture or that not enough support and training was provided in the early periods to help them change their mindsets. Businesses that have successfully introduced departmental self-budgeting have identified significantly reduced budgeting costs (mainly through reduced time spent by management on the process), increased buy-in to the budgets from the business and an increased sense of ownership of the delivery of the financial as well as the technological output of the business. Some have taken the process to the point where the initial briefing is now quite short, the departments being so used to the mechanics that they take over the process from thereon and deliver a complete and cohesive budget to top management in a very short time.

Approaches to creating financial projections

15.9   There are many ways to go about producing projections. What follows is only one method and can be adapted and modified to match personal preferences.

However, there are some common features about any successful approach to turning what has up to this point been largely words, in the form of the strategic and business plans, into figures:

- Rigorous process.
- Development of comprehensive assumptions.
- Regular tying back of the figures into the plans – using the plans as support.
- Regular sense checks on the figures.
- Some form of checklist to ensure that all the areas are considered.

Top down or bottom up?

15.10   These are two terms that are widely used in financial planning. They refer to the two polar extremes of approach to the process:

> **DEFINITIONS**
>
> - Starting with a high level model and drilling down to generate more and more detailed supporting sub-layers (*top down*).
> - Starting with the detailed levels first and consolidating them into a unified whole rather like the normal accounting process itself (*bottom up*).

An extension of the bottom up approach is zero-base budgeting.

> **DEFINITION**
>
> *Zero-base budgeting* is the process of starting from a clean piece of paper and building up a new model for each period.

Zero-based budgeting contrasts with the normal and possibly more practical approach of starting with an existing model and adjusting it into line with expectations. An example of the difference would be staff costs. A normal approach in an existing business would be to take the current monthly cost and only adjust it when staff numbers are expected to change. A zero-base approach would involve looking at the necessary staff numbers first, then the costs per staff level and building a model from that basis.

While this may seem a minor difference it can be significant for two reasons. Firstly, a zero-base approach allows management to check the logic of the status quo rather than just accepting it and, secondly, it helps to ensure that all the costs and revenues have been identified rather than assuming that the current model is accurate.

An initial set of projections is by definition therefore zero-base – regardless of whether it is top down or bottom up.

Cost or revenue?

15.11   The next question is the starting point for the projections. Should this be to work out what the costs are or what the revenue is going to be? To a certain extent the answer will depend on the nature of the business but in general the answer is: Yes!

This seemingly ridiculous answer is actually very sensible for one main reason: it is vital not to let the one drive the other. The projections are one of the key tests of the viability of a business proposition. Hence, revenue and costs have to be realistic and hence, again, these two elements must be assessed separately.

The danger is that, if costs are done first, the temptation will be to ensure that the revenues provide an adequate return on those costs. If the revenues are done first then the costs may be manipulated to generate the right result. Both of these approaches, which are as much the product of human nature as deliberate, have the potential to ignore reality.

Inflating revenues to cover costs, which is generally what happens in the first scenario, is a route to having inadequate capital and, in extreme cases, the business failing at an early stage when it becomes clear that the revenue will not be generated.

Reducing costs to match the revenue, the normal response in the second scenario, may doom the business to never having an offering to sell. Without adequate resources it may be impossible to progress the development to timetable and there is a high level of danger that the business will run out of money before it can start to make sales.

So, the answer is to look at each separately and then bring them together. By assessing the revenue and the costs separately the viability of the whole business can be considered.

This does not mean that it will work the first time. It is likely that the costs will include some 'nice to have' items that could be removed without seriously damaging progress or maybe second-hand equipment would be adequate to start with instead of brand new, generating a saving. Either way, it is likely that some iterations of the two halves will be needed before the two dovetail together. The important thing is that the questions are asked from the perspective of maintaining the whole position of the business, not that one is flexed simply to match the other.

A possible methodology for creating projections

15.12   What follows is not intended to be proscriptive as an approach nor is it intended to be all encompassing in terms of details. Given the wide range of technologies and business models that fall into the definition of technology businesses it would not be practical to provide examples for all of them – it would take several volumes the size of this book.

Instead, this is intended to be more of a thought process with pointers to key areas for consideration and, alongside them, common failings.

Stage 1: Document the assumptions

15.13   Assumptions come first. They drive the models and the formulae that underpin the projections.

DEFINITION

Assumptions are statements of assumed truth. They are unchanging throughout the period covered by the projections, unless there are known factors that are modelled in to change them – but even the occurrence of these known factors may actually be an assumption. Assumptions generally have two implications to them: quantity and timing.

The first source of assumptions will be the business plan. It should be read through in detail and everywhere that there are statements relating to income or expenditure there are likely to be assumptions. Examples of these business plan related assumptions are statements like:

- 'There will be four projects in this area each of roughly equal size.'
- 'Each team will consist of a project manager, a senior technologist, two technicians and a technical administrator.'
- 'A review process will be built in at this stage'.
- 'The development of this product will take six months of work for the team to reach beta.'
- 'A double blind trial will be required with approximately 200 subjects.'
- 'Production models should cost around £150 each to produce using an outsourced manufacturer.'
- 'This initial product will be ready for launch in month 10.'

Each of these statements has a financial impact which needs to be translated into an assumption. The first five items are cost related and, for some of them, timing related. For example, will the four projects in the first statement all run concurrently or sequentially? If concurrently then the timetable is compressed but the cost of running the projects will fall into a quarter of the time period that would be the case if they run sequentially. However, the total cost of the projects may be the same in the long term.

The last item is interesting in that it has both cost and revenue implications. The revenue implications are that, with launch in month 10, revenue should start to arise in month 11. The cost element is less obvious. Launching a technology offering can involve significant expenditure with promotional activities, launch events, sales material to produce, sales teams to train and customers to visit. Even for discovery businesses there are costs involved around their equivalent of a launch. Here, rather than sales and marketing costs, the costs relate to identifying and visiting potential licensees, negotiating with them and drawing up legal contracts – but they are real costs just the same. In both cases the timing implication of the assumption is that the cost will occur in or before month 10 – ie before the revenue starts to be generated.

The next source of assumptions is in the background research information. This will provide information on items such as:

- Likely selling prices.
- Likely markets and profile of sales volumes from launch.
- Certain costs such as approvals, mandatory testing (such as the mandatory EMC testing required for electronic equipment) and intellectual property protection costs.

This is likely to leave a number of practicalities still uncovered either because they are taken for granted in the business plan or because they are potentially too low a level of detail for the business plan narrative. Areas to consider at this stage include:

- Manufacturing costs per unit (particularly if manufacturing in house) including both purchased materials, processing costs and staff costs.
- Premises costs including rent and rates, fit out costs, security and basic desks, chairs and tables.
- Infrastructure costs including heat, light, power, telephones, communications and Internet access and water rates.
- Administrative costs including the costs of the directors, legal advice, accounting advice and audit and tax compliance work, intellectual property protection advice, business and other insurance.
- Marketing budgets and postage costs.
- Capital equipment budgets and timing of requirement including not only laboratory and manufacturing equipment but also computers and other equipment needed by the support staff – associated to this is the setting of depreciation policies (see below).
- Insurance costs, including both insurance for property and physical assets, employer's insurance and insurance related to the business's products or services – it is worth taking advice on what insurance is needed as some forms, such as professional indemnity insurance which is needed by consultants, are specialist areas with potentially significant premiums.
- Initial payments to acquire intellectual property rights and the setting of amortisation periods (see below).
- Joining fees for associations and other bodies.
- Set up costs including company formation costs, rent deposits, other up-front costs and one-off expenditure.

'Depreciation' and 'amortisation' are accounting terms used to denote the charges to the profit and loss account made to reflect the use of capital assets or intellectual property by the business over time. The charge, which reduces the profits of the business, is there to reflect the fact that physical assets are used up over time and that intellectual property has a fixed life (patents being 20 years for example).

Depreciation and amortisation lives are always estimates but should reflect the estimated useful life of the underlying asset and any amount expected to be recovered by sale at the end of that life.

Examples of average useful life estimates include:

Asset class	Useful life estimate
Leasehold premises	The life of the lease.
Freehold premises	25 to 50 years depending on the type of building and the use of the building.
Laboratory fit-outs	The life of the lease of the premises or around 10 years whichever is shorter.
Other leasehold premises fit-outs or improvements	The life of the lease.
Laboratory and test equipment	3 to 6 years depending on the nature of the equipment.
Manufacturing equipment	5 to 10 years depending on the nature of the equipment.
Computers and related equipment	3 years.
Desks, tables and chairs	5 years.
Motor vehicles	3 or 4 years.
Patents	The remaining life of the patent cover.
Trademarks	Case by case consideration (see Chapter 34).
Goodwill	Case by case consideration based on the underlying remaining lives of the offerings acquired with the business (could relate back to patents) or the period of guaranteed retention of key members of staff or contracts with customers.

Items *in italics* are subject to depreciation, all other items are subject to amortisation.

DEFINITIONS

Goodwill is an accounting concept to explain the difference between the total value of all the business's assets less the total value of its liabilities (known as its *net assets*) and the value of the business to a buyer.

For example, if all a business has in its balance sheet are:

- Equipment and other fixed assets worth £10 million.
- Amounts due from products sold of £3 million.
- Stock on hand of £1.5 million at cost.

(Continued)

> • Amounts due to suppliers of £3.5 million.
>
> Then the net assets of the business are £11 million (£10m + 3m + 1.5m − 3.5m). If a buyer is willing to pay £20 million for the business then the goodwill that the buyer would have to recognise in their accounts is £9 million.
>
> Goodwill exists within almost all businesses but for accounting purposes only arises on the acquisition of a business and, under recent UK accounting standards, it must be recognised in the balance sheet and amortised over its estimated useful life. Basically, like patents or trademarks goodwill is an *intangible asset* – one that cannot be physically touched. Goodwill can theoretically be negative – in effect the seller is willing to give away assets to get rid of the business as it is worth less than its net assets.

It is now very unusual for anything other than freehold land not to be depreciated or amortised.

Timings

15.14   The last key area to consider involves certain specific timing issues. These include:

- Payment periods allowed to debtors and how fast they will pay after that time – this is usually done by way of an assumption that sets out what proportion of the debtors will pay in each month after sale.
- Payment periods allowed by suppliers and when their invoices will actually be paid – a similar time profile is often used in models.
- VAT periods – this will vary depending on the type of business and advice should be sought from an accountant on this point.

Building the model

15.15   This takes time, care and attention. Logic checks should be undertaken regularly and key data checked back to the business plan and the assumptions.

Most assumptions translate reasonably easily into figures. The key elements being those of the assumptions themselves: quantity (here reflected by value) and timing.

Formulae can often be developed for repetitive items, such as staff salaries or monthly rent. They can also be extremely useful to build into areas where there may need to be refinements as part of the revenue versus costs comparison. However, be careful not to make the formulae too simplistic in their relationships. It is very easy to drive all the costs from revenue (simply by allocating proportions of revenue to the major cost captions and to profit) but this can lead to unrealistic outcomes if the revenue figures are altered.

Some people will dive in and build the model using the real numbers. Others prefer to build the model and formulae first, test it using simple numbers where they can calculate the outcome easily, or at least estimate it to ensure that the model is making sense, and then go back and insert the real numbers at the end once they are happy the model is working correctly. This second approach has real merits, particularly where the model may be complex with a series of projects or multiple offerings to project.

In the same way, being aware of what sensitivities may need to be run on the model will help in its design.

DEFINITION

Sensitivities are different scenarios that alter either specific numbers or relationships between numbers and therefore give rise to different end results. They are used for a number of purposes including:

- Calculating the impact of delays or changes to the plan.
- Calculating downside or upside scenarios and their impact on cash requirements.
- Calculating whether a specific project is worthwhile to the business as a whole.

Tips and hints

15.16   There are a number of items that tend to get forgotten or overlooked when people work on projections. These are just some points noted from experience:

- Employers' national insurance contributions (NIC) are a cost on top of salaries.
- NIC and PAYE are paid over to the Inland Revenue the month after the salaries are paid.
- The cost of providing pensions in accordance with the Stakeholder Pension requirements needs to be reflected.
- Timing and impact of VAT.
- Recruiting staff costs money – it can often cost 30% of first year salary.
- People cost money – be realistic about their salaries and check with recruitment firms on salaries and packages if you are not sure.
- Generally staff cost twice their salaries by the time that you add in the other direct costs that will be incurred.
- You cannot assume that customers will pay on time and should, somewhere, include a contingency for some not to pay at all – very few will pay up front.
- In the first periods of trading it is more than likely that suppliers will want cash up front from the business until it proves it can pay its way.
- Rent is generally paid in advance.
- Rates are paid over 10 months not spread evenly over 12.
- The timing and profile of hire-purchase and leasing costs may not be even across each month; often there are up front elements or final payments to be made.
- Bank interest is lower on cash in hand than it is on overdrafts so a simple calculation based on the cash, whether positive or negative, will not work – the exception to the basic rule is when the cash is invested rather than just sitting in a bank account when the interest rates may be equivalent.

- Do not squeeze the contingency element out just to make profits – you *will* have forgotten something.
- Do not forget the administrative and general costs – they may not directly add to the development of the technology but they will be incurred.
- The founders need to be able to take something out by way of salary if they are working in the business.

Analysing the Market　　　　　**16**

OBJECTIVES

- To explain the importance of market analysis.
- To provide guidance on market analysis.
- To introduce potential market analysis approaches.
- To provide suggestions of potential sources of market information.

The importance of market analysis

16.1　Market analysis is key from four main viewpoints:

- It supports the revenue assumptions that are part of the proof of whether a technology is commercially viable.
- It assists in the formulation and finalisation of specifications.
- It provides information on competitors and competing technologies.
- It helps to determine the access points and the entry method for the offering.

It is therefore not an area that can be undertaken on the basis of instinct or gut feeling. The results of the analysis will set the direction not only for development of the technology but also for its marketing and thence the revenue of the business itself.

All of which makes the analysis challenging. There is, however, a further challenge: with new technologies there may well be very little obviously available information. Quite often inventors and founders of technology businesses facing this problem have a tendency to say that, after all, if the technology is truly ground-breaking, no-one has been there before and hence the market information cannot exist.

　　This is, however, a dangerous argument on two fronts. Firstly, the statement raises the question as to whether there is a reason why there is no technology already out there and secondly, if you cannot identify the market then you cannot sell to it.

If it does not exist, why not?

16.2 This is the blunt way of asking the first of these two questions. It does need to be answered and the more consumer oriented the technology the more important the answer is. For a consumer product aimed at the mass market the likelihood is that someone has thought of the idea before; and there may therefore be a good reason why the product has not been launched.

This is not to say that there are not a variety of good reasons why the ideas did not make it to the market. The main one is inadequate technology. It may be that the technology that you have is the missing link that makes a mass market application possible. An example of this is the mobile phone. The basic technology for analogue mobile phones had been around for a significant period of time – after all, personal mobile radio systems had been in use well before mobile phones. Integrated circuit technology was available and the concept of cellular network structures was well understood. The problem was power and more specifically battery technology.

The initial mobile phone services were launched in the late 1970s; like the Bahrain Telephone Company's network which went live in May 1978 and which was closely followed by a 10 cell test system in Chicago run by AT&T and an 88 cell system in Tokyo launched in December 1979 and rolled out across Japan in 1984. The phones for these systems were generally either carphones running off the vehicle's electrical supply or bulky portable units quite unlike the compact handheld and pocket-sized devices of today.

The problem was that battery technology had not kept pace with the advances in electronics. What was needed was a twofold solution – lower power systems and better batteries. The first came about through improvements in the cellular infrastructure and, eventually, through a move from analogue to digital transmission as used in GSM, GPRS and UMTS (often referred to as third generation or 3G) systems. But the real advances were in battery technology.

The advances in the technology produced both smaller and more powerful batteries with longer charge lives. Not only that, but the batteries could be mass produced at a price that made them commercially viable. By mid-2001 lithium-ion technology had produced mobile phone batteries with standby times of over 600 hours and talktime of 10 hours plus. All this in a battery that measures 65mm by 40mm by 5mm.

The market opportunity that spurred the development of the battery technology came from two areas. The first was the level of interest shown by the public in the early stage test systems through their exposure in the press and on television. This showed that there was the opportunity to create a viable mobile phone market if the technology could make the phones more practical and easier to carry around. The second was the seemingly unrelated Californian vehicle emission regulations. These required the car manufacturers to start introducing vehicles that did not rely on petrol or diesel for their fuel. The obvious solution was to go for electric cars – they had been around since the nineteenth century – but the problem was battery life.

The combination of these two towering commercial imperatives drove the technology advances.

Who is going to buy it?

16.3 The second half of the dilemma is the key question of where the income is going to come from. It is possible to create brand new markets – the mobile phone industry effectively did that – but it is generally immensely expensive and very high risk. The size of the market has to be significant enough to make it a worthwhile exercise.

Consideration of the issues involved highlights a series of hurdles that need to be overcome:

- The market has to be persuaded that they need the offering.
- They have to be shown that it is worth paying for – mass market creation is easy for a free product but generating revenues is not so straightforward.
- The production facilities have to have adequate capacity to meet a mass market demand but they have to be in place up front.
- The market has to be communicated with.
- The channels to market have to be persuaded that there is a market and that it is big enough not only for them to make a margin but to make enough money to generate the profits they need.
- Sales materials have to be produced and salespeople trained.
- The post-sale support systems and infrastructure have to be in place to support the product in the market.
- Spares and repair facilities have to be set up and personnel trained.

And all of these may need to be done in multiple territories if the product is going to be viable.

In other words, a mass market opportunity may be worth creating but those are few and far between. Even success stories like the Dyson vacuum cleaner actually piggy-backed on existing markets – in James Dyson's case the well developed vacuum cleaner market. Dyson built the business himself because he could not persuade existing manufacturers to acquire and develop his patents. Truly groundbreaking market generation activities have been as momentous as electricity, the car industry, radio and television, personal computers and the telephone. Others, such as video recorders, CDs, DVDs, in-car satellite navigation systems and even the Internet have built on existing identifiable markets.

What is more, the first half of the equation comes back into play. If the market opportunity is really so big why is nobody doing it yet? In Dyson's case they were, but not as well as he believed his technology could.

First mover advantage and first mover disadvantage

16.4 By using the Internet, reading appropriate publications including trade and academic journals, and attending related exhibitions and conferences it is generally possible to identify potential or actual competitors.

The identification of competitors is not necessarily a negative. Indeed, from a potential investors' point of view it can be a positive piece of news. The fact that others are working on the same problem or looking to address the same market can be a confirmation that there is a real market need and, more importantly, a real market.

However, the identification of a competitor does not of itself, provide proof of a market. The competitor may be following a hunch or simply be in a position to take a risk driven on by the desire to see their technology completed.

There can be real negatives, of course, such as the identification of similar technologies where there may be patent conflicts or identification of competitors who are, or appear to be, significantly more advanced in their development.

The second of these may be an opportunity if the patent position suggests that you have prior claim. In this case, it is worth considering whether the competitor should be approached about the potential breach of patents. A strategic decision needs to be made about when to make such an approach. It may be that, by waiting for the competitor to complete development, the eventual deal on the intellectual property can include not only a licence to the competitor with the fees that go with it but also access to their completed version thus significantly reducing development costs.

The concepts of first mover advantage and first mover disadvantage, sometimes referred to as second mover advantage or follower advantage, pick up on these points.

DEFINITIONS

First mover advantage is the benefit that the first person into a market can gain from simply being first. The advantages can include:
- Initially 100% market share but significant market share even after competitors come in.
- Extended revenue periods – if a market has a 5-year life and the first mover comes to market 6 months ahead of the competition they have a 10% longer period to earn revenues in.
- Profile and publicity helping to build brand image.
- Adoption as a standard forcing the other to match the standard and, potentially, therefore to require licences from the first mover.

First mover disadvantage relates to the downsides of being first. Examples include:
- Having to generate the market can have a significant cost where a follow-on business has lower costs as it has, effectively, gained free advertising from the first mover.
- Having to build the routes to market with the associated costs.
- Resistance to a lack of choice and, when the second player enters, significant intial fall off in sales as people try the alternatives.
- Not having anyone to learn from – it is rare for a business to get everything right first time from a zero base position. Followers can watch and learn and avoid the problems while, potentially, thinking of better solutions.
- Customer feedback – this can be positive but it can also be a chance for the follower in that negative feedback builds up in users' minds (even if only minor items) and, if that can be avoided by the follower, they have a perceived quality advantage over the first mover.
- Not having the standard that gets adopted – the functionality or simply the weight of commercial support behind alternative approaches can undermine the first mover's advantage.

(Continued)

> • Loss of momentum – technology businesses often thrive on internally generated momentum (the buzz of the place, the thrill of launching the first product and seeing it taken up) but when competitors enter and market share automatically falls from 100% then morale and internal momentum can slip as well.

There are examples of both first mover advantage and first mover disadvantage in the technology and related arenas. Amazon, the on-line book and now general e-tailer, is often cited as an example of first mover advantage. Certainly, as far as recognition is concerned they seem to hold that position. However, it has been at a real cost with significant losses generated in the first years of trading to build up the business and be competitive.

Netscape has been put forward as an example of first mover dis-advantage. The original internet browser they launched took hold quickly and was widely adopted. However, the recognition by Microsoft of the market potential, and the industrial might that Microsoft could bring to bear, meant that the Microsoft Internet Explorer browser quickly eroded Netscape's lead. The same is true to some extent of Apple and the PC. Apple had, with the Macintosh and particularly the Mac OS operating system, features and ease of use that the PC took many years to come close to. However, the combination of the might of IBM and internal difficulties at Apple led to the PC becoming the more widely accepted personal computing platform, particularly when married to Microsoft's Windows operating systems.

Realistic competitor analysis is both useful and positive. It should identify both the strengths and weaknesses of the competition and provide ideas for the market size and value and the way to enter the market itself.

So how can a market be identified?

16.5   On occasions the market parameters can be relatively easily identified from existing market research, available statistics, or simple research in the market itself.

Other techniques include the *vapourware* approach – announcing the technology well in advance of any likely launch date (but only after patent applications are submitted, of course). The objective of this approach is to flush out basic underlying interest and, potentially, funders for the technology as well.

The announcement should, if the PR is well handled, provide evidence of the level of interest in the offering. The BBC television programme Tomorrow's World is a favourite for this form of early stage publicity which often generates significant feedback. Trevor Bayliss was one beneficiary of the programme. He had struggled to find a manufacturer to produce and promote his clockwork radio but, following an appearance on the programme in April 1994, he was approached by Christopher Staines and Rory Stear who helped set up a company in South Africa.

However, the PR angle has to be carefully thought through and handled if the interest generated is not to be turned into frustration because the product really is a long way from the market.

This last point causes significant problems in the pharmaceutical and biotech arenas. Here, publicly traded companies have to announce the results of the trials that their drugs are undergoing. Announcements usually start with the announcement of a Phase I trial – the earliest involving humans. The announcement of a drug trial for a disease where current treatment is either only moderately effective or is inherently unpleasant tends to give rise to a significant number of calls to the company from people who are themselves sufferers or know people who are. The problem is that the public and the general press do not always understand the time periods to product launch for drugs. Having to inform ill people or their relatives that, far from this being a cure for them here and now, the drug is actually still years away from the clinic is reported to be one of the most harrowing experiences that drug company staff have to go through.

What is worse is that the relatively regular stream of press stories about '*wonder drugs*' and particularly '*cures for cancer*' does not only raise hopes in the sufferers, they also generate frustration, disappointment and ultimately a lack of belief in the sector. The time taken, from the initial press story around the discovery of a potential candidate to it reaching the market means that sufferers may never get to see the product in use. The fallout rates through clinical trials are so high that the new drug may, in fact, never make it to the market at all. Such a climate of disbelief in the ability of a sector to deliver can slow down existing programmes and even stop new programmes of research from being funded.

So, the PR needs to be handled well, and the feedback analysed thoroughly, taking into account that only those people who are both interested and motivated to make contact will provide feedback.

But what if there does not seem to be any market information?

16.6 Where the information appears to be almost entirely lacking there are a number of ways of approaching an estimate of market size and value. These are generally based on a process of:

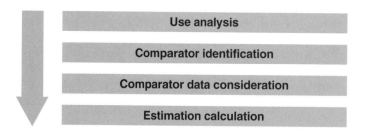

Use analysis

16.7 This exercise identifies the end users of the technology and the use(s) that they will put the offering to.

The outputs of this analysis will include determination of the user type:

- Domestic users (the offering will be used either at home or in another private environment such as in a car).

- Commercial users (the offering will be used in a business but not as part of a further product).
- Industrial users (the offering will be used in the production of another offering).
- Developers (the offering will be built into another offering).
- Research and Development users (the offering will be used by the user to research other technologies or develop other technologies).

It will also specify the use of the offering by the user type and identify any features that may differ between the requirements of different user types. For example, woodworking equipment can be domestic or industrial – both home woodworkers and furniture manufacturers use table saws and bandsaws but the industrial ones are designed to be used throughout the day, five or more days a week, where the domestic versions are designed for lighter use.

This type of comparative difference appears in a whole range of products. The cathode ray tubes in traditional computer screens are, in essence, the same as those used in televisions. However, despite the increased time spent in front of the television, the tubes designed for PC usage in businesses have to be capable of much more extended on-times and on an everyday basis. Likewise, industrial vacuum cleaners designed for use in building or hotel cleaning have to be more rugged and their motors less prone to overheating than those designed for home use.

Comparator identification and Comparator data consideration

16.8   This stage requires some creative or lateral thinking. The object is to identify existing products with similar end user profiles and similar or complementary uses.

Take as an example the domestic dishwasher. If dishwashers did not exist how could you estimate the market potential?

A first estimate might be the number of families with their own accommodation. However, a problem arises in that this is the maximum total population rather than either an addressable market or an estimate of the likely annual volume of sales.

Hence, looking around for a comparator product you could select domestic use hobs and ovens. They have the same end user profile and a complementary use in that, with the exception of the preparation of certain craft materials or fishing baits, they are used to cook the food that will give rise to the pots, pans, cutlery and crockery that will be cleaned in your new dishwasher product. This starts to narrow down the market and provides a first estimate of sales volumes.

But, a significant proportion of hob and oven sales are as packages to builders for new properties. What is more, if your user analysis for the dishwasher is realistic it will have identified that it is a luxury product and not a staple, unlike a hob and oven. Hence, not everyone who has a hob and oven will want a dishwasher and it is unlikely that any but the most expensive houses will therefore be sold as new with dishwashers ready fitted.

However, the number of new houses built each year is a known figure so the new-build related sales can be estimated and deducted from the total sales figure.

The user analysis suggests a certain socio-economic profile of purchase for the dishwasher. This can be used to work out the proportion of the population in the socio-economic bands identified as potential users.

A further simple calculation can be made at this stage by applying this proportion to the sales volumes for the hob and oven. However, a more sophisticated exercise may be possible. If the statistics for hob and oven sales available are analysed into price bands, it may be possible to estimate potential market size by looking at hob and oven sales in the same or higher price ranges to those proposed for the dishwasher.

Again, this is not necessarily a straightforward exercise. For example, it might be that the stratified hob and oven sales information excludes cookers of the Aga/Rayburn type. If this is the case, consideration has to be made as to whether this will significantly skew the market estimate.

Any number of other factors may need to be considered.

Whilst the dishwasher example is, in some ways, frivolous it is indicative of the care and thought that needs to go into the process.

Estimation calculation

16.9   The final step is to take the information and assess it carefully. Out of this process should come a calculation of the estimated market size.

Where possible the process should be sense checked to ensure that no erroneous assumptions have been included. This element is rather like a logic puzzle in that each assumption along the way needs to be re-assessed and the impact of adjustments considered in the light of the differences between the comparator and the actual offering. The logic of the calculation should be laid out clearly so that those making the investment decisions can identify the key elements.

Market research

16.10   There are numerous organisations who undertake market research. Some have a specific technology focus and may well be of use to businesses looking to qualify or confirm internal analyses. The quality of the work done is often a factor of the quality of the briefing, the timetable and the funds available. It is difficult for any organisation to undertake good and extensive market research without adequate amounts of each.

Off-the-shelf research reports can be useful. These vary from industry association data collection through general market research reports or periodic commentaries to detailed sub-sector reports. If the focus is tight enough and the methodology of the research is rigorous enough then these reports can provide very good support for market size and other market information.

Commissioned market research is likely to be both the most useful, but also far and away the most expensive, option. In addition, picking the right firm to undertake the market research can be a difficult exercise. Those with the appropriate knowledge may wish to re-use the information gained elsewhere in their portfolio, particularly if they already undertake research in overlapping areas which is generally available. Alternatively, wholly independent firms may not have access to the knowledge of the technology needed to undertake the work.

Market research can also be a two-edged sword. Good market research identifies not only the strengths in the market but the weaknesses. It should highlight factors that will make either entering the market or market development itself difficult. Examples might include:

- Issues over public perception (such as the problems with Genetically Modified Organisms when applied to food).
- Geographical dispersal suggesting that access to the market may be overly costly.
- Conflict with an existing standard or platform (it will be hard work introducing a software tool running on a Windows NT™ platform into an industry sector that has traditionally run AS400™s or UNIX™ machines).
- Historic acceptance times for new ideas or traditionalist tendancies.
- History of long trial periods or products with low or no sales.
- External factors such as current or potential regulation.

All of these factors need to be appraised, considered and addressed in the business plan. While some of the points may seem insignificant they still need to be thought through as they may be very significant indeed in practice.

Other sources of information

16.11   There are myriad sources of market information. A significant number are now available on the Internet and some are even available free. Others are available by download from the information owner, such as Datastream, or are available for subscription. Libraries can also be useful sources of market information with some of the more expensive reference works available such as the Compass company information materials.

What follows is not intended to be a comprehensive list of resources but should at least help stimulate thoughts on where information may be found:

- Internet search engines such as Google.com or Northernlight.com
- Industry associations – on their web-sites or by direct enquiry.
- Government statistics – from the web-sites or by direct contact with departments, the Office for National Statistics or other agencies such as the Patent Office, local inward investment offices or development agencies.
- Chambers of Commerce.
- Bank of England reports.
- Parliamentary records, such as Hansard or, if you can gain access through your MP, the Palace of Westminster's library or even through written questions in the House.
- Competitor or complementary product web-sites.
- Published accounts of companies in a sector.
- Merchant bank analyst research notes on companies in the sector.
- Market research reports (public and private).
- Consultancy reports such as those published by the major management consultancy firms, the major accounting firms, lawyers and patent agents.

SUMMARY

16.12   Market analysis is a key element both in providing evidence of the viability of the technology being developed and in targeting the technology's development so that it matches the requirements of users. It therefore forms a central plank of the business planning process.

It is not, however, a one off exercise. Market research should be kept up to date as far as possible and certainly reviewed regularly during development and after launch to ensure that the technology is still heading in the right direction and that there are no changes in the market environment that require adjustment to the plan. Examples of the need for change driven by the market range from the negative position of the launch of an alternative technology in advance of yours, or one with better performance characteristics, to the entirely positive such as when a legislative change creates an even bigger opportunity or requirement for the technology.

Too often technology companies skimp on market research – possibly because it does not seem to relate to the technology itself and can even drive changes in the development plan. This is short-sighted given the value that could be lost by making decisions that move the technology away from the market or by developing something that never has the chance of reaching or generating a market of adequate size to support the cost of development.

Tax Strategy $\quad$ **17**

OBJECTIVE

- To provide an overview of the elements of strategic tax planning.

Introduction

17.1 Strategic tax planning is something which far too few businesses consider – whilst tax should not be the driver for the way a business is operated, the tax position of the business can make the business more attractive and more competitive.

The aim of strategic tax planning is to ensure that the tax liability of the business is minimised sensibly throughout the life of the business – as far as possible. The key is tax awareness, rather than tax avoidance.

- **This chapter is not intended to provide you with an absolute method of implementing a tax strategy. Each tax strategy must take into account the needs of the specific business, and should be developed with professional advisors. This chapter aims to give an overview of the areas which need to be considered and the questions and concepts which should be kept in mind.**

Advantages of tax planning

17.2 Tax planning has a number of advantages for a business, including:

- *Lower tax payments* – this is an obvious statement but, particularly in the early stages of profitability, planning will ensure that the business does not suffer from unnecessarily high tax bills; similarly, losses can be maximised to reduce profits later.
- *Investment* – a company with a lower effective tax rate will usually be more attractive to investors as the after tax returns should be higher.

Tax planning strategies

17.3 The overriding aim of any tax planning is to complement and enhance the business objectives; tax should not be the main concern when developing the overall strategy of the business, but it does need to be incorporated within that overall business plan.

When should tax planning begin?

17.4 The answer to this question is: as soon as the business is even thought of – it can be difficult to back-track to place a company in a better tax position if the planning is left too late.

For example, if Company A buys some ideas developed by another company ('Company B') which does not want to exploit them (perhaps because they do not fit the core business of Company B) but, instead, transfers the intellectual property in the ideas to Company A in exchange for a cash lump sum, that has already set out a chain of events which have tax implications:

- Should the intellectual property be brought directly into Company A?
  - (i) Putting the intellectual property in Company A, mixing it with the other assets of that company, may make it more difficult to sell on the same intellectual property later.
  - (ii) Alternatives include:
    - Forming a separate company (a subsidiary of Company A) to acquire and exploit the intellectual property. If the ultimate intention is to sell off or float the business related to that intellectual property, having it in a separate group company already could make the sale or float far easier to achieve – certainly in comparison to trying to unravel that element from the overall business of Company A. If the development costs are expected to lead to losses which are planned to reduce the profits of Company A it is worth noting that losses in subsidiaries can still be relieved against profits of the parent company or other qualifying subsidiaries.
    - Forming a joint venture with Company B. This does depend on Company B's co-operation but, rather than incur the immediate capital expenditure on acquiring the intellectual property, a joint venture would allow Company B to invest the intellectual property in the joint venture in exchange for a share of that joint venture. This requires far less of the capital of Company A and also spreads the risk involved with any new business. However, care needs to be taken that any joint venture structuring does not endanger other areas of tax planning, such as the ability to qualify for investor relief under the Venture Capital Trust (VCT), Enterprise Investment Scheme (EIS) or Corporate Venturing Scheme (CVS). In addition, qualification for the Enterprise Management Initiative (EMI) scheme for share options may be put at risk if the structures are not put together carefully.

- Should the intellectual property be acquired outright?
  - (i) If Company B insists on an outright sale, Company A has no option if it wants to acquire the intellectual property. However, if Company B is flexible on this, other alternatives may be appropriate.

(ii) Licensing the intellectual property may be more tax-effective. This will depend on a number of factors, in particular whether Company A has any trading losses – if it does, and it wants to use up the losses, then it may be appropriate to license the intellectual property rather than buy it outright. In this case, care needs to be taken to make sure that the licensing transaction is not treated as a capital purchase.

And when should it end?

17.5 Tax planning is an ongoing process – a strategy, once put in place, has to be reviewed regularly to ensure that the company is operating the best strategy open to it in the circumstances. External factors can change – new measures may be introduced by the annual Budget or new investors may be brought in. Internal factors may also change – increasing revenues may make some tax planning ideas more cost-effective.

What taxes need to be considered?

17.6 All areas of tax need to be considered in the planning – it may not be possible to do anything to make the company more efficient in each area of tax, but nonetheless, they all need to be considered. It is not possible to give precise details of what is particularly appropriate to consider, as all businesses will have different needs, but the following are general areas of tax that may well apply:

Income tax/Corporation tax

17.7 Reducing an employee's tax bill by, for example, offering approved share options can improve employee retention and make it easier to attract employees. In some industry sectors, employee benefits such as these are expected. Additionally, improving an employee's taxable position will also usually benefit the business by reducing the amount of employer's National Insurance Contributions which need to be paid.

Withholding tax

17.8 Is the business paying royalties to a foreign intellectual property owner? If so, withholding taxes may need to be deducted. The business needs to be aware of this and ensure that it complies with the Inland Revenue reporting requirements.

Where payments into the business may be structured as either capital or revenue, consider which is more appropriate to the business – the way in which contracts and licences are drafted, for example, can make all the difference. Rather than simply accepting the outcome, it is worth considering from the start of a transaction what the best options are for the company.

• For example, a company with capital losses may want to use them by ensuring that payments received for a disposal are capital rather than revenue.

- Conversely, a company with trading losses may prefer to ensure that a licence results in revenue, rather than capital, payments.

Capital allowances and other reliefs

17.9 The business should ensure that it is claiming all available allowances – such as industrial buildings allowance, first year 100% allowance against computers, etc, and general capital allowances on plant and machinery.

Particularly important to technology businesses are research and development allowances – these are only available to companies.

For small and medium-sized technology businesses, research and development tax relief may be available – this should be claimed in order to reduce any taxes, or increase available losses for future relief.

A repayment can be claimed, instead of increasing losses, but this needs to be considered carefully. In particular, balance the *total* cost of carrying the relief forward as a loss against the repayment received. Ultimately, the needs of the business will be paramount – if cash is needed, then a repayment is probably the right option. If, however, the company does not need the improved cash-flow, and the company's cost of capital is not high, then it may be better overall to let the relief be taken forward as losses and used to reduce future tax liabilities.

Capital gains tax

17.10 Ensure that all appropriate reliefs are taken. Balance the benefit of the relief against any future impact – most forms of relief operate by postponing a gain rather than reducing it. Those reliefs give an immediate benefit but a longer-term liability.

For example, the proceeds on the disposal of a business asset can be rolled-over into the acquisition of another asset. This postpones the gain on the original asset. If a business disposes of an asset with significant proceeds, it may not have acquired – or be intending to acquire – enough new assets within the time limits to mop up the gain. One option is to purchase assets to absorb the gain; however, the purchase of such assets may cost more than paying the tax on the gain if they are to absorb the proceeds – if the business does not actually need the new assets, it may be more cost-effective simply to pay the tax.

VAT

17.11 Businesses should consider whether they ought to register voluntarily. Where a significant amount of VAT is being incurred when setting up the business (eg on equipment and services provided to the business) it will probably be worth considering applying for VAT registration voluntarily.

Voluntary registration enables the business to recover VAT incurred; it also requires the business to charge VAT on the VATable goods and services which it sells.

The benefit of the VAT recovered needs to be balanced against the potential competitive advantage of being able to make supplies without charging

VAT – although, if the business is successful, that competitive advantage will be shortlived!

Consider whether overseas registration is appropriate – if the business is making significant supplies to overseas consumers, it may be appropriate to register for VAT in one or more other countries. Once registered, the local rate of VAT can then be applied to sales in those countries.

Other areas of tax

17.12   Other areas of tax which should be considered when planning include business rates, stamp duty (generally, only when considering the tax planning for a specific transaction – day-to-day business operations do not usually incur stamp duty).

Maintain a holistic approach to planning

17.13   Tax planning needs to be part of a holistic approach to business planning for the entity – tax permeates all areas of business, and changing something in one part of the business can affect other, apparently disparate, areas. Tax is not simply a number in the profit and loss account, or the cheques to the authorities.

Practical considerations which need to be included in any tax strategy include:

Keep it simple, and keep it flexible

17.14   It is far easier to defend – and maintain – a tax strategy which is well understood and clearly documented.

Flexibility is essential – whilst all businesses should have some form of goal for their tax strategy (whether short, medium or long-term) reality dictates that things do not always run to plan. A flexible tax strategy will ensure that it is not necessarily financially painful to adapt to changing circumstances.

Consider the sophistication of management

17.15   Complex tax planning requires a degree of experience from the management team who will run the day-to-day operations of the business. In particular, any tax planning which relies on part of a group being non-UK resident will need experienced management to ensure that the non-UK resident companies are not inadvertently brought into the UK for tax purposes.

Consider the needs of investors – present and future

17.16   The business should have some idea of how it wants to develop in future. Often, one or more independent investors will be needed in order to have access to adequate funds to develop the business.

Any tax planning should consider – as far as possible – where and when investment is likely to be needed. If an investor is likely to be located outside the UK, it may be worth planning to locate some or all of the assets of the business outside the UK, in a location that is likely to be tax-efficient for them. This can make the business more attractive to investors. However, this may endanger qualification under VCT, EIS, CVS and EMI schemes.

Consider the overall costs of a tax strategy

17.17 It is not worth saving £100 in taxes if it costs £101 to obtain that saving. The benefit of any tax strategy is the tax advantage gained, *less* the costs of obtaining that advantage.

The costs include not only the costs of compliance with requirements for returns, for example, but also matters such as the cost of capital employed in obtaining the advantage – see the example regarding research and development tax credits above. The cost of capital which needs to be held to support a loss can make all the difference between taking the relief as an immediate repayment or leaving it to roll forwards as a trading loss.

The costs of compliance should not be underestimated – putting into place an employee share option scheme, for example, involves not only the initial professional fees involved in setting up the scheme but also the ongoing costs of maintaining records and (in some schemes) maintaining a trust, with the associated compliance costs.

For *bleeding edge* tax planning, the costs of unravelling the strategy need to be considered. For some companies, generally those with very experienced management who are not risk-averse, a novel tax strategy may be taken as a calculated risk – but the calculation of risk must include all factors. The strategy needs to be such that the tax savings, which may only be short-term, are balanced against the costs of putting the strategy together and then reformulating a strategy once the Inland Revenue has blocked whatever loophole was being exploited.

Match tax planning with commercial reality

17.18 Some tax planning may seem appropriate from the outset – a business developing intellectual property which is believed to be likely to attract an overseas buyer, may want to consider setting up a subsidiary to hold the intellectual property outside the UK from the outset. Generally, the intellectual property would be transferred when worth very little – to minimise the capital gains tax liability in the UK – and then sold once developed.

However, even where this seems to be a good idea, it is generally worth waiting a little while to ensure that – apart from any other considerations – the intellectual property is actually worth developing. It is not unheard of for a project to have to be abandoned because of some technical difficulties with aspects of the idea. In that case, the costs of setting up overseas and dealing with overseas tax issues such as transfer pricing and controlled foreign companies, will have been wasted.

It is often worth waiting for some proof of concept, developing the intellectual property a little further, before making the related tax planning more complex – this approach may cost a little more in terms of capital gains tax, but is likely to cost less in compliance and professional fees overall.

SUMMARY

17.19 Overall, tax must be considered as an essential part of the business's strategy – tax strategy should not drive the business but, equally, it cannot be tacked on as an afterthought to the business planning. It should balance the needs and resources of the business with the potential tax advantages – long- and short-term – always keeping the overall strategy flexible.

Strategy for E-business $\qquad$ 18

OBJECTIVES

- To provide an overview of e-business.
- To help in the consideration of the extent to which e-business is appropriate for the business.
- To highlight the risk areas.
- To highlight technical concerns, particularly over the tax and legal implications of e-business.

Introduction

18.1   E-business – electronic business – is a fundamental shift in the way in which businesses operate; e-commerce is a very small part of e-business, and certainly not the most significant. E-business permeates the whole of a business, throughout the value chain from raw materials to customers.

E-business is about using Internet technology to do business, including:

- Reducing cost throughout the value chain.
- Improving customer relationships.
- Speeding up the business.

Despite the spate of publicity over dotcom failures in late 2000 and 2001, the Internet is not dead. Far from it. Now that the rush of blood to the head seems to be over, the value of the Internet to business is beginning to be explored properly, in depth, and with due consideration to the requirements of businesses.

Essentially, the Internet is no longer an optional extra – businesses cannot afford to ignore it. It may not need to be the cornerstone of the business – and, in most cases, should not be – but nonetheless is a business tool in the same way as the telephone and fax machine. Increasingly, customers expect to be able to at least find information about the business on the Internet.

Developing an e-business strategy

Why go online?

18.2   The first question in developing any e-business strategy is straight-forward – why does the business want to be online?

The answer may be as simple as this – 'because it's expected' – or as complex as this – 'because we want to develop a fully integrated end-to-end business solution which services global customers seamlessly'.

The question needs to be considered carefully – why does the *business* want to be online? It is not enough to go online just because the IT department want to be allowed to play with webservers – in fact, that's a good reason not to go online.

Areas which need to be reviewed include:

The business environment

18.3   Consider whether the business is operating in a sector where most customers or suppliers routinely use the Internet for researching purchasing decisions, even if they do not actually place the orders online. Without an e-business strategy, the business's reputation and goodwill – part of the brand of the business – will suffer if the business environment expects a particular minimum deployed level of e-business.

The business needs

18.4   Any strategy – e-business or otherwise – needs to be developed to complement and enhance the business objectives. A strategy that is developed for its own sake, without close reference to the business strategy, is pointless and unlikely to be effective.

E-business can result in savings for the business – for example, by using e-procurement, or by improving the delivery of digital products. The competitive advantage that may be available through e-business improves the business's value to investors and founders.

The actions of any competitors

18.5   A business cannot ignore the actions of its competitors – that is not to say that everything a competitor does should be copied or reacted to but, equally, if a competitor is having a degree of success with a particular business model then the model should be analysed to determine what can be learnt from it.

What customers are demanding

18.6   An increasing number of customers, particularly overseas, prefer to communicate via e-mail – it is far easier than using the telephone where there can be a language difficulty (most people can read a foreign language better than they can understand it spoken) and/or a time zone obstacle.

Some customers have begun to demand that their suppliers deal with them electronically, usually via an extranet. Such customers (including, for example, many supermarkets) may have used an earlier form of electronic communication (such as EDI) with some suppliers. This was rarely forced on all suppliers because, before the advent of internet technology, the systems were expensive to implement. The relative inexpensiveness of the Internet means that these businesses can now refuse to do business with a company that does not follow its requirements. Where the customer forms a significant part of a company's business, the company needs to implement e-business or lose the customer.

What is the business trying to achieve?

18.7 Having established why the business needs to go online, the next consideration is what the business expects to achieve from doing so – identifying these targets will help to establish the basis for the e-business strategy.

Increased speed

18.8 Internet technology allows a business to respond to customers – and the market in general – far more quickly.

Reduce costs

18.9 Using internet technology can reduce the cost of a number of elements of the business, including:

- *The sales process* – if customers can, in effect, serve themselves by using e-business the cost of processing sales to those customers can be cut considerably; the savings compared to dealing with mail or telephone orders can be significant;
- *Stockholding* – creating an integrated supply chain through the business can significantly reduce the need to maintain high levels of stock; linking the purchasing system through to the ordering system can allow for a much more sophisticated approach that is also more cost-effective to the business;
- *Operations* – particularly for large companies, using internet technology allows for centralisation of a number of functions. Having a single, central, unit is generally far more cost-effective than duplicating the function in each location.

Connectivity

18.10 Being closely integrated with business partners within a strategic alliance network can provide significant advantages – including increased loyalty and knowledge-sharing. The co-operation between companies in a network is much more efficient than the closed protectionism of a single company; each link in the network will have its own distinct competencies that are enhanced in the network by the complementary competencies of the other network members. E-business technology allows the network to communicate and interconnect fluidly.

Service

18.11   Customers increasingly expect to be able to communicate with their suppliers whenever necessary – perhaps even 24 hours a day, 7 days a week. E-business allows the business to meet those expectations without the cost of maintaining a physical contact.

E-business can also enable a business to remain active 24 hours a day, 7 days a week – this is particularly the case for international businesses, who can maintain contact between the group companies by using e-business technology – such as an intranet, where the business knowledge can be stored and developed as part of the Knowledge Management activities, available for all parts of the business at any time.

Reach

18.12   E-business gives small businesses – and even larger business – a global reach that previously required considerable expense to establish and maintain. This can be important in enabling the business to survive market cycles.

Delivery

18.13   More and more, e-business is being used to deliver the products and services of a business – particularly in the software sector but, increasingly, in all knowledge-based sectors. The costs of delivery are nominal – once a digital product or digital version of a product has been developed it can be delivered at effectively no cost. Using this mechanism will also help to improve the customer relationship – it allows for a much faster delivery, and also enables the business to supply enhancements and additional material in a pro-active manner.

Data collection

18.14   E-business is a growing mechanism for collecting business-critical information – this need not be simply customer information; increasingly, e-business is being used to collect technical information, such as patient record data in clinical trials.

The ability to collect data in this way is invaluable – it reduces the time delay between the data being gathered and being available for processing; it also minimises errors in re-entering information because it reduces the number of times the information needs to be entered.

Sample results

18.15 E-business is playing a larger role in conducting drugs trials and developing treatments; the potential cost savings make the move to e-business essential: getting a drug to market one day earlier by saving one day in the clinical trials process is often equivalent to generating an extra $1m in revenue.

E-business technology can be used, as described above, to collect patient data for processing. This allows such trials to be considerably more global than before – trials have traditionally been conducted in a relatively small geographic area to deal with the problems of communicating with the doctors involved in running the trials.

Now, the trials can be truly multi-centre; this will be particularly important when testing the newer generations of drugs which are tailored to the individual. Testing globally will allow the effectiveness of the tailoring to be measured and confirmed.

Integration of e-business to diagnostics/treatment methods is not far off – trials have already been conducted which allow surgeons to perform operations remotely, using e-business technology to manipulate instruments in an operating theatre in another country. Eventually it should be possible to use technology to directly diagnose certain conditions and prescribe treatment.

Collaborative work, using the Internet, will improve speed of analysis – and this is not limited to collaborative work between universities and other research centres. Trials involving a significant amount of computer processing can be carried out using a multitude of computers in parallel; these need not all be connected with the research operation. For example, a recent experiment looking at developing a cure for cancer required the use of substantial computing power – it found it online, in the idle processing time of thousands of private computers connected to the internet. The owners/users of the computer signed up to receive data for processing – sent directly over the Internet – which was processed by the computer automatically whenever the computer was not otherwise busy. The results were returned to the project co-ordinators – again over the Internet, and another set of data sent out to be processed.

Formulating an e-business strategy

18.16 E-business implementation can range from a simple web-site which effectively acts as advertising to a fully-integrated business which is capable of executing and fulfilling the orders without the need for any intervention. There are several stages in between – a business can be placed anywhere along the curve: strategic planning ensures that the e-business element is where it needs to be, not simply pushed into a possibly inappropriate place.

E-business is an *extension* of the business – not an entirely new creation. There *are* a very few businesses for whom e-business is the business, but these are rare. Even Cisco, one of the most developed online businesses, still relies on partners for a significant proportion of its business and makes a significant amount of its money through selling hardware.

Four principal stages of e-business are set out below, ranging from a business that makes no use of e-business technology to a business that, through e-business technology, operates in a way not previously possible.

Description	Traditional	Twin track	Technological	Totally digital
Proposition	E-business is not a necessity.	What *could* we do with e-business?	What *can't* we do with e-business?	If we can't do it with e-business, we don't do it!
Product	Tangible – even if the product is intellectual property, this is recorded, published and delivered in physical form	Still tangible – new product lines are increasingly delivered digitally in parallel.	Product can be delivered both in tangible format and/or digitally, depending on the type of product.	Product is digital.
Processes	Traditional – little if any use of electronic processes other than for communication.	Use electronic processes for communication and new business processes.	Electronic processes actively introduced.	Purely digital processes as far as possible.
Position	No use of internet technology made.	Limited use of internet technology.	Some degree of internet based technology.	Internet technology used throughout the business, underpinning the business model.

None of these models is necessarily intrinsically better than the others; each is appropriate in different businesses and different sectors. The traditional model may become less relevant as businesses become more interconnected, particularly within the area of high technology. Some businesses will remain largely traditional – a small independent company producing medicines, for example, will have little need for e-business beyond communication – medicines cannot easily be digitised!

Businesses need to consider which description best fits their *current* position, and then determine whether that is in fact their *optimal* position – in either case, they will need to implement an e-business strategy to ensure that their approach to e-business reaches and/or maintains that optimal position.

Systems and business

18.17 The business needs to review whether the systems and the business itself are properly aligned with the optimal position. This includes staff – whilst some e-business changes can be outsourced, the business will still need to have some staff who are able to implement and develop the approach.

Flexible approach

18.18   E-business is notoriously fast moving, and an approach that is appropriate today may well not be appropriate in three months time. Technology changes – what is not possible now, because the technology is too expensive, may become commonplace tomorrow as prices fall. For example, the price of computer memory has fallen by 75% in the last few years.

   This rate of change also needs to be factored into each *make versus buy* decision. Research is particularly important in the infrastructure areas of the business as software and systems that cost many thousands of pounds to develop in-house may be available off the shelf in six months time for only hundreds.

   New business models are being developed based on e-business – once a pioneer has developed a business model that works and generates a real return, elements of the model may be incorporated into the planning as appropriate. Alternatively, the business may want to be the pioneer, exploring new business models – these should be developed in a separate part of the business. This contains the risk involved, to avoid affecting the rest of the business.

Customer/supplier relationships

18.19   If the customers/suppliers of the business are unable to deal with the business electronically, the approach will need to take this into account. There are two options – if the business is strong enough, the customers/supplier may be able to be forced to accommodate an e-business strategy. However, few businesses are in that position. The more realistic option is to ensure that the strategy will be able to scale up when each customer or supplier does become able to do business electronically.

   The customer or supplier may demand e-business capacity – if essential to the business, this may force the strategy to accommodate a faster change to incorporate e-business than may otherwise have been contemplated.

SUMMARY

18.20   E-business is now a fact of life for companies. It is easy to rush into e-business decisions on the basis of the excitement around the technology. Instead, e-business decisions should be based on an e-business strategy that sets out where e-business fits into the overall business plan.

   When selecting e-business solutions or developing them it is important to take into account the sophistication of the communications and IT equipment that actual or potential customers, suppliers or partners use. Some technologies work wonderfully well over 100BaseT networks inside the business or even over cable or DSL. However, they may not be so useful and may not even be viable if the other party uses a 56Kbps modem.

Of the four types of adopter the Traditional business is becoming a less and less acceptable position – particularly in the technology field. Even in the life sciences e-business solutions are bringing about rapid change in areas such as bioinformatics and collaborative computationally based drug design.

   Few businesses can now afford to ignore e-business and many find that the benefits go far beyond their initial expectations.

Intellectual Property Strategy

19

OBJECTIVES

- To show how the different areas of intellectual property fit together.
- To introduce the concept of IP walls.
- To introduce the concept of an intellectual property strategy.

Introduction

19.1   Chapters 22 and 23 in *Technical considerations* section of this book on intellectual property set out both the different types of protection available depending on the nature of the intellectual property and the process for applying for a patent under the UK system.

They also make the point that not all IP has to be protected and that some that technically could be protected may be better treated as being trade secrets.

This chapter looks at the need to set out a policy for which areas should be protected and which should not. In addition, it considers the strategic background to that policy.

IP areas

19.2   A single piece of technology can include a number of different pieces of intellectual property. The IP broadly falls into five types:

- Hardware
- Development and process
- Software and presentation
- Manipulation and testing
- Combination of the above

Figure 19.2 (overleaf) gives examples of these different types of IP and the way that they overlap in some real world examples. The common feature in the real world examples is the combination.

The diagram also includes two other aspects of an IP strategy: public and private managed knowledge.

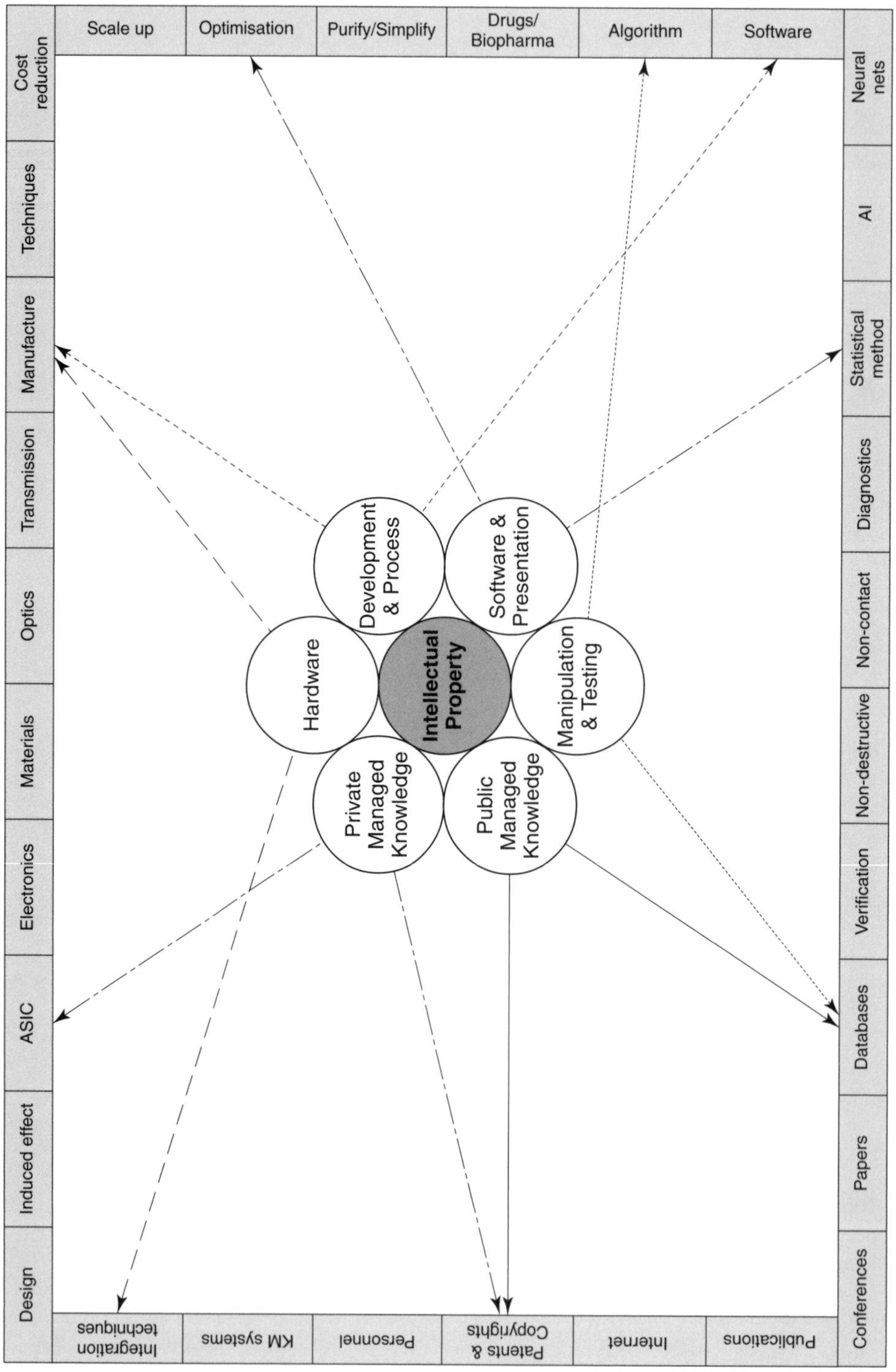

Figure 19.2 – IP interrelationships.

Source: PKF

Public managed knowledge

19.3 This is where, after gaining formal protection, the business allows people from outside to have effectively free access to the intellectual property. This can either make the information generally available, as with a patent, or available to selected groups, as through a conference or a trade journal.

Private managed knowledge

19.4 In contrast to public managed knowledge, private managed knowledge is where the business has made a positive decision not to allow third parties to see the detail of the IP.

Building an IP wall

19.5 IP protection can involve difficult decisions. There are a series of balancing acts to be undertaken. For example, with a patent a decision has to be made on the breadth of the patent and, in particular, the claims. Too broad a patent, even if granted, may not be defendable. Very broad patents run the risk of being challenged under:

- Effective infringement of another patent.
- Prior art – in that others may seek to show that areas that the patent claims to cover are actually in regular use already.
- Obviousness – the broader the idea the more likely a court might judge it not to be really novel.

On the other hand, too narrow a focus can either leave room for others to 'engineer around the patent' or form such a small part of the solution that others may be willing to risk breach in the expectation that any retrospective license fees will be low.

One approach that companies have adopted to address this problem is to build IP walls.

DEFINITION

An *IP wall* is a set of interrelated blocks of IP some or all of which may be formally protected. By building the wall the company aims to reduce the risk that by challenging, say, one patent a competitor can knock out the technology.

To achieve this the company looks to split up the technology into its component elements and then considers whether to seek formal protection for each element or whether to keep that element as a trade secret.

The number of IP bricks in the wall will be a key consideration; there is always a trade-off between sub-dividing the IP to enhance protection and the cost of maintaining each of the individual patented elements.

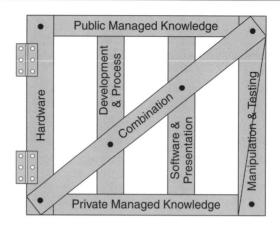

Figure 19.5 – the five bar gate approach to intellectual property

Source: PKF

IP protection strategy

19.6   The concept of building an IP wall gives rise to frameworks such as the Five Bar Gate illustrated above. The idea of the gate model is that by splitting the technology up into its component IP elements and then protecting some, but probably not all, of those elements the protection is effectively stronger than it would be with a single all-encompassing patent.

In the exampleillustrated by Figure 19.5 the key element is the hardware – that is why the gate hinges on that element. When graphically representing other pieces of technology the vertical slats might be re-arranged so that the appropriate key element is the hinged one.

In this model, private and public managed knowledge are always the top and bottom rails of the gate as they tie the other elements together.

Models such as these are intended to help in the development of the IP protection strategy and the policies that flow from it.

Developing the strategy

19.7   The strategy is based on an analysis of the underpinning technologies of the business. This analysis needs to consider:

- The elements of the IP within the technology.
- The types of protection that would be available for the elements and the strength of the protection that could be attained.
- Where protection is available whether the disclosure required to gain the protection actually gives away more useful information than the protection is worth.
- Which elements are vital to protect (generally those where protection is available and where it would be relatively simple to reverse engineer the solution from looking at the final product).
- Which elements would be difficult for a competitor to ascertain from dissecting the product.

The last item is particularly interesting as anything identified as falling into this category has the potential to be most valuable if it is *not* protected, particularly if it is not patented.

This may sound counter-intuitive but an example may help. A piece of testing equipment, particularly one that provides a diagnosis of errors, may relay on an algorithm.

The temptation would be to work on the principle that, as the algorithm is central to the functionality of the equipment, it should be protected and preferably patented. The problem is that the patent would end up disclosing commercially sensitive information about the way that the equipment works. In addition, the problem with algorithms is that the function of the algorithm can often be either recreated by using different techniques or adapted. Therefore, the risk is that by ensuring that the detail of the algorithm is different enough it may be possible to bypass the patent.

A similar problem arises over the value of copyright over software code. The functionality of a product can generally be recreated without breaching copyright on the code. See, for example, Microsoft Office™ and Star Office™, which perform essentially the same functions.

From this analysis flow decisions on which IP elements of the technology should be treated as private and which as public knowledge. Within the public knowledge elements there may be further decisions on the type of protection to be sought and the type of IP that should be protected.

IP policy

19.8 The analysis will feed into an IP policy. The objective of the policy is to help in deciding on a day-to-day basis whether IP protection should be sought for individual pieces of IP developed.

The policy should be available to developers and the knowledge management teams. Reference to it may also assist in setting development plans as focus can be placed on the key elements.

Certain elements may need additional work and development over that strictly needed for the offering. These are likely to be either:

- those elements that are to be protected and where extra work is needed to assist in the protection process; or
- elements which will not be protected where extra effort may be needed to make them less obvious in the finished product.

An example of this second class could, again, be an algorithm. It may have been decided that this should not be protected. However, it is possible that the algorithm itself is visible in, say, software. In this situation the decision may be to spend time making the appearance of the algorithm more complex so that it becomes difficult for a competitor to analyse which part of it is actually doing the work.

Protecting the private knowledge

19.9 This may seem like a contradiction in terms. However, the private knowledge is unprotected and resides in the heads of the development team and others around the business. Having made the decision not to formally protect this IP some other way of ensuring that it does not simply walk out of the door with the employees needs to be deployed.

Basically, the business has to work hard on motivating and retaining its people. There are a wide range of ways of doing this such as:

- Share ownership plans and share options.
- Loyalty bonuses and promotions.
- Other non-cash benefits such as cars.
- The quality of the working environment.
- Providing interesting work.

Whichever option or combination of options is used, the business has to keep the position under review.

Other techniques to retain this private knowledge include contractual terms in employees' service contracts and particularly non-compete and non-disclosure clauses for employees that leave. Legal advice should be taken as these clauses have to be carefully worded to be valid and not open to challenge on the grounds of restraint of trade.

Good knowledge management and knowledge sharing systems also help by ensuring that the IP is not concentrated in the heads of one or two people.

SUMMARY

19.10   IP protection is a key part of a technology business's strategy. If it is done well the business can gain significant commercial advantage. If it is ignored or done badly the business can put itself at risk.

Developing the strategy and the policies is a complex process. It may well need to be undertaken for each technology that a business develops. Having been developed the policies have to be implemented and monitored for reasonableness. In this, IP protection is no different from any other part of the business plan and the strategy.

Brands and Intellectual Property   **20**

OBJECTIVES

- To explain the concept of brands and brand value.
- To differentiate brand value from name recognition.
- To explain the inter-relationship between brands and IP.

Brands

20.1 Brands, branding and brand building were common themes throughout the late 1980s and the 1990s. The concept of a brand is:

DEFINITION

A *brand* communicates a set of values to a consumer and attaches to the offering a series of meanings beyond its own simple use or enhances the status of a business or offering in the consumer's eyes.

Hence, a strong brand is one that is rich in positive associations to the target customer group. A weak brand comes in two forms:

- one that has few if any positive associations; or
- one where the associations do not create perceived value for the target customer group.

A concern about some branding exercises is that, in common with a number of areas of pure marketing, the perceptions and intangible associations may have little to do with the reality of the situation. While this may help to enhance initial sales it can lead to real issues further down the line when the unreality of the associations becomes obvious to customers.

Worse still are the occasions when a brand begins to carry negative connotations for the target customers or their influencers. Recent examples of this phenomenon include:

- Businesses hit by allegations of the use of third world child labour.
- Claims of environmental damage from products or processes.
- Quality questions being asked about brands built on a quality cornerstone.
- Political or socio-political issues – such as a decision to move manufacturing out of a country or to retrench from a territory thereby creating job losses.
- Changes in fashion leading to a reversal of the brand image.
- The actions (legal or otherwise) of directors and staff bringing the business into disrepute – recent examples have included inaccurate publicity, questions over share dealings, and executives' and non-executives' pay.

So what is the objective of branding?

20.2   Branding is used for a number of purposes. At its most basic level, branding is a mechanism for supporting the revenue stream: both in the short and longer term.

Hence, brands operate on a series of levels:

- At the offering level (as in confectionery brands).
- At the target customer level (as where car manufacturers split their ranges for the US market into different brands to appeal to different users).
- On the general perception level (as where fashion designers/houses build a brand around the name that can be transferred to a range of loosely or seemingly un-related products).
- At the business level (an extension of the general perception level as here the group name becomes the brand and a set of related products gains kudos by association).

The last of these, the business level brand, can be a very powerful tool. VAG (the car group that includes Volkswagen and Audi) has used its own brand strength to significantly alter the views of the public about both its SEAT and, more impressively, its Skoda subsidiaries.

Offering level

20.3   At the offering level branding is used to:

- Provide product differentiation to avoid sales loss to other similar products.
- Support pricing differentiation policies.
- Generate customer loyalty.
- Sell in add-on or complementary offerings.

This type of branding has been used very creatively for everyday products: Ariel brand image as a reliable washing powder has been used to create a market for washing-up liquid while Fairy Liquid has gone in the other direction. Confectionery products gain ranges of similar products: Mars and Galaxy now exist as ice creams as well as ambient chocolate bars, Aero is available in a range of flavours and Polo mints now need not be mint flavoured, don't have to include sugar and can even be the holes rather than the ring around the hole.

Target customer level

20.4 This level is often used as the basis for price differentiation. As well as the car marques mentioned earlier airlines, railways and cruiselines use this level of branding.

Airlines are particularly interesting because they use a hybrid of this level and the business level. Certain airlines, such as easyJet, Ryanair and Go are aiming at very particular sectors of the public with Go using its links with British Airways as an added level of branding. The other companies ensure that the business level brand is in line with their target market – projecting a simpler, more down-to-earth and slightly more basic image than Go with its Jasper Conran designed uniforms.

In the same way, Virgin uses both target customer level branding and the Virgin name to create an image of the business. Virgin actually takes the process a stage further with clearly defined targeting that presents quite different images to the economy and premium price passenger markets. A further interesting element is the way that the Virgin name is used – clearly linked to the economy end but, while present, not emphasised to the premium market. So, while Go and British Airways combine target customer and business levels Virgin combines the target customer level with a general perception level branding based on the Virgin name and its associations – particularly with the group's founder Sir Richard Branson.

Another interesting use of target customer level branding is the ability to collect information from the target customers. At this level feedback is garnered in a variety of ways, not all of them obvious to the customers themselves.

Examples of this information collection include:

- Linked web-sites that require registration information.
- Sponsoring of magazine surveys or exhibition surveys.
- Entry to benchmarking activities (a favourite of PC hardware manufacturers).
- Sponsoring events likely to attract the target audience, especially those where attendees have to write in for tickets.

General perception level

20.5 This is perhaps the most difficult level to achieve and is also the most precarious to maintain depending, as it often does, on a form of the *cult of personality* for its basis.

It has been said that the best of these brands are those where the originator is now dead. In these circumstances any drop off in form can be blamed on the present incumbent and does not, per se, damage the brand itself.

It can be difficult for technology companies to achieve this type of brand image but it is not impossible. Hewlett Packard is perhaps the best known example. With a range of offerings covering computing, peripherals, chip and component design, medical and scientific equipment and many other areas the group has an image that underpins both the value of the offerings and the likely acceptance of them by users.

Other examples include the Phillips group where a range of offerings, covering white goods as well as industrial and medical equipment all carry the perceived quality and value for money image of the group.

Again, TAG McLaren has used this approach – taking its known excellence in leading edge design and electronics, built up in the motor racing field, and transferring that image to the hi-fi equipment arena through its rebranding of Audiolab.

Over recent years this approach, often referred to as brand extension, has been popular with an ever widening range of businesses. One can now buy:

- Porsche designed pens, watches, kettles, blenders and coffee makers.
- Swatch cars.
- BMW skateboards.
- Virgin mortgages and other financial products, rail tickets, perfumes, and airline tickets – all this from a brand originally based on selling records.

However, general perception can be fragile. It only takes one public or publicly exposed slip by the person or business at the centre of the brand to cause a change in customer perception and therefore a failure of the central tenants of the brand image.

It may not even need a slip; sentiments can change leaving the brand behind. This happened to conglomerates in the mid-to-late 1990s. The brand (which effectively attached itself to management or even to CEOs/Chairmen) had been seen as being the ability to manage any business and drive value from it but the market moved to wanting to do its own risk diversification. Hence, when investors want to choose the range of businesses they invest in, conglomerates go out of fashion and the associated brands become devalued.

Business level

20.6 This is the highest level and is differentiated from the general perception level by the fact that the business brand tends to relate to a specific and closely related set of offerings.

Examples of this type of brand include:

- Financial institutions (banks, insurance companies, etc).
- Utilities companies.
- A number of technology companies.

IBM was one of the best known examples of this in the 1980s. At that stage whenever IT projects came up one heard the phrase 'no-one ever got sacked for choosing IBM'. Indeed, it has been argued that the success of the personal computer is largely down to the fact that IBM threw its weight behind the concept. Certainly, Steve Jobs at Apple, amongst others, had moved to the concept earlier but, without the weight of the IBM brand, did not instigate the wave of public acceptance that was seen from the late 80s.

Again, the brand has to be carefully nurtured and looked after. IBM's problems both in product development and financially in the early 1990s damaged the brand significantly. It took a change of management and a biscuit maker (Lou Gerstner, formerly of RJR Nabisco) to turn the position around and, even then, IBM has never recovered its once pre-eminent position across all fields of computing.

Microsoft is another company with a business level brand. Most users, and probably most purchasers are not aware of the alternatives to Microsoft's products. Indeed, they are probably not aware of what the products they use

174

actually do beyond the very basics. Yet the name and the brand are powerful persuaders to a wide range of people to rely on their products.

Like IBM, Microsoft's image has been tarnished in recent years. In Microsoft's case by allegations over trading and anti-competitive practices brought first by Netscape and then by the US Government. What is interesting is that, by the time the allegations arose, the brand was so dominant in its key target sectors that competitors seem to have been unable to take significant advantage of the situation. This is, however, a particularly unusual situation and certainly is not one that other businesses should look to rely on.

Brand versus name recognition

20.7 The dotcom explosion in the late 1990s and 2000 saw much talk about marketing spend being focused on brand building.

Brands carry meaning: they bring with them associations and implications of values such as quality, price, exclusivity, design or technological advance. They also bring with them a degree of customer trust and acceptance that allows the brand holder to support and enhance their revenues.

By contrast name recognition is just that; the ability of potential customers to remember or produce the name of the business or offering when prompted.

As the dotcom companies discovered, name recognition is not, of itself, a guarantee of income to follow. Just because potential customers can remember the name of the business does not mean that they either know what the business is about or trust it to deliver. Indeed, it has been argued that name recognition that is not backed by a developed brand is dangerous to a business – if customers do not know what the brand stands for they are unlikely to pick it in preference to a brand with meaning.

In retrospect, some dotcoms gained their name recognition simply because of the amount they spent on getting their names known. Customers only associated the businesses with marketing spend and adverts and not with any specific activity or with an offering they wanted to purchase.

Which is not to say that name recognition is not important and that time and effort does not have to be spent on maintaining the business's name in the customers' psyche.

The head of one technology business complains that the business lost the chance to tender for a replacement for a system they had installed because the system worked so well that they never had to visit. So, when it came time to tender, and management at the customer had changed, they got missed off the list – they were just invisible to the customer.

In the same way, names themselves can be very important tools. A business's name can communicate a lot of the qualities and principles that underpin the brand. For technology companies the choice of a name can be particularly difficult. Tempting as it can be to pick a name that is current or suggestive of leading edge technology, such a name can age badly.

Again, the dotcom boom saw a large number of companies appearing with '.com' in their names. With the collapse of investor confidence in the sector from the middle of 2000 this suffix became not a benefit but a handicap to some companies being taken seriously.

The rush to change names that often comes with a merger, a change of management or a realignment of strategy can overlook the value in the name and the difficulty of building up a new name.

Qualities of a brand

20.8 So, brands are a complex combination of aspirations, perceived status and implied values. Can these qualities be planned for? The answer is yes, to some extent.

In Chapter 4 of the *Lifecycle* section of this book on the *Pre-formation* phase of a business the strategic challenges included answering the big questions:

- *What is the business?*
- *What will it do?*
- Who are its customers?
- *Why will they buy from the business?*
- *What will it be known for?*
- *How will it do it?*
- Who will run it?
- How will it make money?
- What is its lifespan and can it be regenerated?

Those in italics above are elements of the brand. The reason for including them so early on in the strategic process is that one key element of a brand that got overlooked by the dotcoms is that brands develop and are accepted *over time*.

It is interesting to look at the age of the best known confectionery products on sale in the UK:

Brand name	Year launched	Top ten best sellers in the UK in 2000
Rowntree's Fruit Pastilles	1881	
Cadbury's Dairy Milk	1905	2nd
Milk Tray	1915	
Jelly Babies	1918	
Cadbury's Flake	1920	
Milky Way	1923	
Snickers	1930	10th
Mars bar	1932	3rd
Aero	1935	
Quality Street	1936	
Maltesers	1936	7th
Kit Kat	1937	1st
Trebor Extra Strong Mints	1937	
Smarties	1937	
Cadbury's Roses	1938	8th
M&Ms	1940	
Polos	1948	
Galaxy Bar	1958	4th
Twix	1968	5th
Wrigleys Extra	1990	9th
Celebrations	1997	6th

The average age of the top ten brands is over 50 years (given that Celebrations is actually a selection of miniature versions of other brands the underlying age is even older) – but these potentially elderly brands generated upwards of £975million in sales in 2000. The average of this whole list is an even more startling 64 years.

The qualities of the brand that underpin its selling points take time to communicate to customers. More time is then needed for customers to accept those qualities and identify with them. This is why businesses can often find it hard to win repeat orders early on. Customers need to live with the offering and see if it lives up to the brand image portrayed during the sales process.

Hence, setting out the brand – at least at business level – needs to start very early on. For a lot of technology businesses the answers to these questions go back to the very reason for founding the business.

Everything else in the strategy is driven by the answers to these questions – they are what the brand is intended to become.

As set out in Chapter 12 in the overview of the strategic process, these answers become the elements of the strategy and business plan of the business. They should also underpin the business level brand and any offering or target customer level branding.

Understanding these qualities and communicating them internally is a vital part of building the business. David Packard of HP is quoted as saying that HP's *'main task is to design, develop and manufacture the finest electronic [equipment] for the advancement of science and the welfare of humanity'*. That could easily be a description of the HP brand but is also, apparently, well understood within the organisation.

Brand value

20.9 The concept of brand value springs from the basic premise that a brand exists to support and enhance the current and future revenues that can be generated from offerings.

Many specialists have attempted to quantify this value and, as explained in Chapter 34 on the accounting issues around *Brands, intangible assets and aquiring goodwill*, arguments have raged over whether brand values should be carried on the balance sheet of companies.

There are, however, a series of difficulties surrounding the valuation of brands – ranging from the purely technical, such as the choice of method and discount rate to apply, through to the philosophical, such as how to differentiate the revenues relating to the brand from revenues that would occur naturally.

However, it is clear from a range of transactions, from car manufacturers to shampoo, that brands do have value.

Applying absolute values to brands is a notoriously difficult area but some commentators take the view that relative values are easier to ascertain. To do this they look at peer groups of brands and make relative assessments of aspects such as:

- Customer acceptability.
- Market share over time.
- Name recognition.
- Perceived quality and value for money.

In this way they rank the peer group and can even attempt to compare different products.

This exercise often takes place as part of the justification for or against a takeover. It becomes part of the valuation process for goodwill – there is an argument that goodwill is the sum of the values of the product and business brand value.

Brands and IP

20.10   The inter-relationships between brands and IP are complex.

In common usage it can be hard to see where the line falls between brands and intellectual property. For many people brands are a form of intellectual property just like patents or copyrights. However, brands are fundamentally different in that a brand per se not only has no existence without the offering or business to which it is attached but also a brand on its own does nothing for the customer – customers may love Ben and Jerry's ice cream, for example, and they may even love the concept of the related philanthropic activities – but they don't love the brand in isolation. What is more, they do not buy the application of the brand the way that they buy the application of the IP.

Graphically the different types of intangible can be shown as follows (value relates to the notional enhancement to a company valuation that an investor places on each type of intangible):

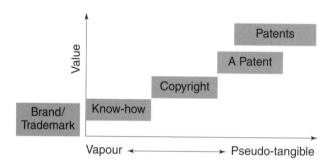

Figure 20.10 – relative value of intangibles

Source: PKF

So, at one level brands and IP seem unconnected in that IP and technology can be seen to exist in a vacuum – they are there whether or not customers need them. Certainly, the relationship seems tenuous when viewed from the IP standpoint.

However, looking in the opposite direction, brands can enhance IP and IP can enhance brands. For example, by building a patent wall with multiple patents Dyson is able to claim that their vacuum cleaners are based on hundreds of patents. The combined patent portfolio is reflected in a brand with qualities of scientific rigour and backed by quality and original thinking. This is further enhanced by the fact that James Dyson went through 5,127 prototypes before launching his first machine.

What is clear is that technology companies, despite their focus on IP, cannot afford to ignore the brand that will develop alongside their technology.

Strategic Alliances

21

OBJECTIVES

- To introduce the concept of strategic alliances.
- To consider the range of alliances available.
- To consider the intellectual property aspects of the options.
- To consider the alliance process.
- To introduce the concept of strategic networks.

Strategic alliances

21.1 The concept of a strategic alliance or a series of alliances is now prevalent in the technology sector. Partnering recognises that certain businesses have certain strengths but also that very few have such a complete set of skills, capabilities and intellectual property that they can undertake everything on their own.

DEFINITION

Strategic alliances are arrangements between businesses under which they agree to work together and share information at a level that implies a much closer relationship than a normal commercial relationship between, say, a company and a supplier.

Businesses enter into strategic alliances for a wide variety of reasons including:

- Gaining access to technology.
- Solving a development or other problem.
- Gaining access to skills, capability, equipment or capacity without direct investment in them.
- Gaining access to markets or countries.
- Better funding opportunities.
- Their fundamental business model (for example biotech companies in the

drug development area form strategic alliances with big pharma companies in order to generate revenues).

Whatever the reason for it, the alliance must be mutually beneficial to the parties involved. If one party gains all the benefits then the other will require payment, turning the arrangement back into a more normal commercial trading relationship.

Looking at the examples given above, the give and take often looks like this:

Reason for partnering	*Mutual benefit*
Access to technology	Must be two way or potentially partner providing the technology has partnering as a fundamental element of their business model.
Solving a problem	Must be two way or at least there must be a way in which the technology provider gains value from helping to solve the problem that it would not have gained through other means.
Access to skills, capability, equipment or capacity	Generally this is about volumes through a business combined with the ability for the partner providing the capabilities to build a better case for investment in equipment, people or quality.
Access to markets	Revenue for both parties.
Funding opportunities	Funding for both parties that might not be available separately – for example through UK or EU grant schemes.
Fundamental to business model	Must deliver technology or solutions that are valuable to the other party.

A number of these, such as the first and last reasons, are clearly complementary and certainly the reasons are often different on the two sides.

This culture of partnering, of creating value and businesses through bringing the skills and abilities of different entities together saw its zenith in the 1990s with the creation of virtual companies.

DEFINITION

Virtual companies are companies where only a very small core staff, often purely administrative, build and manage a set of relationships in which the activities of the company are effectively outsourced to others who have the specific skills required. The object is to use the business equivalent of the old saying that the whole is greater than the sum of the parts. In virtual businesses the whole brings together exactly the skills needed and can therefore pick the very best partners to put together, with the aim that the offerings created will be enhanced by the involvement of so many specialists.

The spectrum of alliances

21.2   The term strategic alliance is vague. It does not imply any particular form of arrangement nor does it even imply the closeness of that relationship. In fact there is a broad spectrum of different alliances and arrangements that fall under the caption of strategic alliances, each used for different reasons and with different implications both commercially, for tax purposes and for intellectual property ownership purposes.

In addition, the level of control over the technology being developed and the responsibility for the eventual offering differs between the options. In turn this means that the level of risk relating to the alliance changes and so does the level of return required from the parties.

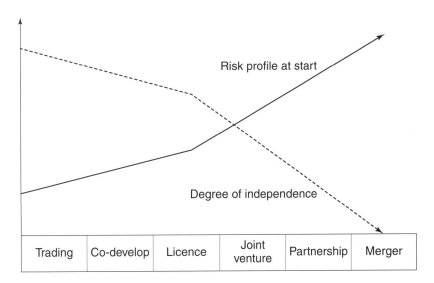

Figure 21.2 – the spectrum of strategic alliances

Source: PKF

Each of the options has different features:

Trading

21.3   Trading relationships are the simplest type of alliances. While they can be built up over long periods of time they are, at their core, transient. The clothing manufacturer William Baird discovered this when Marks and Spencer ended a long-term trading relationship and started sourcing their clothing from outside the UK.

Each transaction can be on the same or different bases. It is rare, though not impossible, for the supplier to develop an offering specifically for the customer – the main exception being contract based work such as systems integration. More often an offering can be adapted or tailored to a customer's needs. Automotive components, particularly items such as spark plugs, lights or even turbochargers are either selected from a range of standard offerings or, as in the case of turbochargers, can be a standard unit with fittings developed for the specific customer preference. Either way, no intellectual property rights change hands as part of the process.

Co-develop

21.4 Co-development has increased significantly in recent years. In the technology area, development groups have been formed around certain pieces of technology. The idea of these groups is to ensure common standards, interoperability, common interfaces and, in some cases, open standards.

Examples of development groups include those related to:

- Bluetooth – one of the range of competing 2.3GHz wireless networking protocols.
- TETRA – the digital mobile radio and datacoms network.
- Linux – the alternative operating system.
- Human Genome Project.

Development group activities live in a semi-formal world. Set-up and entered into through a document such as a Memorandum of Understanding (or MoU) they are a pooling of mutual interest. Each business does its own development work implementing the technology in the way it sees best but all subscribe to a set of common goals and standards.

On a smaller scale basis co-development can also take place on individual projects. Where two or more businesses have complimentary technologies they may work together to produce a joint product that both can sell. Often these projects are a form of integration or convergence activity with both companies looking to serve separate markets either by industry sector or territory. Alongside some form of MoU or co-development agreement there will be a degree of cross-licensing allowing each company to market the final unified offering including the IP that belongs to the other party.

Licence

21.5 In a licensing relationship the developer passes over the right to utilise, and possibly to further develop, the technology to the licensee. However, it is rarely the case that the arrangement stops there. Generally, there will be an ongoing relationship attached to the licensing. This may cover areas such as:

- Development of the technology by the developer to meet the licensee's specific needs.
- Rights to further developments of the technology, or even a requirement for the developer to continue development.
- Close involvement in trials and approvals, as in the case of drug development.
- Creation of joint development teams.
- Sharing of intellectual property on complementary technology developments.
- Royalty payments to the developer.
- Co-marketing of the products.

Entering into a licensing arrangement can be a relatively high risk activity for both sides. The developer is placing at least some of their future income into someone else's hands – they will be dependent for the royalty income on the licensee completing the development of the products and then marketing them successfully. The licensee has to take technology that they have not developed and, potentially, integrate it with their own, take it through the testing phase and then market it. All this and they may well be paying access fees up front, milestone payments along the way and royalties for the life of the product.

Some of the relationship extension items mentioned above, such as co-marketing, are designed to help even out and mitigate the mutual risk positions.

The acceptance and integration of third party technology can be both technically and psychologically challenging and should not be under-estimated. Technologists can have firmly fixed views on what is and what is not good technology. More than that, they may have had their own ideas on how the piece of the jigsaw that is being filled by the developer's technology should be filled. Where there are differences of view, or even where there are few, if any, technical differences of approach, human nature can take over.

A syndrome referred to as '*Not Invented Here*', or NIH for short, can arise. In NIH the licensee's team is at first suspicious and can become actively hostile of the licensed technology. Research suggests that this is a combination of uncertainty due to the knowledge of the newly introduced technology being significantly lower than the knowledge level of the licensee's existing technology and insecurity over position. This second point relates to a natural human concern that, if a new technology is brought in, the incumbent team may not be the one charged with implementing the integration or, at the other extreme, may be criticised for a failure that they put down to the licensed technology.

Either way NIH can be crippling to the project and, if it becomes culturally ingrained, to the business as well. It is hard to track down verifiable examples of NIH but apocryphal stories of potentially world-beating technologies being shelved or projects falling by the wayside due to NIH abound.

Joint venture (JV)

21.6 A JV is generally a specially created legal entity, often a company, set up by two or three businesses to develop and produce a jointly developed offering. JVs arise for a number of reasons:

Reason	Comments
Non-core activity	While the offering may not be core to any of the businesses it is seen as profitable enough to be worth maintaining and not selling off. Critically, the entity needs to be self-supporting in the medium to long term for this to be worth while. If not it will either not be undertaken or will be spun out quite quickly.
Need for equal input	Where the offering needs equal input in terms of skills, time, funding or capabilities and the market opportunity is significant enough a JV may be the answer. Generally there is the added element that this is the only, or one of very few, points at which the JV partners' activities dovetail together.

(Continued)

Reason	Comments
Mutual benefit	Examples of this type of JV arise when one company has the technology and the other has, say, funding available and sales and marketing capabilities. Here, neither of the JV partners could succeed on their own – the funder does not have the technology and the intellectual property owner does not have the funds or sales and marketing infrastructure.
Off balance sheet activity	Historically joint ventures were not treated as being subsidiaries of either entity. Hence, they could, at least to some extent, avoid presenting too much bad news about them in the early stages. Current UK accounting standards make it more difficult, but not necessarily impossible, to achieve this 'off balance sheet' status for a JV.
Funding vehicle	This has historically occurred more in the US than the UK due to differences in both accounting and the legal philosophy about groups*. The concept is that two or more companies put elements of technology into a vehicle that is funded either by a third company or by a consortium of venture capital funds.
Shareholders would not accept a merger	Realistic management teams may recognise that, either for historic rivalry reasons or because the area of overlap between two companies is relatively small, a full scale merger is not a practical option. What may then happen is that they move the areas of overlap into one or more joint venture vehicles. An example of this in the UK was GPT which was a group of technology companies set up as a JV between the then GEC and Siemens of Germany.

US law and accounting tend to look at groups as single entities whereas in the UK the view, driven by the development of tax legislation, has been more that groups are collections of individual legal entities. This gives rise to differences around items such as the rights of shares. In the US, for example, it is possible to have staple stock or tracking stock – shares that only really have an interest in the earnings of a part of the group's activities yet without those shares being a minority interest in the companies that undertake that activity.

The diversified biotech company Genzyme is an example of a US company which has taken tracking stock to its ultimate logical extreme. Tracking stock corporations such as Genzyme, the telecoms companies AT&T and Sprint and the Walt Disney Corporation are almost turning the JV model on its head.

JVs come with a series of issues that need to be addressed at the outset, and normally are either through the memorandum and articles of association of the JV entity or through a shareholders agreement. The items typically covered include:

- Relative shareholdings and types of shares held.
- Board representation.
- Funding allocation both initially and in future.
- Expenses that the JV partners can look to recover from the JV entity.
- Rights of the JV partners to sell their shares.
- Levels of commitment (time, facilities, etc) that each party will put in.

- Intellectual property rights injected into the JV or licensed to it and the ownership of any intellectual property created by it.

A JV is therefore a long-term relationship that ties the partners together, in which both have a real and vested interest and which both need to see succeed for either financial, strategic or technological reasons.

Partnership

21.7 Until very recently true partnerships have been rare in the UK due to the difficulties of aspects like unlimited liability. However, with the introduction of Limited Liability Partnerships, or LLPs, to the UK this position may well change.

LLPs are a form of halfway house between a traditional partnership and a company. Legally it is a body corporate, like a company, with a separate legal personality and unlimited contractual capability. However, it is taxed as a partnership. It will have to produce accounts, like a company, and again like a company, it will be able to create fixed or floating charges as it will be able to own assets in its own name – the security that banks need for providing overdrafts or loans.

The liability of the partners, who can include companies, is, in most cases, limited to the capital they put in plus any additional payments agreed.

Available as an option from April 2001, case law and practice is yet to arise and it will be interesting to see how LLPs, which were largely developed for the large legal and accounting partnerships, will be used. The tax transparency of an LLP could well make it an attractive option for consortia or other joint development projects.

Merger

21.8 The ultimate alliance. The term 'merger' is often mis-used as it implies that the two parties are of equal strength before the combination and share responsibilities after. In practice this rarely happens and, as is now recognised by UK accounting standards, in reality one company actually takes over the other.

Takeovers are permanent alliances. With very few exceptions taken-over companies become absorbed into their new parent. Most recent exceptions, such as the telecoms business Orange (which was acquired by the German Mannesmann only to be demerged after Vodafone Group acquired Mannesmann) or elements of pharmaceutical giant GlaxoSmithKline (the combination of GlaxoWelcome and SmithKline Beecham), arose when the competition commissioners either in the UK, Europe or the US demanded the disposal of specific businesses. The reason for the demands was that, without the disposals, the combined businesses would have had an effective monopoly position in the activities that those businesses undertake.

As with all alliances there can be a variety of reasons for takeovers. In the main they arise when the purchaser has a business requirement for some facet of the target. Examples include

- well-developed distribution networks;
- market share or geographic presence;
- offerings to complete a range;

- technologies required for future products; and
- processes or relationships with suppliers or customers,

that are vital to the purchaser's continuing development and where the purchaser calculates that it is cheaper to acquire the target than to develop an equivalent capability in house.

Alongside this is the potential for synergies between the two companies to be exploited with the effect that the market capitalisation of the combined entity exceeds the sum of the market capitalisations of the individual companies. Factors giving rise to synergies include an easier supply chain being obtained by undertaking vertical integration, the possibility to pool premises and release value by selling premises or immediate penetration into a specific geographical market. Other synergies generally sited relate to the reduction in central administrative and other support costs – duplication can be removed saving money.

Because of the combination of all the interests of the businesses, mergers take a significant length of time. A period of due diligence – basically, investigation of the other business from commercial, legal and accounting viewpoints – is usually undertaken. The process of drawing up an acceptable sale and purchase agreement can also be lengthy involving as it does elements such as:

- Valuation of both businesses and calculation of the price to be paid.
- The form of the payment (cash, shares, loan notes or a combination) and the timing of it – often an element of the payment is deferred and may be dependent on the performance of the acquired business after the acquisition.
- The split of ownership of the new enlarged entity.
- The ongoing involvement of key people in the acquired business and the terms.
- Taxation issues.

Once all of this is completed shareholder approval may be required on both sides.

All this assumes that the proposed takeover is both friendly and does not fall under the conditions of the Takeover Code – the rules that govern the way takeovers have to be handled for certain, generally larger, companies such as quoted companies.

Reasons for such takeovers range from the defensive to the offensive:

- ● Removal of a competitor — Defensive
- ● Avoidance of others acquiring the technology
- ● Build an entity that is commercially fundable
- ● Getting over a development hurdle
- ● Filling a hole in the product range
- ● Kick-starting a product range
- ● Adding to an existing product to extend functionality, life and market share by leap-frogging a competing product
- ● Combining technologies to gain a market lead or allow a spin-out of a new business
- ● Providing funding to potentially world-beating technology — Offensive

The alliance process

21.9   The process of identifying, negotiating and consummating a strategic alliance is a long and often exhausting process. Any alliance needs to be part of the strategy and needs to add to the achievement of both the strategic aims of the business and the business plan of the business. The takeover option, from a seller's viewpoint, may also be the strategic exit that the founders or funders envisaged.

The slides that follow over the next few pages have been adapted from a presentation given by one of the authors at the Southern Bioscience international partnering conference *Pulling Together 2001* held at Henley on Thames in 2001. They are included here as thoughts and guidance on going through the alliance process from a practical and commercial viewpoint.

During the negotiations

Are you really doing as well as you think?

✓ DOs	✗ DON'Ts
✓ Think positive	✗ Get competitive
✓ Take breaks	✗ Force the issue
✓ Think post deal	✗ What's In It For Me?
✓ Be creative	✗ Forget the people
✓ Be flexible	✗ Ignore the objectives

✓ Remember your initial drivers for being here

During the negotiations

The key is to know:

- your parameters

&

- your strategic pluses and minuses

✓ DOs	✗ DON'Ts
✓ Think positive	✗ Get competitive

It's all in the training

- **Prepare!** Talk to your shareholders

- **Prepare!** Set your criteria

- **Prepare!** Practice and script

Picking the team I

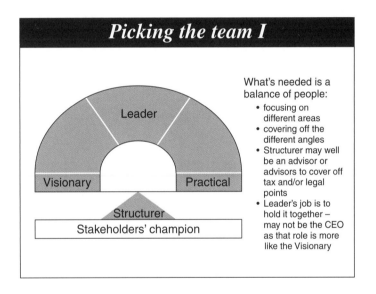

What's needed is a balance of people:

- focusing on different areas
- covering off the different angles
- Structurer may well be an advisor or advisors to cover off tax and/or legal points
- Leader's job is to hold it together – may not be the CEO as that role is more like the Visionary

Team characteristics

- Experience – needed to get the deal done

- Blooding – give the less experienced experience

- Internal agreement – vital or the team and deal will fall apart

- Enthusiast v Stoic – you need a balance to keep on track

- Knowledge of the business – if your team doesn't understand what you are trying to achieve and how the deal fits your strategy, **FORGET IT!**

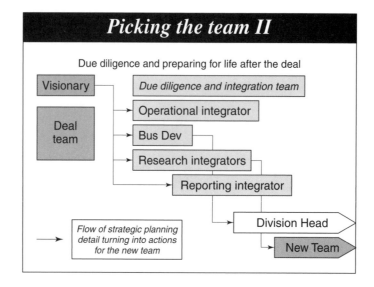

Picking the team II

Due diligence and preparing for life after the deal

Activities before completion

- Due diligence
- Funding/shareholder issues will need CFO and CEO input plus advisers
- Deal finalisation – get the lawyers in early; it really will save you money. The later advisors are brought in the more they have to catch up and the more that it will cost.
- New IP package review – acquisitions and disposals? Is this the opportunity to refine your Intellectual Property portfolio by selling non-core IP or do you need to license in to enable the alliance to really spring forward?

Funding issues

- Review against promises – what have you told your investors you will achieve and does this match it?
- Milestones and working capital – do they leave you with a working capital exposure?
- Timing to raise cash – is now the right time and even if it is, do you have the time needed to raise the cash?
- Dilution and major holders – a chance to raise cash? – if major shareholders don't want dilution will they put up cash to keep their stake up?
- Share option planning for everyone – dilution effect and incentives
- Tax – think about it first not afterwards, so get advisors in early!

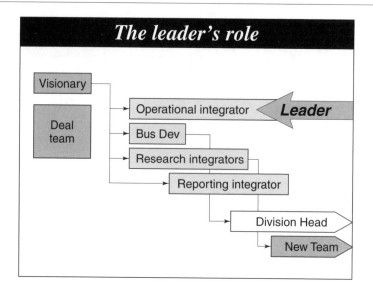

Once the decision to go ahead is made

- Draw up the plan based on objectives

- Pick the team

- Drive the process and call the pace

- Monitor progress

- Hand on the tiller – someone has to oversee and ensure the alliance stays on course from both sides' viewpoint

Remember

> Plan first:
> Then execute your plan with the utmost vigour
>
> **AND**
>
> A plan without actions is just paper

Practicalities

- Be ready for timetable drift — it's likely to take longer than you think but if it's going faster, watch out that you're still on course for the destination you want

- It's hard to juggle too many balls — don't overload people with too many alliances each. Every business has a different culture and processes and remembering who does what can be difficult but is key

- Someone has to be in charge

- Changing course is painful but may be necessary — keep the alliance under review and be willing to make hard choices to renegotiate if needed

- Build a team across the partners

Megaphone needed?

- Communication is key
- Don't be fooled into doing everything in meetings
- Use the latest tools – there are lots of useful IT tools to help you broadcast progress internally and help you communicate across the spaces between the partners
- Beware email/voicemail – you can't assume they've been checked
- Think *message: message: message* – *when communicating to the team*

Before the dust settles ...

- Know where you want to get to and have a clear view of the likely obstacles
- During the negotiations focus on the main goals, don't get drawn into artistic touches
- Once the deal is agreed set up the team to drive the due diligence/completion/integration process
- Take the time to sell the plan internally as well as externally
- Don't rely on nudges and winks – make sure the message is clear and has been understood

Adapted from the Session '*Setting the Stroke Rate*'.

Source: PKF

Strategic networks

21.10 Traditionally strategic alliances were seen in isolation. A business might have a series of strategic alliances but they would be in different areas of activity or interest and were separate from each other. This approach mirrored the very task focused approach that research and development based businesses had adopted over the years.

As communications have improved, and increasingly with the arrival of the Internet, broadband communications and video conferencing, this view of business as a set of separate relationships has evolved. Technology businesses now set out to build alliances from an early stage and expect more from those alliances.

While historically alliances short of mergers might involve activities such as short-term secondments, unless the alliance partners were located close together the practicalities were that the two businesses continued to run separately. Indeed, their individual elements of the project would take place independently and be brought together only at a fairly well developed stage. Possibly apocryphal stories of the building of the Concorde supersonic jet tell of the British and French working from plans that differed in a major way – the Brits were working in feet and inches while the French used metric measurements. There must have been a lot of nervous people when the elements of the body were brought together for the first time!

More recently companies have come to recognise that they may have been missing out on additional benefits from their webs of alliances – by getting their alliance partners to work together there is the opportunity for everyone

Figure 21.110 – Diagrammatic representation of a strategic network

Source: PKF

to benefit, and to benefit to a greater extent. This has given rise to the concept of strategic networks.

The concept behind a strategic framework is that the Originator business builds up a network of alliances and at the same time ensures that all of the partners are in contact with each other. Because of this interwoven structure the Originator business does not have to act as central clearing for all activities. More than that the partners are free to work together to solve problems on a pro-active basis providing the solution to the network as a whole. Hence, the idea is that not only is the process speeded up by having one-to-one direct relationships but also the final offerings are stronger from the close involvement of all the parties.

Clearly there are logistical issues to be handled but the use of modern communications should allow quite large groups to interact without the need for constant and interminable meetings – the bane of many business people.

Also, it should be realised that not all activities may be susceptible to a strategic network approach. It might be difficult, for confidentiality or other commercial reasons, to involve multiple sales and marketing partners, particularly where they are part of the group to achieve different aims or offerings. However, where the sales and marketing partners are territory or sector focused it can be immensely beneficial to have them all involved.

For example, by bringing all the country requirements to the table at the same time (regulatory, testing, legal, etc) significant redesign work can often be avoided. Rather than designing for country A and then having to redesign for country B it may be that an adaptable design can be created in the first place with small adaptations to meet the individual country requirements.

Some may question the involvement of the lawyers, accountants, patent agents and other advisors in the network. However, their input on a range of issues from regulations to royalty rates to joint ownership of intellectual property may often change the structure or approach to markets and intellectual property protection. As with so many things in business, maintaining a running dialogue with advisors really does add value and, in the medium and long terms, reduce overall costs.

SUMMARY

21.11   As technology gets more and more complex, as markets become more sophisticated and as regulations get stronger, strategic alliances become more and more important to success. They are a fact of life for most areas of technology and the development of webs of alliances is seen by some commentators as a sign that a specific technology sector has come of age.

Based on a realisation that few businesses can do it all, alliances need to be approached positively but with care. Getting the right partner – one who brings more than just their technology and with whom you can work – is the first step. Doing the right deal and setting up the right structures for working together is next. Ensuring that you have aligned your alliances with your strategic and business goals is a more serious challenge, as is putting the alliance together in a tax efficient way.

Strategic networks are beginning to appear and represent a further realisation of the value in the alliance approach.

Strategic alliances are a fact of life and it is likely that most technology businesses that want to be successful will enter into at least one at some stage in their development.

Technical Considerations

Intellectual Property # 22

OBJECTIVE

To describe:

- Copyright, including database rights.
- Patents.
- Trademarks.
- Designs – design rights and registered designs.
- Other intellectual property.

Intellectual property (IP) rights – an introduction

22.1 High-technology companies are, under the author's definition, dependent on IP for their existence; during the early part of the lifecycle of the business it may be the only asset that the company has, in the midst of a sea of losses and expenditure. Further into the lifecycle, it is the IP of the business that defines and differentiates it from competitors.

IP rights are generally monopolistic; they give the owner the right to prevent others from exploiting the rights, rather than specifically conferring on the owner the right to exploit it. As with all legal rights, IP rights are generally considered to be assets – they are intangible assets, in contrast to the tangible assets, such as property, which may be owned by a business. Intangible assets cannot be touched – or kicked – but are equally important to a business. However, as with other assets, they are capable of being transferred (in full or in part), and can also be mortgaged as security,

There are several types of IP; the two most usually applicable in high technology businesses are copyright and patent rights. Other IP, such as trademarks and design rights, are generally less important although still useful in building up the asset base of the business if there are assets which could be protected by registration as a trademark or design right. Finally, non-registerable assets such as trade secrets (know-how) are also IP; protection of these assets is more difficult.

IP may be created or acquired; generally, IP is developed in the early part of the lifecycle of a business and then exploited later on. Often, complementary IP is acquired or developed to broaden the scope of the company's offerings.

Some businesses exist to create IP and then licence or sell the resulting rights – the *research outfit* business model. For these businesses, the IP rights which they create are not regarded as assets of the business – instead, they are more usually classed as 'trading stock'; the company trades the IP developed, rather than using it to trade in a physical product. Many biotechnology companies, particularly in biopharmaceuticals, operate on this principle, preferring to create new IP which may then be licensed to a major pharmaceutical company (often referred to as a 'big pharma') for late-stage development and sales and marketing. The big pharma trades in the physical product, the biotech company trades in the IP. The biopharmaceutical industry is sometimes referred to as the 'outsourced R&D department' for big pharma.

Copyright

22.2   There are two types of copyright – *artistic* (covering visual works) and *literary* (covering written works). Literary copyright covers computer software, presumably because it is capable of being written down.

DEFINITION

Copyright is an automatic right, which is created when the work is created and recorded in some way (on paper, electronically etc); there is no registration required for copyrights in the UK. Copyright covers only the expression of an idea; it does not cover the idea itself. Copyright protection lasts for the life of the author, plus 70 years. There is no need to renew the protection – it automatically extends from one year to the next.

Copyright gives the creator the right to control use of the copyright material in a variety of ways – making copies, issuing copies to the public, performing in public, broadcasting, adaptation (including the conversion of a piece of software from one computer language to another) and use online. Copyright also gives the creator the right to object to distortion or mutilation of the copyright material. There are exceptions to copyright protection – for example, limited use of material for review purposes, or for reporting of current events, is allowed without the permission of the copyright owner.

Ownership

22.3   Copyright belongs to the creator of the work, or to their employer if provided for under the contract of employment – businesses need to ensure that their contracts of employment *and* contracts with sub-contractors explicitly provide that any IP created as a result of the contract will be the property of the business.

Protection

22.4 It is good practice to record the fact that material is copyright, by adding the © symbol followed by the name of the owner and the year of creation to the work, but, in the UK, it is not legally necessary in order to protect the work. Some countries do require that the © symbol and information is attached to the work; if a business plans to publish any copyright material on the Internet it should ensure that such information is included on the material, to ensure that copyright protection is available outside the UK.

As there is no registration process for acquiring a copyright, it can be difficult to prove when a copyright arose if a legal challenge is made to the use of the copyright material. As far as possible, a date should be fixed for the initial existence of the copyright – this can be done in a number of ways, including depositing a copy of the copyright material in a safety deposit box or, for software, through one of the recognised code depositary schemes, or by the creator mailing a copy to themselves by recorded delivery. This can then be produced to rebut any challenge to the copyright.

Database rights

22.5 There is also a form of copyright known as a *database right* – it provides 15 years protection, from the creation of the database (or from the date of later publication), against unauthorised extraction and reuse of the contents of the database where there has been substantive investment in the creation of the database contents. The database right protects the contents of the database; the selection and arrangement of the contents of the database may also be capable of being protected by copyright. Database rights are not universally recognised, although most of Europe does recognise some form of database right.

Patents

22.6

DEFINITION

A *patent* gives the inventor of the subject of the patent a monopoly right to stop others from making, using or selling the invention; if a product or process is not patented, it is harder to protect it from unauthorised use. The protection is for industrial products and processes – functional and/or technical – and most patents are, in fact, given for new developments of existing technology.

There is no particular requirement for the product or process to be complex, only that it be novel, involved an inventive step and is industrially applicable.

What can't be patented?

22.7 Patents are not given in the UK or Europe for business methods – unless they are specifically technological. In contrast, the USA does grant patents over business methods even where they are not technological (for example, a process for allocating staff to a project can be patented in the USA. The UK would not grant a patent over that process).

Software

22.8 Computer software may be patented, but only in exceptional cases where the program produces an improvement in technology (for example, a program which improves the rendering speed for graphics might be patentable. A program which translates text from one language to another is not patentable). As with business methods, the USA has a more liberal approach and often grants patents for software which is not patentable in the UK or Europe.

Biological material

22.9 Biotechnology products involving biological material may be patentable, as may processes by which biological material is produced, processed or used. However, plant and animal varieties are not patentable and neither are essentially biological processes for the production of plants and animals. Plant varieties may be separately protected under UK or European plant variety rights. However, inventions relating to plants or animals may be patentable if the technical aspects are not specific to a particular plant or animal variety.

Gene sequences – full or partial – may be patentable. However, the simple discovery of the sequence or partial sequence of a gene is not a patentable invention. Isolated from the human body or otherwise produced by a technical process, the reproduction of a sequence may be a patentable invention, even if the structure of the final product is identical to that of a natural element.

Ownership

22.10 In general, in the UK, the right to apply for and own a patent belongs to the inventor or inventors. However, the inventor can sell or give away that right (in addition to being able to licence or sell the patented product or process once the patent has been granted) or, in certain circumstances, the law may determine that someone else has that right – generally, this will be the case where a patent results from an invention made by an employee in the UK. Unless the employee and the employer agree otherwise, if the invention is made in the course of an employee's duties then the invention belongs to the employer either if:

- it is reasonable to expect an invention to result from the employee's duties (for example, if they are employed to carry out research and development); or

- if the employee had a particular obligation to improve the employer's interests (for example, as a company director).

If the invention is made overseas, the laws of that country apply instead, and may be different from those in the UK.

Applying for a patent

22.11   Patent rights are not created automatically, unlike copyright. To be able to claim the protection of patent rights, the patent needs to be registered. In the UK, registration is with the UK Patent Office (www.patent.gov.uk/patent/index.htm) or through the European Patent Office (www.european-patent-office.org/).

Patent strategy – is a patent the most appropriate protection?

22.12   As discussed in Chapter 19 on *Intellectual property strategy*, it may not always be appropriate to apply for a patent on a product or process; the application procedure for patents requires the disclosure of a considerable amount of information which is then published by the Patent Office. This information is available to anyone who cares to look for it – including competitors. Included in the information must be the industrial application of the product/process. Depending on how the application is made, the public information may provide a blueprint to the product or process which can be used to recreate the product/process outside the territorial protection of the patent; in this case, the patent rights provide no protection unless the product/process is resold into the UK (or into other areas where a patent right has been granted).

Public information

22.13   Once a patent has expired, the information in the patent application can be used by anyone – generic pharmaceuticals usually appear immediately after the patent on the original drug has expired; as the information is publically available, the manufacturers can get ready to produce the drugs whilst the patent is in force so that they can sell immediately it expires (this is dependant on the generic drug being able to demonstrate bioequivalence – ie show that it performs in the same manner – with the original patented drug). Ultimately, a business will need to balance the protection given by a patent application against the requirement to publish potentially sensitive information.

A patentable product/process may still be protected by copyright and/or design rights, or protected by confidentiality agreements, even if the patent is not applied for. If it is important that details of the product/process are not disclosed to the extent necessary to apply for a patent, then it may be commercially more effective to rely on those rights instead.

For example, Coca-Cola has not – and will not – patent its recipe; if it were to do so, it would be required to disclose the ingredients. Given the mystique with which Coca-Cola and folk history has endowed the secret recipe, this could be a commercial disaster for the company.

In particular, if a product or process is expected still to have significant value at the end of a patent protection period, it may be more appropriate to rely on treating it as a trade secret and protecting it by confidentiality agreements – these may be more difficult to enforce than patent rights, but the product or process remains secret as long as the confidentiality is unbroken. Using Coca-Cola as the example again, if it had patented its recipe more than 20 years ago, it would now be unable to prevent a competitor from using the recipe.

Protection

22.14   A patent right does not last as long as a copyright; in the UK, patent rights are granted for 20 years from the date the application is filed. The right is also restricted to the UK; if patent protection is required elsewhere, then patent rights will need to be separately acquired in the relevant countries. Alternatively, a European or international patent can be obtained. The Patent Co-operation Treaty provides for a single application procedure for an international patent; application in the UK is via the Patent Office and the application must list the Treaty countries for which the patent is to apply. Over 70 countries are currently signed up to the Treaty, and an international patent is treated as a series of patents, one for each country, each subject to national law in the country in which it is valid.

A European patent is valid in most Western European countries, and application can be made in any country in Europe, or via the European Patent Office. In the UK, application is usually made via the UK Patent Office. The countries for which the patent is to apply must be listed on the application and a fee paid for each country listed; this is usually a cheaper route than opting to make separate patent applications in each country. The resulting European patent is treated in the same way as an international patent – as a series of national patents, each subject to national law in the country in which it is valid.

Renewals

22.15   Although a UK patent right is granted for 20 years, it must be renewed annually after the fifth anniversary of the filing of the application for grant of the patent right. If the patent is not renewed within six months of the renewal date it will expire, although the patent holder can apply for the patent to be restored within 13 months of the expiry date.

The cost of renewing patents should be considered; if the patent is not actively being exploited, it may not be worth the fees involved in the later years. Renewal fees for patents increase each year – the payment on the fifth anniversary is currently £50 whereas the payment on the twentieth anniversary is currently £400. For a company with a portfolio of patents, the renewal fees can be a significant cost.

Indeed, the cost of maintaining patents is often cited as a barrier to innovation in the UK.

Trademarks

22.16

DEFINITION

A *trademark* is a sign or mark which distinguishes the products of one trader from those of another. The trademark can include words, signs, logos, slogans, and sometimes sounds and gestures. It is primarily a marketing tool, and must be capable of being graphically reproduced (in words or in pictures) in order to be registered in the UK. Once registered, the owner of the trademark has the exclusive right to use that trademark – it is not mandatory to register a trademark, but it is easier to protect a registered trademark.

The ™ symbol does not denote a registered trademark; it indicates that the word or logo is used as a trademark, but not necessarily that it is registered. The ® symbol, however, does indicate that the word or logo is protected by registration somewhere in the world.

Registration

22.17   In the UK, the Patent Office (www.patent.gov.uk/) is responsible for dealing with applications to register trademarks. As with patents, once an application is made a search is done to ensure that the mark is unique. The mark must also not be confusingly similar to existing registered trademarks. A European trademark, giving protection throughout the European Union, can be registered at the Office for Harmonization in the Internal Market (http://oami.eu.int/). Trademark or patent attorneys can assist with making the application. The Institute of Trademark Attorneys (www.itma.org.uk/) and the Chartered Institute of Patent Agents (www.cipa.org.uk/) can both provide directories of appropriate attorneys.

Once registered, a trademark can be licensed or sold in the same way as other pieces of IP; registration also makes it easier to protect the mark – it provides evidence of ownership of the mark, and provides protection throughout the territory. It is more difficult to defend an unregistered trademark, as there is no proof of ownership and it is much harder to prove that there is a trading reputation related to the mark throughout the UK (or in whichever market it is necessary to defend the mark).

Renewal

22.18   Trademark rights do not expire, unlike patents and copyrights. However, they need to be renewed every ten years to maintain the rights; if not renewed, the mark will expire – an application to restore the mark can be made within a year of expiry. Unlike patents, the cost of renewing a trademark remains the same no matter how long the trademark has been protected – currently, the renewal fee for trademark protection is £200.

Designs

22.19 Designs are increasingly important; the shape or overall appearance of a product can have an appreciable commercial function. Designs may be protected either by registration or by design rights.

Design rights

22.20

> **DEFINITION**
>
> *Design rights* are similar to copyright in that they arise when the design is created and no application is necessary to grant them. They apply to original, non-commonplace designs of the shape or configuration of an article. Only three-dimensional designs are protected; two-dimensional designs (such as textile patterns) are not protected, although they may be protected by registration.

A design right is rather shorter than copyright, lasting for 10 years after an article with the design is first marketed (or, if shorter, for 15 years from the creation of the design). Protection is given in the United Kingdom for individuals and companies in the European Union, or nationals from New Zealand or United Kingdom colonies. As with copyright, a date for the creation/existence of the design right should be established as far as possible by keeping a record of when the design was first recorded in material form and when articles with the form are first sold or rented. A prototype and/or example of the finished product could also be deposited – if feasible – in a safety deposit box.

Licences of right

22.21 Design rights are not as extensive as copyright; only the first five years of existence of the right provide a monopoly on exploitation for the creator. For the remaining five years of the right, it is subject to licences of right – anyone will be entitled to a licence (subject to paying appropriate royalties) to make and sell articles copying the design. The owner is not, however, required to make drawings or other know-how available to the licensee. The exception here is in the design of semi-conductor chips; to fit with European law, the design right in semi-conductor chips lasts 10 years in full with no licences of right available at any time in those 10 years.

Exclusions

22.22 Design rights are not available for objects that are required to fit or match one or more other items – this ensures that competition is not stifled in trade in, for example, spare parts for cars. Competitors cannot be prevented from copying features of a protected design that are necessary to allow them to produce something to be fitted to or matched to the design. However, copying features where there is no need to do so is not permitted.

Registered designs

22.23

> **DEFINITION**
>
> New, aesthetically appealing, designs may be registered to protect them; this gives the owner of the *registered design* an effective monopoly over the design for the registration period.

To be registered, a design must

- have significant eye appeal (there must be design freedom – articles whose design is dictated purely by function are not protected; car panels, for example, are not protected).
- be new (the design must not previously have been published, other than by exhibition in certain approved exhibitions not more than six months before application, and must not be materially similar to an already registered design).
- not be excluded (certain articles are automatically excluded from registration, including sculpture, medals and printed materials which are primarily literary or artistic – this includes advertisements and dress patterns).

Registration

22.24   Registration is by application to the Patent Office; as with application for other rights, the assistance of a patent or trademark attorney may be worthwhile. Where a set of articles is produced, one application may be made to register the set, rather than making individual applications; this will only be possible if the articles in the set have sufficient commonality of design. Protection for the design overseas is only available by making separate applications to each country; there is no international treaty which permits an application in one country to cover several countries. Registration does not eliminate any copyright or design right existing in the same article. Once registered, the design can be sold or licensed in the same way as other IP.

Renewal

22.25   Registration of a design gives a monopoly on the outward appearance of a manufactured article; it is valid for up to 25 years from the date of registration, but it must be renewed every 5 years to prevent the registration from expiring. As with patents, the renewal fee increases with the length of time the design has been protected – currently, the first renewal fee (on the fifth anniversary) is £130; the renewal fee on the twentieth anniversary is £450.

Compulsory licence

22.26 If a registered design is not used, an independent party can apply to the Patent Office for a compulsory licence to be granted to them so that they can exploit the design.

Other intellectual property

22.27 Trade secrets – also described as 'know-how' or 'show-how' – are not specifically protected but do need to be included in a discussion of intellectual property; whilst copyright and other such assets are valuable, the expertise to use and develop the rights is perhaps more valuable. This is why *private managed knowledge* forms a core part of the intellectual property strategy discussion in Chapter 19. It is certainly something for which businesses can and do pay significant amounts of money. Know-how is protected commercially by maintaining security within the business and by the use of confidentiality agreements; there is no statutory protection for them. Payments for know-how need to be distinguished from payments from any associated intellectual property, as the tax treatment will be different.

Confidentiality

22.28 Relying on protecting a product or process as a trade secret – for example, where the commercial risk from disclosure of the details of that product or process via a patent application is unacceptable – requires detailed adherence to confidentiality. A business relying on maintaining confidentiality should ensure that there are procedures in place to protect that confidentiality. In particular, the following need to be considered:

- document confidentiality procedures to be able to enforce them;
- ensuring employees are educated about the procedures relating to confidential information, and include restrictive covenants relating to any confidential information in contracts of employment;
- keeping confidential information locked in files, and encrypted if held on computer;
- restricting the number of people who know the confidential information;
- putting in place non-disclosure agreements with third parties to whom information is – or may be – disclosed.

SUMMARY

Characteristics of intellectual property

Intellectual property	*Include:*	*Owner (subject to alternative agreement)*	*Length of protection*	*Automatic protection*
Copyright	Literary and artistic works; computer software	Creator or employer	Life of owner plus 70 years	Yes
Database rights	Contents of database	Creator or employer	15 years from creation	Yes
Patents	Novel product/ process capable of being applied in industry	Inventor or employer	20 years from application for patent (but must be renewed annually after fifth anniversary of application)	No
Trademarks	Words or symbols distinguishing the products of a business	First applicant	Indefinite, but must be renewed every 10 years	No
Design rights	Original, non-commonplace three-dimensional designs	Creator or employer	10 years from first marketing (to a maximum of 15 years from creation)	Yes
Registered designs	New aesthetically appealing designs	First applicant	25 years from date of registration, but must be renewed every five years	No

Patent Process

23

OBJECTIVE

- To describe the process involved in applying for a patent in the UK.

Introduction

23.1 Patent rights are not created automatically, unlike copyright. To be able to claim the protection of patent rights, the patent needs to be registered. In the UK, registration is with the UK Patent Office (www.patent.gov.uk/) or through the European Patent Office (www.european-patent-office.org/). The application procedure is complicated and most applicants will use a patent agent to assist with the preparation and submission of the application. The Chartered Institute of Patent Agents (www.cipa.org.uk/) maintains a directory of patent agents and can also provide information about the patent process.

Papers to be filed

23.2 Two papers need to be filed with the Patent Office to apply for a patent; the *specification*, and *Patents Form 1/77*.

Any *claims* and an *abstract* can be filed later in the process.

Specification

23.3

> **DEFINITION**
>
> The basis of the application is the *specification*; this is a document which describes the invention. The specification needs to include a full
>
> *(Continued)*

> description of the invention, including drawings where appropriate – the drawings help to describe the invention but do not need to be technical blueprints; the Patent Office do not want engineering diagrams.

The description must be as complete as possible because changes *cannot* be made to the specification once it has been submitted to the Patent Office. Additionally, a patent application will fail if there is not enough information in the specification to enable others to carry out the invention for which a patent is applied – it is this level of disclosure that can make applying for a patent a commercial risk.

The specification should include the following to be complete:

- The background to the invention, explaining the problem addressed.
- Essential features of the invention.
- Detailed description of the invention.
- Examples of how the invention may be used.
- Important features in the drawings should be indicated by reference numbers, which are then cross-referenced in the text of the description, where the features are described.

The specification needs to be typed/printed, and submitted on white A4 paper. The paper should be typed/printed on one side of the paper with a wide margin. All drawings need to be in black and white, printed clearly so that they can easily be photocopied.

Two copies of the specification and related drawings need to be filed.

Claims

23.4   The specification can include a claim, which gives a precise statement of the invention – it must define the invention by setting out the distinctive technical features. The claim should not include any commercial or other non-technical advantages of the invention.

The claim should not include restrictive terms, or non-essential technical features. Subsidiary features should be set out in dependent claims. The claim cannot include anything that has not already been referred to in the specification. A claim cannot be used to amend or add information to a specification.

Claims do not need to be included in the specification when it is filed. If not included in the specification, they must be filed at the Patent Office (in duplicate) within 12 months of filing the specification.

Abstract

23.5   An abstract is a brief summary of the invention; when the Patent Office publish the patent application (about 18 months after filing) the summary is used as the front page description.

The summary should include all the most important technical features; it may also suggest a drawing from the specification which is appropriate to illustrate the invention – this drawing should be referred to in writing (using any reference numbers relating to the drawing). New drawings cannot not be included in the abstract.

Two copies of the abstract will need to be filed with the Patent Office within 12 months of the filing of the specification.

Patent Form 1/77

23.6 This form needs to be completed and submitted with the specification – it is relatively straightforward, providing the Patent Office with contact details for the inventor and any agent acting for them.

No prior disclosure

23.7 Once an application is made, the Patent Office will do a search to make sure that no patents have already been granted for the product or process and to ensure that there has been no prior publication of the information; it can often be necessary to negotiate the scope of protection with the Patent Office before the patent is granted. There should be no *public* disclosure of the invention before filing an application; any type of disclosure (including word of mouth, demonstration, advertisement or article in a journal) by an applicant or anyone acting for them, could prevent the applicant from getting a patent. It could also be a reason for having the patent revoked if one was granted. Any disclosure should be made only under conditions of strict confidence.

When should a patent be applied for?

23.8 Application for patent protection can be made at any time; there are advantages and disadvantages regardless of what the state of research is at the time of application. An application when the invention is still in the early stages of research may ensure priority over anyone else who files a similar application; however, if there are changes to the invention as the research progresses, the application will need to be refiled. A later application, while it runs more risk of a competing application having been made during the research process, may be more commercially advantageous – it may be preferable to wait to file an application until a prototype has been tested and the invention is ready to be marketed.

Business Practicalities

24

OBJECTIVE

- To give an overview of the practical aspects of setting up a company and dealing with required administrative matters, particularly:
  - Types of legal entity.
  - Forming a company.
  - Companies House requirements.
  - Directors and company secretaries.
  - Company meetings.

Warning:

- **This chapter contains only a brief overview of these matters; for more detail, see the guidance leaflets available from Companies House, either by post or via their website (www.companieshouse.gov.uk) or discuss it with company/commercial lawyers or accountants.**

Is a company needed?

24.1   It is not necessary to set up a company in order to run a business; partnerships and sole traders can operate as effectively.

Most businesses do use the company format, but there is no simple answer as to whether a company is better than the other models.

Benefits of a company

24.2   Companies do have the advantage of a lower tax rate than either partnerships or sole traders, and this may be a motivation. There are also certain tax reliefs that are available only to companies, not to other types of business.

Using a company can limit the liability of the owners of the business although, in practice, this is not as helpful as it might seem – lenders will often want personal guarantees from shareholders of small business which negate the limited liability of the company.

Disadvantages of a company

24.3   The company model generates additional administration – the statutory requirements for accounts and returns are more involved for companies than for other models. An unincorporated business does not generally need to file accounts (although some form of accounts will be required with the tax return).

Other options

Sole trader

24.4   In this case, the founder of the business is self-employed – the income of the business is his income, and there is no real distinction between the business and the person. This is the simplest form of business and, generally, is only practical for small businesses. Once a business starts to grow, and in particular when it starts to require external funding, the sole trader will need to seriously consider incorporating the business.

Partnership

24.5   Where more than one person is involved in the development of the business, a partnership may be formed between the founders. A partnership is not a legal entity in its own right; it is best described as a relationship between the partners – the existence of a partnership is regulated by the agreement between the partners.

Partners are jointly and severally liable for the debts of the business – there is no limitation of liability available.

Limited Liability Partnerships (LLPs)

24.6   These are a new form of entity in the UK; unlike partnerships, this is effectively a separate legal entity, which needs to be registered with Companies House – this means that it can, for example, own property in its own right and borrow in its own right. Traditional partnerships cannot do either – partnership property is owned by the partners, and borrowing is undertaken by the partners, not the partnership.

As a separate entity, an LLP will continue to exist even if the members change – in contrast, traditional partnerships technically cease to exist and are re-created each time the membership changes.

The liability of the members is limited to the capital contribution which they agree to make to the partnership; an LLP effectively acts as a form of company which is transparent for tax purposes – unlike a company, which is directly taxed on its profits, the profits of an LLP are taxed on the members of the LLP. This can allow for some more flexible tax planning than is generally available to companies.

Choice of entity

24.7   There is no single answer as to which type of entity is the best way to do business – the decision will depend on the type of businesses and the expectations of the market and investors. In general, however, most businesses in the technology sector operate as a company and, accordingly, the rest of this chapter looks at the practical aspects of running a company.

Types of company

24.8

DEFINITION

A company is a *legal person* – an entity that exists separately from both the shareholders and the directors of the company.

Why set up a company?

24.9   As the company is a person in its own right, for legal purposes, it can hold property and can also give security for any debts against such property. In any disputes, the company is the person that either sues, or is sued – the owners of the company are not usually liable for the actions of the company. The company is also not tied to any changes in its membership (shareholders); it will continue to exist until it is wound up.

There are various types of company; the principal distinction is whether or not a company is limited.

Unlimited companies

24.10   Unlimited companies are rare – the shareholders of the company are not protected against the liabilities of the company if the company is wound up. Whilst the company is still a going concern (ie able to pay its way and continue in existence) the members are only liable for any unpaid element of their shareholding. However, if a creditor issues a winding up order against the company to recover a debt, the shareholders will be liable for the entire debt.

Limited companies

24.11   The majority of companies are limited liability companies; the shareholders (or other members) are protected from the debts of the company if it is put into liquidation.

Companies limited by guarantee

24.12 A company limited by guarantee has no share capital; instead, the members give guarantees instead – their liability is limited to the amount of the guarantee. These companies are not generally used for commercial enterprises; they are more commonly used for non-profit organisations.

Private company limited by shares

24.13 A company limited by shares is the most usual form of company. The shareholders' only liability is the amount (if any) still unpaid on their shares.

Public company limited by shares

24.14 A public limited company ('plc') is one which – subject to certain regulations – is allowed to offer its shares to the public. As with private companies limited by shares, the liability of the shareholders is limited to any amount unpaid on their shares. There are some requirements which need to be met for a company to be public; the main requirements are:

- that the authorised share capital is at least £50,000. Of this, at least 25% must be paid up. If any premium is charged (over the nominal value of the shares) this must be entirely paid up; and
- the company must state that it is a public limited company – the name must finish with 'plc' or 'public limited company'; and
- the company must have at least two shareholders (private companies need only have one).

Plcs are subject to additional rules and regulations, and are more tightly controlled than private limited companies. Consequently, investors will usually insist on investing in a plc; it may be necessary to create a new plc to act as the holding company owning an existing limited company before an investment is made.

Note that plcs do *not* need to be listed on a stock exchange – the vast majority are not listed.

Forming a company

24.15 A company is formed either by buying an 'off-the-shelf' ready-made company or by setting up the company from scratch.

'Off-the-shelf' company

24.16 This is the fastest way to set up a company – the company will already have been formed, all that is required is to transfer the subscriber shares from the company formation agents, register the change of directors and shareholders, and (usually) to change the name.

It is not essential to change the name, but most ready-made companies have names which are not particularly memorable. The name will also have nothing to do with the business for which the company is to be used.

Other matters which may need to be altered include the articles of association and any share capital – most companies are set up with £100 of share capital divided into £1 ordinary shares. Depending on the needs of the investors, additional share capital and different classes of shares may be required.

Setting up a company from scratch

24.17 This is usually done with the assistance of a lawyer; in most cases, companies are set up from scratch when there is something particularly complex about, for example, the articles of association or memorandum of association (see below).

Company name

24.18 All companies need to be named; there are some restrictions on what can be chosen but these are not very onerous. The company name must be registered with Companies House.

Requirements

24.19 The name must end in either:

- Limited
- Unlimited
- Public Limited Company

The ending depends on the type of company; abbreviations (such as 'Ltd' and 'plc') can be used, as, for companies based in Wales, can the Welsh equivalents.

The name chosen may be rejected by Companies House if:

- another company with exactly the same name is already registered; or
- it includes the words *limited, unlimited* or *public limited company* anywhere other than at the end of the name; or
- it is considered offensive; or
- its use would be a criminal offence.

Approval

24.20 Some names need approval from the Secretary of State before they can be used – these are names which include certain specific words (such as 'British' or 'chemistry') or suggest a connection with government or royalty.

Passing off

24.21   Even if a name is registered, if it is similar to the name of another company already in existence then the company is at risk of a 'passing off' action from the first company and may be liable for damages. Generally, the names need to be similar enough to potentially mislead the public. The two companies also need to be in the same area of business – a tailor is unlikely to be able to stop a biotechnology company from using a similar name, for example.

Documents required

24.22   Several documents are required to form a company; these need to be submitted to Companies House for the company to be formed and registered.

Memorandum of association

24.23   The memorandum of association of a company is the charter document of the company; it sets out the following information:

- the name of the company; and
- where the registered office of the company is located; and
- what the company will do (this is usually stated in very wide terms, to allow the company freedom in its business dealings – it is possible to state that the company will simply carry on business as a general commercial company); and
- any share capital of the company (the value and the number of shares).

Articles of association

24.24   The articles of association set out how the company will operate internally. Most companies base their articles on one of the model sets of articles defined in regulations and amend it as necessary.
   The articles generally cover information such as:

- how directors are to be appointed and when they are to retire;
- the procedure for altering share capital;
- the procedure for holding company meetings;
- the restrictions (if any) on the issue and transfer of shares.

The contents of the articles of association may be complemented by a shareholders' agreement, which sets out the way in which the shareholders will deal with each other and the company. A shareholder agreement is recommended for joint ventures; it is particularly useful where the shareholders are contributing non-cash assets, such as intellectual property, to the company in exchange for shares.

Companies House forms

24.25   In addition to the memorandum and articles of association, two forms must be submitted to Companies House to form the company.

Form 10 gives details of the first director(s), company secretary, and the address that will be the registered office.

Form 12 confirms that the companies legislation requirements have been followed.

Companies House requirements

24.26   Companies are required to publish a certain amount of information; they are also required to submit specific documents to Companies House on a regular basis.

Publishing information

24.27   A company must state its name in certain places, as well as on company documents. Additional information is also required on business stationery.

Company name

24.28   The name must be displayed:

- outside every office or place of business of the company – including the homes of directors, if business is carried on there;
- on all business letters;
- on all notices;
- on all invoices, receipts and letters of credit;
- on all cheques, money orders etc.

Business stationery

24.29   The following information must be included:

- the place of registration;
- the company registration number;
- the address of the registered office;
- either all or none of the directors' names – it is not possible to show only some of the names.

Documents to be submitted

24.30   The main forms which need to be filed with Companies House on a regular basis are:

- the accounts
  - (i) all companies – including non-trading companies – need to keep accounting records and file accounts for each accounting period;
  - (ii) exemptions from filing are available for small- and medium-sized companies, and dormant companies.

- annual returns
  - (a) this provides general information about the company, including the directors and shareholders;
  - (b) usually, the return is provided by Companies House. The company secretary will need to check it and make any necessary amendments before returning it;
  - (c) failure to file an annual return can lead to prosecution of the directors and company secretary by Companies House.

- forms recording changes of
  - – accounting date;
  - – directors (change of address, appointment and resignation);
  - – company secretary;
  - – allotments of shares;
  - – registered office of the company.

- resolutions of the company in general meeting;
- mortgages and charges over property.

Directors and company secretaries

24.31 All companies require at least two formally appointed company officers.

A private company requires:

- one director; and
- one company secretary – this cannot be the same person as a sole director, although the company secretary may also be a director. No formal qualifications are required.

A plc requires:

- two directors; and
- one company secretary – this may be one of the directors, and must be formally qualified (generally, the secretary must be a member of one of a number of specific professional organisations).

Directors

24.32 The directors manage the business of the company, and exercise the powers of the company – as defined in the articles of association. Generally, anyone can be a company director. There are some exceptions:

- Undischarged bankrupts.
- People disqualified from being directors.
- For plcs and their subsidiaries, anyone over 70 years old.

Appointment

24.33 Directors may be appointed either when the company is first registered or, later, in accordance with the requirements of the articles of association.

Retirement

24.34 A director can resign at any time, subject to the terms of any service contract.

The articles may require directors to retire and offer themselves for re-election on a regular, rotating, basis; this is more common in plcs than in private companies. In small companies it would generally be impractical and largely pointless for the directors to put themselves up for re-election in this way.

Additionally, directors of plcs are required to retire at the annual general meeting following their 70th birthday.

Removal

24.35 A director can be removed by ordinary resolution of the company, subject to special notice of at least 28 days. A director removed from office may be able to claim compensation.

Disqualification

24.36 A director may be disqualified from office either by:

- the articles of association – these may require a director to leave office in certain circumstances (eg ceasing to hold shares in the company);
- law, for
  - (i) misconduct (eg convicted of an offence in connection with the company);
  - (ii) unfitness (eg persistent failure to deliver returns to Companies House);
  - (iii) other matters (eg fraud).

Directors' duties

24.37 Directors have two primary duties – a fiduciary duty, and a duty to use skill and care in the company's management.

Fiduciary duty

24.38 The fiduciary duty of a director is owed to the company. In general, it requires the director to act in the best interests of the company. In particular, directors should not put themselves in a position where personal interests may conflict with the duty to the company.

Duty of care

24.39   The duty to use skill and care in managing the company, whilst important, is reasonably straightforward. In particular:

- There is no requirement to have any greater skill in management than anyone else with the same knowledge and experience.
- A director's duties are exercised at board meetings – there is no requirement to be continuously involved with the company unless required by, for example, a service contract.
- A director can rely on employees to carry out the day-to-day running of the business.

Directors' liabilities

24.40   Directors are not, generally, liable for the actions of the company. However, there are some circumstances in which a director may become personally liable for those actions – for example, when a director does not act in the best interests of the company.

An action which may result in a director being personally liable may be validated – removing the liability – by the shareholders of the company. This will not always be effective; it depends on the extent of the breach of fiduciary duty, for example.

Company secretary

24.41   The company secretary's general duties are set out in a service contract, and will vary from company to company. However, there are certain duties which are usually carried out by the company secretary on behalf of the company.

These duties include:

- Maintaining statutory registers (register of members, of directors etc).
- Ensuring that required documents are filed at Companies House.
- Providing members and auditors with notice of meetings.
- Keeping the minutes of board meetings.

A company secretary does not have any powers granted by legislation, other than to be able to sign Companies House forms on behalf of the company. However, as an officer of the company, the company secretary is liable with the directors for defaults of the company – such as failure to file an annual return with Companies House.

Company meetings

24.42 Company meetings are held to allow shareholders (*members*) to decide on actions to be taken by the company; whilst the day-to-day running of the company is in the hands of directors, there are some decisions which need to be confirmed by the shareholders of the company to be valid.

There are two types of company meetings:

- annual general meetings; and
- extraordinary general meetings.

Annual general meeting (AGM)

24.43 These must be held every year, within 15 months of the previous AGM. At least 21 days written notice of the AGM must be sent to every member of the company, although shorter notice is acceptable if the members entitled to attend agree.

Extraordinary special meeting (EGM)

24.44 An EGM is a general meeting other than an AGM; it is usually called by the directors to deal with some aspect of the company's business that requires the approval of members.

Members may also force the directors to call an EGM, although the members need to have at least 10% of the voting rights of the company in order to be able to do this. Generally, 14 days notice of the EGM is required, although this is increased to 21 days where a special resolution is to be passed at the meeting. Again, shorter notice may be given if the members agree.

Resolutions

24.45 Resolutions are matters agreed by the members, usually authorising the company directors to carry out a particular action or series of actions. Once the resolution has been passed, the company is bound by it.

Ordinary resolution

24.46 This requires a simple majority of the votes of the members attending. These are used for more straightforward matters – including the appointment of an auditor, the removal of a director, an increase in share capital.

Extraordinary and special resolutions

24.47 These require at least 75% majority of the votes of members attending the meeting and entitled to vote.

Extraordinary resolutions are mostly used in insolvency matters – they sanction a creditor's voluntary winding-up, for example.

Special resolutions are used for matters affecting the company directly – including the amendment of articles, or increases or reductions in share capital.

Written resolutions

24.48   It is not always necessary to hold meetings to pass resolutions; private companies can pass resolutions provided that all the members who would be entitled to attend and vote at the meeting sign the resolution. A written resolution cannot be used to dismiss a director or auditor.

A written resolution takes effect when the last member signs. The resolution must be filed at Companies House in the same way as other resolutions.

Employees and the Employer's Responsibilities

25

OBJECTIVES

To give an overview of the issues (legal, tax and practical) involved in employing people. In particular:

- Employee or contractor?
- Employment contracts.
- PAYE and National Insurance.
- Employee incentives.
- Dismissal of employees.

- **This chapter is not intended to provide you with a complete guide to dealing with employees, and cannot replace a professional advisor. This chapter aims to give an overview of the areas which need to be considered and the questions and concepts which should be kept in mind.**

Employee or contractor?

25.1 Distinguishing between an employee and a contractor is critical; the regulations relating to employees are far stricter than those relating to contractors. It is not unusual in certain industries for businesses to prefer to use contractors rather than employees – particularly for specific projects. Contractors are less of an administrative burden to businesses – there is no requirement to operate the Pay As You Earn ('PAYE') tax collection system, nor to account for National Insurance contributions. Contractors also have far fewer rights against a business.

The status of a worker is not entirely decided by the business; once an employer has determined whether an employee or a contractor is needed, it is essential that the employer ensures that the worker is treated in a manner consistent with the status required. The description of the worker as 'employee' or 'contractor' is not decisive and there are a number of tests which have developed over the years to distinguish between them. No single test is decisive, and it is often necessary to consider them in conjunction – each case will depend on the facts specific to it.

The more important tests include:

- The control test: the level of control which an employer has over the worker – both in terms of the work to be done and the way in which the work is done. The greater the degree of control, the more likely it is that a worker will be an employee.
- Risk and reward: whether the worker carries any risk in respect of the work done (for example, is required to provide tools at his own expense) and whether the worker has the opportunity to make any additional profit (for example, by finishing the work ahead of schedule on a flat-fee contract).
- Integration: the more essential a worker is to a business, the more likely they are to be an employee.

If the business requires the worker to be a contractor, legal advice should be taken to make sure that the contracts and working conditions are such that the worker can maintain that status. If, for some reason, the worker is found to be an employee the Inland Revenue can generally take action against the company for failure to deduct tax through PAYE, for example. If the worker is operating through a personal service company, however, it is the personal service company that is responsible to the Revenue for PAYE and other such payments.

Employment contracts

25.2 An employment contract can be written or oral; besides the terms specifically agreed between the employer and employee, it will also include a number of terms which are implied by law where they are not included in any formal document.

Implied terms of employment

25.3 The following are among the terms generally implied in any contract of employment:

- Both employer and employee:
  - To give reasonable notice of termination of employment.

- Employer obligations
  - (i) To provide a written statement of terms and conditions of employment – where an oral contract of employment is made, it must be followed up by a written statement. The written statement must include certain pieces of information, including holiday entitlement and rates of pay.
  - (ii) That the employer will provide work for the employee – this is generally implied where the employee's pay is related to the amount of work done.
  - (iii) Health and safety – this is a duty owed by an employer to all employees.
  - (iv) To follow legislation with regard to statutory sick pay, maternity rights, holiday entitlements, redundancy payments and discrimination.

- Employee obligations
  - (a) To follow an employer's instructions regarding work.

(b) Due diligence and care – an employer can be liable for negligence of employees.

(c) Not to disclose trade secrets – this should be reinforced with express terms in the contract, where the employee works with trade sensitive information, be it public or private managed knowledge.

Non-competition and non-disclosure covenants

25.4 Any high-technology business will have certain employees – if not all employees – who are involved with the know-how that is at the centre of the business model.

Whilst some protection is available to the business by way of patents, copyrights and other intellectual property rights, often it is the technical know-how contained in the employees' heads that is the most valuable asset of the business.

In order to protect the business, therefore, it is usual to include some form of restrictive covenants in the contracts of employment to prevent the employee from either taking the technical information of the company to a competitor, or personally starting up in business in competition.

These covenants will only be upheld by a court if they are reasonable – particularly with regard to the length of time after employment which is covered by the covenant, and the geographical area within which the covenant will operate. There is no absolute rule as to what is appropriate – it will depend on the company and the trade protected.

PAYE and National Insurance

25.5 The Pay As You Earn system is used to administer income tax payments by employees. The shorthand 'PAYE' is generally used to refer to the income tax deducted as well as to the system of deduction.

Instead of an employee being required to account for income tax on employment income at the end of a year of assessment, the employer will deduct tax from any relevant payments as they are made during the year.

Some businesses use a third party to deal with payroll matters, including PAYE; it is important to remember that, even though the business is not directly administering PAYE, it is still treated as the administrator for tax purposes. A business which plans to outsource its payroll function will need to be aware of this and, if possible, ensure that the contract with the company dealing with payroll on its behalf allows the business to recover any penalties or fines charged by the Inland Revenue for errors in administering PAYE.

What does PAYE cover?

25.6 PAYE must be deducted by an employer (for the purposes of this section on PAYE, 'employer' includes any third party to whom the PAYE function has been outsourced) from all income assessable under Schedule E – broadly, all salary or wages payments, together with any taxable bonuses (including gains on certain types of share options) and benefits in kind.

Benefits in kind

25.7 PAYE is deducted on the cash value of a benefit in kind; generally, most forms of payment other than in cash will be a benefit in kind, including gifts of shares in the company or the opportunity to buy shares at a discount. The PAYE on benefits in kind must be deducted from any cash actually paid to the employee, in addition to PAYE on the cash itself.

Lower-paid employees

25.8 Employees earning *less* than £8,500 a year are taxed only on benefits in kind which can be turned into cash. Other benefits, including beneficial loans and medical insurance, are not taxable on these employees.

Payments which are not benefits in kind

25.9 Certain payments will not be a benefit in kind for any employees. These include:

- Contributions to approved pension schemes (within certain limits).
- Staff canteen facilities (provided that all staff are eligible to use the facilities).
- Workplace nurseries (these must be directly provided by the employer, alone or jointly with other businesses – cash allowances to pay for child-care *are* taxable).
- Relocation expenses of less than £8,000.
- Computer equipment – the first £500 of the cash equivalent of any computer equipment given to an employee is not taxable.

Accounting for PAYE

25.10 Employers must account to the Inland Revenue for PAYE deducted from employees within 14 days of the end of the tax month in which the deduction was required to be made. Where the employer deducts less than £1,500 a month in PAYE, the employer can elect to pay it over on a quarterly basis instead.

National Insurance

25.11 National Insurance contributions ('NICs') are collected by employers, and paid by employers, on payments to employees during the year.

Employees' NICs

25.12 An employer must deduct NICs on payments (including benefits in kind) to employees between the lower and upper limit, at the rate of 10%. The limits change annually. Once payments have reached the upper limit, no additional NICs need be deducted.

Employers' NICs

25.13   Employers are required to pay NICs on payments to employees (including benefits in kind) over a specific amount. There is no upper limit on payments; employers will continue to have to pay NICs on payments even if there is no additional liability on employees.

Employers' NIC payments are *in addition* to the deduction of NICs from employee payments and cannot be recouped from employees.

Employee incentives

25.14   Over the past decade or so it has become increasingly common for employees to be given incentives related to both their own and the company's performance; most of these remain taxable (cash bonuses and similar gifts). However, it is possible for both the employee and the company to gain a tax advantage with certain types of incentive. These include:

* Save As You Earn schemes
* Share option schemes
* Enterprise management incentives

Save As You Earn ('SAYE') schemes

25.15   These are schemes, which must be approved by the Inland Revenue, through which employees save money on a monthly basis in order to buy shares in the company. The shares are normally acquired by the employee free of income tax.

All employees and directors must be eligible to enter the scheme, although the company can set a qualifying period of service which must be completed before the employee can join the scheme.

How does the scheme operate?

25.16   Through the scheme the company grants an employee an option to buy shares in the company in 3, 5 or 7 years time at a price between 100% and 80% of the current market value of the shares.

Tax effect

25.17   No income tax is charged on the grant of the options over the shares, even if granted at less than 100% of the current market value.

The employees will not generally be taxed when the savings are used to buy the shares; capital gains tax will be charged when the shares are eventually sold by the employee.

Share option schemes

25.18   Under a share option scheme, a company will grant an employee the option to buy shares in the company at a future date for a price fixed when the option is granted. If the share price of the company improves, the employee is able to buy the shares cheaply when the option is eventually exercised.

Unapproved share option schemes

25.19   There is no requirement for share option schemes to be approved, unlike SAYE schemes. If a scheme is not approved, income tax and National Insurance contributions may be charged on the grant or exercise of an option.

If the option must be exercised within 7 years of the date on which it is granted, there is no income tax due on the grant. If, however, the date on which the option can be exercised is capable of being more than 7 years from the date on which the option is granted, income tax is chargeable on the difference between:

• the market value of the shares at the date of grant of the option; and
• the exercise price of the shares (plus anything paid on the grant of the shares).

The company must deduct PAYE from any amount taxed. No NICs are due on this amount.

On the exercise of the option, the employee will be subject to income tax on the difference between:

• the market value of the shares at the date of exercise; and
• the price payable for the shares on exercise.

The employee is not actually required to sell the shares acquired although, in practice, some or all of the shares may be sold on exercise in order to pay the income tax due.

The company is required to deduct PAYE and (if the upper limit has not been reached) NICs on the amount taxed on exercise. The company will also have to account for employer's NICs on the amount taxed – however, it is possible for the employee and employer to agree that the employee will pay some or all of the employer's NICs instead. This provides the company with more certainty over its future costs – in late 1999 and 2000 some companies, particularly those in the technology sector, were in danger of being forced into liquidation because of the cost of NICs on share options at the point when technology stocks were rising rapidly in value.

Approved share option schemes

25.20   Approved share options schemes are, as the name indicates, approved by the Inland Revenue and, as such, carry tax benefits in comparison with unapproved schemes.

In general, there is no charge to income tax or liability to NICs when options are granted or exercised under an approved scheme; the only tax charge should be capital gains tax when the shares are eventually sold.

Options cannot be granted at a discount to the market value of the shares on the date of grant. They are, therefore, only worth exercising if the shares rise in value.

There are limits to the value of options which can be held by an employee (currently £30,000 – the value of an option is the cumulative market value of the shares on the date of each grant; existing options are not revalued each time new options are granted). Once options have been exercised they are no longer counted towards the total.

For the tax benefits to be available, the options must be exercised only between three and ten years after the date of grant.

All-employee share option schemes (AESOPs)

25.21   These are a relatively new form of Inland Revenue approved share option scheme. Tax advantages are available for shares purchased by or given to employees through the scheme. The scheme must be open to all employees of the company.

Employees can acquire shares in four ways through the scheme:

- Free shares – a company can give employees up to £3,000 of shares in any one tax year (6 April to 5 April). The number of shares given may be linked to performance targets.
- Partnership shares – these may be bought by employees from gross (pre-tax and NICs) pay – this reduces the amount of tax and NICs payable. Up to £125 (or 10% of gross pay if lower) may be bought each month.
- Matching shares – an employer can give an employee up to two shares for every one partnership share bought.
- Dividend shares – once an employee is a shareholder in the company, the employee can choose to take dividend payments in the form of additional shares in the company. Up to £1,500 of shares can be acquired this way each year. No income tax will be due on the dividend represented by the shares as long as the dividend shares are owned by the employee for at least three years. If the employee does *not* choose to take the dividend in shares, income tax will be due on the dividend in the usual way (through the employee's tax return, not through PAYE).

No income tax or NICs will be due on any free or matching shares acquired through the scheme – normally, shares given to an employee are subject to both.

Shares acquired by employees under the scheme are held in a trust; free and matching shares must be held in the trust for at least three years (the company can increase this holding period to five years). If the shares are taken out of the trust earlier, some tax and NICs will be due on them.

If the shares are held in the trust until they are eventually sold, no capital gains tax will be due on them – the employee will be able to take the proceeds of sale free of tax.

Enterprise Management Incentives

25.22   Enterprise Management Incentives ('EMI') are share options which are designed to help smaller companies reward employees – these companies may not be able to match the cash-in-pocket pay offered by larger companies, but the EMI options mean that a smaller company can ultimately offer a greater potential reward.

EMI options over shares with a market value of up to £100,000 may be granted to any number of employees of a company, subject to a maximum share value of £3 million under EMI option to all employees. The options can be exercisable up to 10 years from the date of grant.

- **Eligible companies** – The company granting the EMI options must be a trading company with gross assets of less than £15 million (if the company is part of a group, the gross assets of the entire group must not exceed £15 million).

- **Tax advantages** – The grant of an EMI option is tax-free and there will normally be no tax or NIC for the employee to pay when the option is exercised. There will normally be no NIC charge for the employer either. When the shares are eventually sold at a gain, capital gains tax will be due – this may be reduced because taper relief (a tax relief that reduces the capital gain of shareholders actively working in the company they hold shares in) will normally start from the date that the option is *granted*, not the date on which the option is exercised. Shares acquired in this way may qualify as business assets which are eligible for accelerated taper relief.

Taper relief is discussed in more detail in Chapter 30 in the *Basis of taxation*.

Pension schemes

25.23 These can be tax-effective for the business, allowing it to reward employees without incurring employers' NIC. Setting up a pension scheme is a complex operation, beyond the scope of this book – most companies will outsource their pension scheme provisions.

The regulations regarding pension schemes are in the process of changing – the introduction of the stakeholder pension schemes by the Government mean that any employer which does not currently offer a pension scheme to its employees will need to at least provide access to a stakeholder pension scheme for those employees, as well as collecting the employees' contributions to the scheme by deduction from pay. The new rules do not apply to businesses that employ four or fewer people.

Dismissal of employees

25.24 An employment contract can be terminated in a number of ways, although the most usual are:

By notice

25.25 Either party gives notice under the contract of employment. If the contract does not set out a notice period, the statutory notice periods will apply – these increase with the length of service.

Expiry

25.26 A fixed term contract automatically terminates at the end of the specified term.

On breach of contract

25.27 Certain types of conduct constitute a breach of contract; the employee can be dismissed without notice following such a breach. The type of conduct which can lead to a breach includes theft (of the employer's property) and gross insubordination.

Employee rights

25.28 An employee whose employment has been terminated has three options available for compensation.

Unfair dismissal

25.29 An employee has the right not to be unfairly dismissed. If an employer is found to have unfairly dismissed an employee, the Employment Tribunal may order the employer to reinstate the employee or – more usually – to pay compensation.

The employer needs to show that the dismissal was fair – there are a set of statutory rules which are generally considered to be fair reasons for dismissal; the employer needs to establish that the dismissal was for one of those reasons. Once established, the court then considers whether the dismissal was fair in all the circumstances.

Certain types of dismissal are automatically unfair – these include dismissals on the grounds of maternity, Sunday working, trade union membership and redundancy (where the employee has been unfairly selected).

Redundancy payment

25.30 Minimum payments are set by statute; if not paid automatically, an employee can make a claim to the Employment Tribunal for payment.

Damages for wrongful dismissal

25.31 Wrongful dismissal occurs where an employer breaches the contract of employment in dismissing an employee; the employee can then make a claim for damages.

A breach of contract will occur, for example, where inadequate notice has been given, or where an employer fails to follow disciplinary procedures set out in the contract (whether contained within the contract or within a handbook referred to in the contract).

Sources of Funding

26

OBJECTIVES

- To set out the various sources of business finance.
- To provide a brief overview of each.

The range of options

26.1   There are various sources of funding for a business. They vary in terms of:

- The level of risk accepted.
- The length of time the funding is provided for.
- The terms on which it is supplied.

The range is as follows:

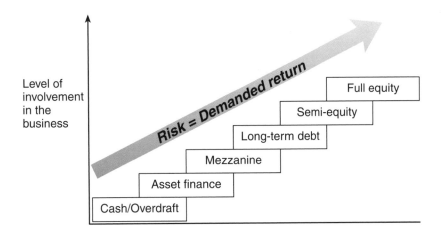

Figure 26.1 – the spectrum of funding options

Source: PKF

A comparison of the nature of the different options highlights the differences between the options. It should be noted that conceptually there may be overlaps between the different types.

Option	*Characteristics*
Cash/Overdraft	Actual cash already in the bank or generated from activities or an overdraft facility that is available but can be recalled at any time.
	A day-to-day financing approach.
Asset finance	Borrowing secured on specific assets such as debtors or stocks. Generally, a proportion is available up front with the rest paid over by the asset finance house when the debtor pays or the sale is made, less the charges being levied.
	Asset finance can also be used to purchase fixed assets such as plant and equipment.
	A short- to medium-term financing approach.
Mezzanine finance	A formal loan that needs to be repaid over time such as a mortgage or other loan. Security is required that backs up the capital element of the loan. Generally, mezzanine finance is provided in relation to asset purchase arrangements.
	A medium-term financing approach.
Long-term debt	A more risk-based loan sometimes in the form of a bond which can be bought and sold by the bondholder. May be issued with only limited or even no formal security underpinning the loan. The debt carries interest at a higher rate to reflect this increased risk.
	A long-term arrangement where the repayment profile may not start for some time and where there may be more to the repayment than simply paying back the capital element.
	Examples include bonds and loan notes as well as senior debt.
	A medium- to long-term financing approach.
Semi-equity	Often semi-equity can look very like a long-term loan in terms of the fact that the funds are provided with the intention of them being available for some time. Semi-equity has, however, some of the characteristics of full equity in that it is in the form of shares and therefore the return is dependent on the profitability of the company. If the company has no profits, the semi-equity holders get no return.
	An example of a semi-equity is preference or fixed dividend shares. These get dividends out of profits in advance of ordinary shareholders or get a fixed dividend per share if there is a profit that can be distributed.
	A long-term funding approach.
Full equity	Shares or partnership capital that have a direct interest in the profits of the company and the assets of the company on any winding up. The return is not guaranteed and the risk is therefore highest with this form of funding. If and when sold, however, the shares can also benefit from the goodwill in the business in that the value of the share may exceed its share of net assets.
	The longest term funding approach.

It is worth noting that the Companies Act requires limited liability companies to have at least some full equity shares in issue at all times.

Conversion

26.2 Some types of finance may be set up in such a way that they can be converted into other forms. Normal examples of this include:

- Long-term debt that can be converted into equity.
- Semi-equity that can be converted into Full equity.

The reasoning behind this is relatively simple – the conversion option allows for the funding provider to share in the capital growth (that is the increase in value of the business as a whole) but retain their actual or potential revenue stream (interest or preference dividends for example) until the capital growth is realised.

Redemption

26.3 Redemption is the ability of the company to buy back and cancel the funding instruments. Overdrafts, asset finance, mezzanine finance and some forms of long-term debt are redeemable by their nature. Shares can also have redemption rights attached to them. However, the Companies Act does require that companies retain at least some non-redeemable shares in issue at all times.

Sources and further comments on the different options

26.4 Set out below are some overview comments on the different types of funding available to companies.

- **The different combinations and options that can be created mean that readers should take this section as an overview only and should seek advice before entering into negotiations regarding any form of new funding arrangement. Such advice can be gained from your accountants or lawyers.**

Cash/Overdraft

26.5 Cash can only really come from existing activities in the business itself. Any other source of cash is going to fall under one of the other headings. The one exception is an overdraft which a bank may be willing to advance if adequate security is available.

The difference between an overdraft and a loan is that, with an overdraft, you only pay for the amount you need to borrow at any one time. This contrasts with a loan where you receive a set amount of cash on day 1 and pay for it until the loan is repaid even if the cash is sitting in the bank to start with.

Key points to remember concerning bank overdrafts are:

- The banks back management teams they believe will be able to repay the overdraft.
- The average bank manager is not employed to take risks with the bank's money so . . .
- . . . they will only 'invest' in clearly viable propositions.
- To avoid risks the security provided for the overdraft must be reasonably easy to realise.

Some venture capitalists will provide a guarantee to a bank on an overdraft as part of their investment. It is worth remembering when this is offered that you may need to give away equity to the investor as the quid pro quo for them signing up to the guarantee. This may mean that if the overdraft is not used then you have given the investor equity in the business without them actually taking a risk.

Asset finance

26.6 Asset finance is an extension of the secured finance approach of the overdraft. It comes in four different varieties:

Variety	Characteristics
Property finance	• Generally 65-75% of value but can be up to 90% on certain properties. • Can be used as a sale and leaseback (ie turning an owned property into a rented property) to free up cash. • Can include re-purchase options. • Interest rates generally driven by the bank base rates. • Available from banks and certain specialist lenders.
Plant and machinery finance	• Generally 80-90% finance available. • Equipment has to be relatively general so that the lender has some comfort that they can resell if necessary. • Specialist lenders available for certain sectors can provide very flexible approaches. • Equipment manufacturers often set up large scale vendor financing arrangements (backed with borrowing from merchant banks) to provide attractive rates to purchasers of their equipment. • Length of repayment periods and levels of risk on resale drive the interest rates. • Most banks have plant and machinery finance divisions together with equipment vendors and certain other specialist lenders.
Debtor finance	• 65 – 90% of good debtors available from lenders as an advance on cash. • Will be heavily dependent on the quality of the debtors and their payment histories. • Available on a one-off basis (often used as part of the finance for management buy-outs on this basis) or as an ongoing facility.

(Continued)

Variety	Characteristics
	• Quality of order to invoice systems within the business is very important to the lender – no cash will be advanced before an invoice has been raised. • Lenders can often offer collection facilities. • Type of invoicing undertaken is also important. • Again, the banks have debtor finance businesses as well as a number of major independent lenders.
Stock finance	• Becoming more common to be able to raise money on stock-in-hand. • Can get 30 – 40% of resale value. • Tends to be limited to resale stock and even then stock which should be easy to resell. • Banks will consider this and there are other lenders who specialise in stock finance activties.

Mezzanine finance

26.7 Mezzanine finance generally has a medium-term repayment period of around five years. The banks specialise in this type of lending to growing companies and most have specialist departments that look at mezzanine finance proposals.

One area of interest is the Government backed Small Firms Loan Guarantee scheme (SFLG). Here the Government guarantees 70-85% of the loan to the bank helping to reduce the bank's requirement for security.

The loan application has to be supported by a business plan and, as ever, the bank is going to look hard at the quality of management and there are limitations on the use of the scheme.

SFLG loans can be up to £250,000 but banks will have internal procedures for approving different levels of loans and all requests for loans over £50,000 will need higher levels of approval than most local branches hold and some applications may need to be referred to the DTi for approval.

It is well worth getting professional advice on an SFLG or mezzanine loan application to ensure that you provide the bank with the information it needs and also present that information in the most appropriate way.

Long-term debt

26.8 Long-term debt is generally the reserve of bigger and more well developed companies. These longer term loans are either put in as senior debt, with some form of security, or in the form of bonds. The security for bonds is, in effect, the quality of future revenues and earning streams.

Generally it is difficult for early stage businesses to use long-term debt as the basis for funding given the lack of security available. The bond approach is also difficult as early stage businesses, and particularly those developing offerings, have little if any track record of revenues.

As with all funding the level of return (in this case interest) required increases as the risk increases. Because of this the cost of long-term debt or bonds, even if they are available, is unlikely to be commercially viable for early stage businesses.

The exception to the rule is loan notes which may be provided by a venture capitalist as part of their investment. Loan notes look to a certain extent like bonds in that they may well have little or no security. They are used by venture capitalists as a way of generating a return during the development phase of an investment when losses are being generated and dividends cannot be paid.

Semi-equity and Full equity

26.9   These two types can be addressed together as they often come from the same sources. The key feature of both classes is that there can be significant risk associated with the investment.

As noted earlier there is a range of types of equity that goes from equity that looks like debt to equity that is almost permanent:

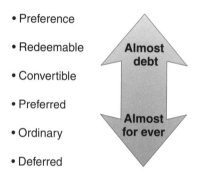

- Preference

- Redeemable

- Convertible

- Preferred

- Ordinary

- Deferred

Figure 26.9 – the range of equity types

Source: PKF

Share type	Features
Preference shares	• A fixed rate of dividend, often set out as a percentage of the nominal value of the share. • The dividend can be cumulative, that is, if a dividend cannot be paid in a year (because the retained profits are not adequate) then the next time a dividend can be paid not only do the preference shares get their dividend for that period but they get a dividend equal to the dividend that could not be paid in the previous period(s).
Redeemable shares	• They can be bought back at an agreed price by the company at some point or points in the future. • The redemption right can belong to either or both of the shareholder and the company but will be specified in the rights of the share.
Convertible shares	• They can be converted into a different type of share. • The conversion calculation is set out in the rights of the share. • Often the trigger is a transaction of some sort like a sale or flotation of the business.

(Continued)

Share type	Features
Preferred shares	• When a dividend is declared they get their dividend ahead of the ordinary shareholders. • Dividend is not, however, fixed by value but can be fixed as, for example, a proportion of after tax profits.
Ordinary shares	• Ordinary shares with standard rights sharing in the profits of the company through dividends, as and when declared, and in the assets of the company on a winding up. • The ability to vote on resolutions in General Meetings and, dependant on the holding, other rights to call General Meetings.
Deferred shares	• Generally shares with very few rights often including no dividend or voting rights. • Come bottom of the pile on a winding up – often deferred shares only get paid out if the ordinary shareholders have received extremely large amounts per share which can be £10m or more per share. • Often created as part of a mechanism to reduce the nominal value of the ordinary shares to avoid issuing new ordinary shares at below nominal value.

The rights of shares are often a combination of the above classes so companies end up with classes of shares such as:

- Cumulative, convertible, redeemable preference shares of 9%.
- Redeemable ordinary shares.

In addition, venture capitalists often have specific rights they like to hold (such as the right to appoint a board member) and this can lead to multiple classes of the same type of share. It is not unusual to see, say, 'A' ordinary shares, 'B' preferred ordinary shares and 'M' ordinary shares in the balance sheets of venture capital backed companies where:

- The 'A' shares carry preferential rights to repayment of capital on a winding up.
- The 'B' shares have a preferred right to a dividend (if a dividend is to be paid, they get it first even if that means that there not enough profits left to pay dividends to other shareholders).
- The 'M' shares have no enhanced rights and are held by the management team.

Sources of equity funding

26.10   Equity funding comes from three main sources:

Source	Timing	Characteristics
Founders and friends and family	Generally at start-up and early stages of development.	Invested through belief in the person and their 'dream'. Often done informally and with little or no thought on valuation.
Business angels and venture capital houses	Can be at start-up if the fund or individual provides seed capital. Then goes through Development Capital to the Expansion/pre-IPO stages depending on the use and scale of the funds being provided.	Business angels often want some active involvement in the business. They are usually entrepreneurs who have made money in previous businesses. Venture capitalists are professional investors who are investing someone else's money, often from a fund raised for the purpose or risk funds provided by institutions. They may well have a requirement for a board seat but are unlikely to be active in the business itself on a day-to-day basis.
Institutions and the public	Generally on a float but could be earlier through a private placing exercise.	Tend to want to have a mechanism to be able to sell their shares when they want, hence the float timing. Institutions can provide very substantial amounts of money. Most will be passive investors but they will want to be kept up to date on progress in the business.

There are a number of venture capital houses and business angels who specialise in investing in technology businesses. It is worth taking advice on which to approach from someone who is used to dealing with them. As with the SFLG schemes, venture capitalists and business angels will want to see certain information and see it in certain formats to help them with their investment decisions.

The options for flotation are considered further in Chapter 8 on the flotation stage of business growth.

Funding and taxation

26.11 There are important tax issues surrounding funding, mainly from the investors' viewpoint. However, as the business needs the investors' cash they impact on the company as well.

When looking at a funding structure it is worth ensuring that every effort is made to allow investors to benefit where there are or may be tax reliefs available. In order to stimulate investment in private companies, successive Governments have introduced and developed schemes that provide some form of tax relief to investors to help mitigate some of the risks of investing in private enterprises such as:

- lack of liquidity in the shares meaning that it may be difficult, or impossible, to sell shares as and when the investor may wish to;
- the higher risk associated with private companies in their early development stages – most business failures occur in the first two years of trading.

The current schemes are focused on assisting UK-based businesses raise money – companies or groups with significant operations outside the UK may not qualify for the schemes. The three schemes are:

- Enterprise Investment Scheme (EIS)
- Venture Capital Trust (VCT) scheme
- Corporate Venturing Scheme (CVS)

The key points of each scheme are as follows:

EIS

26.12   The Enterprise Investment Scheme (EIS) is designed to help certain types of higher-risk small unquoted companies to raise capital. The assistance is given by way of tax relief to investors in those companies. In particular, investors get income tax relief on their investment at the start and may be exempt from capital gains tax when they sell the shares, if they have owned them for more than five years.

VCT

26.13   The Venture Capital Trust (VCT) scheme is also designed to help small higher-risk companies. VCTs are similar to investment trusts; investors buy shares in the VCT which, in turn, invests the money in small companies. By investing in a VCT, the investor can spread the risk on their investment. Investment in a VCT gives some tax relief to the investor – income tax relief on the original investment, and on dividends from the VCT, and capital gains tax relief on the sale of the shares in the VCT.

CVS

26.14   The Corporate Venturing Scheme (CVS) is aimed at larger companies which invest in small independent higher-risk companies. Investing companies are given a number of tax reliefs, including corporation tax relief (up to 20%) on the amount invested, deferral of chargeable gains on disposal of shares, if the gain is reinvested, and loss relief against income for capital losses of disposal of shares.

There are a number of detailed rules around qualification for the schemes, including such areas as requirements regarding the level of holdings in subsidiaries and the fact that certain business activities are specifically excluded.

♦ **Given the complexities of the detailed regulations, which are outside the scope of this book, advice should be sought from an accountant or tax advisor prior to any funding exercise if any of these reliefs are likely to be important either as part of the current, or as part of any future, funding round.**

SUMMARY

26.15 Sources of funds vary widely depending on the use of the funds, the time the funds will be needed for and the risk associated with the business. Most angels and venture capital houses receive significant numbers of approaches and therefore knowing what they are looking for is very important in gaining their interest.

One key area of interest in any of the equity options is valuation which is the subject of the next chapter.

Valuation Issues

27

OBJECTIVES

- To introduce the concept of valuations.
- To give an overview of the methodologies employed.

Warning

♦ **This chapter is not intended to provide you with a cast-iron method of valuing a technology business. Valuation is a technically demanding activity which is heavily dependent on an understanding of methodologies and their application and which relies on experience and background knowledge including the state of the markets. As such, any valuation beyond a very basic one, and certainly any valuation that will be used as the basis of a funding round or for submission to the Inland Revenue, should be discussed with professional advisors.**

Overview

27.1 As stated above, valuation is somewhat of a black art with a series of different methodologies which can be applied depending on the company, its sector and stage of development. In addition, it is worth remembering that a company without funding to develop its products may be worth very little, if anything at all.

DEFINITION

The real difficulty in valuing a business or a technology or a piece of intellectual property is that the valuer is attempting to estimate the likely price that a willing buyer and a willing seller would agree on in an open market transaction.

There are a number of assumptions here:

- That there are willing buyers and sellers (ie there is no compulsion on either side).
- That they have full knowledge of the relevant facts.
- That the technology or intellectual property could be sold at all in its current state of development.
- That a transaction would take place as an open market transaction, without any additional external factors that would impact on the price or ease/difficulty of sale.
- That the transaction takes place at a specific point in time.

On this basis the objective is to place a value on the future economic benefits of ownership of the business/technology/intellectual property.

Use of the valuation

27.2   The use of the valuation has an impact on the details of the methodology used and it is quite normal for a valuation to be given as a range rather than a single figure. For example, in a sale situation a valuer might provide a range of valuations in terms of:

- An opening negotiating position – generally, if working for the seller, an aggressive, but still supportable, view of the upsides; if working for the buyer an aggressive view of downsides.
- A baseline valuation – a view on the lowest realistic value.
- An assessment of the other side's likely starting point.

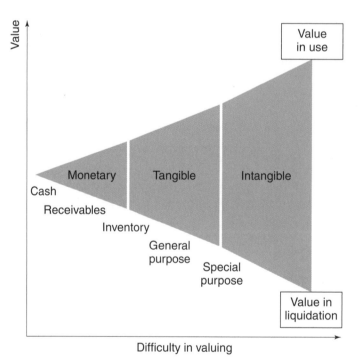

Figure 27.2 – difficulty of valuation and range of values that can arise for different types of asset

Source: PKF

Type of asset being valued and condition of the business

27.3 Both these factors have an impact on the valuation and the range of values that could be calculated.

Valuation methods

27.4 There are three basic valuation methods:

- Cost
- Matching to market
- Income base

Cost

27.5 A cost-based value looks at the cost to replace or reproduce the item. It is often used for items such as very specialist production facilities or other assets where a normal open market transaction is unlikely to occur. It can also be a useful basis when performing a valuation for a *make versus buy* decision. For example, it is possible to assess the potential of an acquisition opportunity in part from the point of view of what it would cost to build the capabilities in-house.

Generally the valuation has to take into account aspects such as the condition of the item being valued and therefore the straight replacement cost may need to be adjusted to reflect any physical depreciation of assets, functional and economic obsolescence.

Cost is not often used in the technology sphere but can be a way of valuing certain pieces of technology from a buyer's perspective and other elements such as brand values.

Matching to market

27.6 The object here is to identify comparable transactions that set a price for the item. The difficulty with technology and intellectual property transactions is finding comparable transactions where:

- The values are in the public domain.
- The technology or intellectual property is truly comparable.
- There were no special factors that influenced either party to do the deal.
- The transaction took place recently enough for the market not to have moved.

The last two points can be particularly difficult. Often in a technology transaction the buyer has a specific reason for wanting the deal such as:

- The need to overcome a specific problem.
- The need to get a product to market quicker than they could by in-house efforts alone.
- The need to complete a range of scaled or complimentary products.
- The need to take out a competitor product.

All of these could lead to the buyer being willing to pay more than a strictly equitable open market price. A similar danger is that where there are two or more potential buyers a bidding war pushes the price up above a normal open market value.

It could be argued that these situations do set a market price but the question is then whether those market conditions would recur if the property being valued were put onto the market now.

The timing of the transactions is also important. The interest of the markets can ebb and flow and with that so can prices. As an example, the valuation of telecoms-related business was high in 2000 with market interest around local loop unbundling, the 3G wireless licenses and the rolling out of DSL and other broadband technologies. However, by the middle of 2001 the market had become concerned about the amounts paid for 3G licenses, the speed of uptake of DSL and broadband technologies and the levels of debt that some telecoms companies had taken on. As a result the valuation of telecoms companies fell dramatically.

In a situation like this picking a transaction from mid-2000 as the basis for valuing a telecoms business could, from a 2001 perspective, drastically overvalue the business.

The list of items requiring comparability is therefore quite lengthy and includes:

- The specific industry sector.
- The market share held by the technology.
- The level of profitability of the business and its access to funds.
- New technologies that have been launched or are expected to be launched.
- Barriers to entry to the market.
- Growth prospects of the business or technology.
- The strength of legal protection for the technology.
- The remaining economic life of the item being valued (for example, the remaining patent life).

The challenge is therefore quite significant when searching for comparative transactions to match against.

The P/E method

27.7 Another method of matching to market valuation for entire businesses is to use a price to earnings (or P/E) ratio. It is important to recognise that this method only works with businesses that are generating profits.

The method is to identify comparable businesses whose shares are traded on a stock exchange. The P/E ratio of the business is likely to be published in newspapers such as the Financial Times and is calculated as:

Market capitalisation/after tax profits

Hence, by finding a comparable company P/E, an estimate can be made of the value the market could place on the business by applying the P/E ratio to the last full year's post-tax profits.

There are caveats to this approach, however:

- The comparability of the company or companies selected is very important.
- It is important to ensure that any unusual reasons for the P/E ratio of the quoted company (such as actual or potential bids for the company) are taken into account.
- The P/E assumes a public company with a market for its shares whereas shares in a private company may be very difficult to sell.
- The P/E will fluctuate with market sentiment and, to some extent, with expectations of future profitability.

In each of these cases adjustments may need to be made to the P/E ratio or the raw calculation to take account of the different circumstances of the business being valued.

Some valuers will use a P/E approach based on projected profits. This adds in more factors for consideration – the risk of the actual profits varying from the projections and also the impact of the profits arising in the future rather than having been achieved through past trading.

Other ratio style measures

27.8 Some sectors have well documented and understood valuations based on measures such as multiples of turnover, multiples of fees or return on net assets. These can be a useful starting point for a valuation but, as with other market-based approaches, the specific situation of the business needs to be taken into account.

Income

27.9 The third method is to use an estimate of future economic benefit as the basis for the calculation.

This has three major difficulties:

- Identifying the revenues that are generated or related to the item being valued.
- Obtaining reasonable estimates of the future revenues.
- Taking account of the time value of money.

Correlating revenues back to intellectual property can be difficult. Often the best that can be done is to estimate the cost savings of owning the intellectual property rather than having to license it and pay royalties. Other factors on similar lines, such as savings in production costs through applying the intellectual property, can also be taken into account.

Estimates of future revenues are just that: estimates. As such the one thing that can be said with certainty about them is that they will be wrong. Significant review and consideration of a set of financial projections being used for valuation purposes is needed to ensure that the valuer feels comfortable that the projections are a realistic approximation of the likely outturn. Valuers may well be sceptical about the basis of projections created specifically for valuation purposes as it may be felt that they have been manipulated to produce the valuation answer desired.

The time value of money is a concept that reflects the fact that investors or purchasers could use their money for purposes other than the acquisition of the item being valued. A calculation is therefore needed to reflect the value that could be generated from other uses of the cash or the average return that is demanded by investors.

As a simple example, if an investor can achieve a 5% return by simply keeping the money in the bank, an investment must offer a return higher than 5% for it to be worthwhile investing in. In addition, any risk associated with the investment will increase the rate required as the return now also has to cover the risk that the return will not actually arise.

The rate of return per annum required by the investor is referred to as the discount rate. Clearly, the further away the return is, the less value it is to the investor now: a pound now can be invested to create a return where a pound in a year's time cannot be invested until it is received. So, at the most, the pound in a year's time is worth a pound less the return that could have been earned on the pound in the meantime.

The discount rate is an annual rate and therefore the impact of the discount compounds the further away from today the cash inflow occurs. For example, at a 20% discount rate £1 in one years time is worth 80p (a 20% discount being 80% of the original amount) but £1 in two years time is only worth 64p (being 80% of 80% of £1 as the discount compounds each year).

As the discount rate percentage increases, the rate of decline in the present value of a set cash flow at a specific point of time in the future increases exponentially as can be seen in this graph:

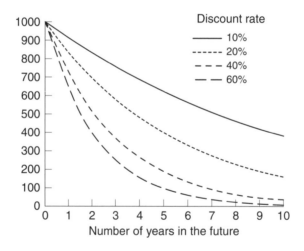

Figure 27.9 – the present value of £1,000 using a range of discount rates

The graph sets out the present value of £1,000 arising at the end of a specific year in the future. So, for the points above 'Year 5' the value indicated for each discount rate is the current value of £1,000 received at the end of a 5-year period using the different discount rates.

The important message here is the inverse relationship between the discount rate and the present value of future cash flows. Because of this fact, the final valuation is highly sensitive to the selection of the discount rate. In addition, the calculation of appropriate discount rates is not a simple matter but can involve complex calculations such as that to identify the Weighted Average Cost of Capital (WACC):

DEFINITION

$$\text{WACC} = w_E k_E + w_D k_D (1 - t)$$

Where:

w_E = weight of equity in the capital structure

k_E = cost of equity

w_D = weight of debt in the capital structure

k_D = cost of debt

t = marginal tax rate

Even here, the cost of equity and cost of debt figures need to be calculated before the WACC can be estimated.

For most equity investments, and certainly those in private companies, bank interest rates are far too low to reflect the levels of risk involved. Indeed, even the interest rates on bonds can be significantly lower than the return rates that equity investors would be looking for. This is due to the risk inherent in the investment decision. As an example of the rates of return that can be achieved, Warren Buffet is quoted as having achieved an average annual return of 30% through investing in the stock markets over a 47 year period. While his investment record may be unusually high (an average may be nearer to 10-15% across the whole of the economy) it does reflect the levels of return available to investors in the public arena.

For venture capital houses the risk element is increased by the need to make a return across a portfolio and therefore the return rate required can include a factor relating to the acceptance that some investments will not make the basic required return and some may make no return at all. In the same way, technology investments are seen as being more risky than other investments due to the risks around development, IP protection and computer technologies, pushing up the risk element in the calculation.

Drug development valuations

27.10 One particular variant of the income-based valuation process relates to biotech companies. There are relatively well accepted success rates depending on the stage of development the drug has progressed to:

Stage	*Success rate*
Pre-clinical trials	Around 5%
Phase I trials	Around 20%
Phase II trials	Just under 30%
Phase III trials	Around 60%
Approval	Around 90%
On the market	Around 99%

The success rate is used as a risk factor in the calculation. It is applied to the estimated annual sales value of the drug, discounted back from the expected year of launch to the date of the valuation, to generate a theoretical value for the drug itself.

The total of the values for each drug in trials gives the value of the company.

This approach places very little value on early stage drugs for two reasons:

- The length of time until launch.
- The high level of risk involved in progressing through trials.

This method is a shorthand approach that avoids the complexity of estimating the net impacts of:

- The timing of any licensing deal during the development or clinical trials process.
- The clinical trials costs saved by any licensing deal (these are normally borne by the pharmaceutical company that licenses the drug).
- The manufacture, distribution and sales force costs saved through using the big pharma company's facilities.
- The milestone payments that would be received by the biotech company during the development and clinical trials process.
- The royalty rate on product sales that the biotech company would receive from launch.

The underlying concept is that, while the milestones and royalties the biotech company receives through a licensing deal will be lower than the revenues it would generate if it sold the drug itself, the biotech company saves an amount equivalent to the reduction in turnover from not having to fund the trials, the manufacture and the sales effort.

SUMMARY

27.11   Valuation is a particularly difficult area. There are so many factors to take into account that the range of valuation for a single business or piece of technology may be very wide. Any valuation that is undertaken is therefore only an estimate and is based on a series of assumptions. The reality of value in a sale situation may vary dramatically from the theoretical valuation due to any number of external factors – from the purchaser's need for the technology to the state of the markets when the deal takes place.

Project Management

28

OBJECTIVES

- To introduce the concept of project management.
- To give an overview of the process.
- To highlight tools available.
- To highlight the risks and rewards of the process.

A massive topic

28.1 Project Management is a massive topic. There are hundreds of books available on the subject – a search under the topic on Amazon.com currently produces a list of 1,334 different matches – and this chapter is only intended to act as a very high level overview.

Large organisations have departments dedicated to project management and professionals with project management skills are greatly in demand. So, what is project management?

> **DEFINITION**
>
> *Project Management* is the process of controlling, driving forward and measuring performance on a project.

It involves:

- Planning out the stages and actions of the project.
- Budgeting their time and cost.
- Identifying the critical path – those items that have to be completed before the next stage can begin.
- Monitoring progress on a number of levels such as:
  - (i)   Technical and functional
  - (ii) Financial
  - (iii) Timetable
  - (iv) Customer satisfaction

- Liaising with internal resources.
- Liaising with external resources.
- Liaising with the customer and/or a prime contractor.
- Monitoring quality and interacting with internal and customer quality personnel.
- Ensuring that actions are taken to maintain or regain momentum.
- Working with the sales, finance and other departments to ensure that invoices are raised and cash collected, including discussing any changes in the specification or difficulties encountered where excess costs can be recovered from the customer.

So the project manager sits at the centre of the entire project web controlling the progress of the project.

But we are small, surely we don't need a project manager?

28.2 This is an oft repeated question from early stage businesses. The answer is that while the business may not need a dedicated full-time project manager someone has to undertake the role.

The danger of not having a formal project management process is that efforts are diverted onto development that, while interesting and often challenging, may not be on the critical path to commercial success. One of the biggest differences between commerce and academia is that while academia values the time spent going down blind alleys and simply learning about what happens if things are tried, commerce sees this as wasting resources that could be focused on launching the product.

In addition, someone has to keep measuring performance against the agreed or targeted standard. Without this measurement the temptation is always to spend that bit more time on areas to make them either 110% right or to add in elements that 'might be useful'. In both cases the question has to be: will customers pay for the extra 10% or the added functionality? If not, then the product should be issued, at least as version 1 with the extra work and time market-tested for value before it is undertaken as part of the development of v1.1 or v2.

What is involved?

28.3 Project Management, at its simplest, is the process of mapping out what needs to be done and monitoring its progress. This involves:

- Up-front analysis of the steps required.
- Mapping of the steps and identification of the critical path.
- Creation of an action plan to get to the end point.
- Monitoring of progress against the steps.
- Drawing up of actions to correct slippages or take account of faster than expected progress.

The other aspects of the role mentioned above are really adjuncts to this process.

Levels of plan

28.4 Sometimes project managers refer to different levels of plan. In broad terms these are:

- Level 1 plan – the highest level setting out the areas of the project that need to be addressed.
- Level 2 plan – sets out the individual sub-projects that need to be undertaken.
- Level 3 plan – sets out the tasks within the level 2 plan sub-projects.

Further levels add ever more detail to the level above.

This hierarchy of plan levels is useful for maintaining an overview whilst not loosing sight of the detail and vice versa.

Tools

28.5 There are a number of tools available to assist in project management. They range from the simplest which is a pencil and paper approach, through wall planners, to ever more complex software tools designed to be used as stand-alone systems or across a network or the Internet.

These more sophisticated tools are useful where multi-company projects are being undertaken as they allow all the different teams involved in the project to see the current status and where they are within the project. This can significantly increase efficiency and cut down on lengthy meetings and travel time.

At the early stages of a business's development relatively straightforward tools such as Microsoft Project™ can be valuable. This provides graphics in a number of formats, allows identification of the critical path and has built-in budgeting and monitoring features. The different levels of plan can also be rolled up so that the process of either drilling down to the detail or rolling up to overviews is made easy.

Other more sophisticated tools, including systems that feed information into accounting and other management information systems or use information from those systems to automate monitoring may be useful further down the line or if the projects are particularly complex.

SUMMARY

28.6 The value of Project Management in a business is easily understated. When done well the process is almost invisible. Indeed, as with many of the support functions, Project Management is most noticed when things go wrong. Project Management is a key skill for any modern business and someone within the organisation needs to take charge of it.

Ignoring the process can lead to a range of problems from unidentified slippages to technology that does not match requirements. Using the process properly can help reduce the risk of these issues occurring. This means that the Project Management process can both save money for the business and help to maximise returns both by minimising costs and by getting the offering to market as early as possible.

The key points to consider throughout the process are:

- Someone needs to be looking ahead.
- Progress needs to be monitored.
- Where variations from the plan arise they need to be investigated and actions put in place to either capitalise on unexpected gains or correct problems.
- Project Management is about ensuring that actions are taken.

Accreditations

29

OBJECTIVE

This chapter describes various types of accreditation which a business may apply for, including:

- Investors In People
- ISO 9000:2000
- TickIT
- Other accreditations

Investors in People

29.1   Investors in People (IIP) is a UK standard which sets a level of good practice for the training and development of people within a business.
   The standard is based on four key principles:

- Commitment – to invest in people.
- Planning – how to develop the skills, individuals and teams.
- Taking action – in a well defined and continuing programme.
- Evaluation – of outcomes of training and development.

Why apply for accreditation?

29.2   The IIP standard can provide commercial advantage – particularly in earnings, productivity and profitability. Investment in staff will improve their skills and motivation.
   The rapidly changing technology sector can benefit from accreditation because, to meet the speed of change and the attention to detail required, well-motivated and skilled staff are essential to the business.

Who should apply for accreditation?

29.3   Accreditation is open to all businesses – the smallest business to have achieved IIP accreditation so far has only three employees.

How is accreditation gained?

29.4   Once the business has put in place the procedures and systems to meet the standard, an external auditor will review the business. Unlike the procedure for ISO 9000:2000 set out below, the auditor is less concerned with the documentation than with the outcome – accreditation will depend on interviews with staff.

IIP accredited businesses will be periodically re-assessed to ensure that they have maintained the systems and standards put in place.

ISO 9000:2000

29.5   ISO 9000:2000 is one of the most important international management standards. It is a development of the quality standards published by the International Organisation for Standardisation ('ISO'). The standards were first published in 1987, and have revised since then, with 9000:2000 being the latest revision.

The ISO 9000:2000 standard is, in fact, a family of related standards related to quality management. For example, ISO 9001:2000 sets the standard for quality management systems; ISO 9004:2000 sets the standard for quality improvement strategies. ISO 9001:2000 is the most widely implemented standard. Where this section refers to the 9000:2000 standard, all the standards within that family are included.

The ISO's aim in developing the standards was to facilitate international trade; by implementing a set of standards aimed at controlling the quality within a business's operations, that business can save money and attract customers.

Why apply for accreditation?

29.6   The standard gives customers – especially those overseas – confidence in the business. ISO 9000:2000 accreditation may be a requirement and not a choice – if the customers require that the business be accredited, then accreditation will have to be obtained. This is particularly the case when dealing with governments – most will insist on the business being accredited. Additionally, potential customers who are themselves ISO accredited will need to ensure that their suppliers are – as far as possible – accredited. If the target customer base of a business includes businesses that are accredited, gaining accreditation will give a competitive advantage.

The ISO 9000:2000 standards may also be met to fulfil an internal need of the business as the process develops a management system aimed at ensuring that the business controls the level of quality in its products and services.

Who should apply for accreditation?

29.7   The ISO 9000:2000 standards can be implemented in almost any business, whether product or service oriented, and regardless of the size of the business.

How is the accreditation gained?

29.8 Once a business has decided to seek accreditation a management system needs to be put in place which meets the ISO 9000:2000 standards; the system needs to be documented carefully. External consultants should be brought in to assist with the process – the standards are comprehensive, and the experience of consultants should ensure that the system gains accreditation.

When the system is in place, an external auditor will evaluate the effectiveness of the system – if they consider that the system meets the standards for the particular accreditation within the ISO 9000:2000 family then an official certificate to confirm this will be issued. Once the certificate has been obtained, the business can begin to state that it is accredited.

As with other accreditations, ISO 9000:2000 status is subject to periodic audit.

TickIT

29.9 TickIT is a software quality accreditation, supported by the UK and Swedish software industries. The quality of software is key to business operations – most businesses will utilise software in some way to maintain or develop information.

The TickIT accreditation requires implementation of a quality system which covers all the essential business processes in the lifecycle of a software product. TickIT is related to the ISO 9000:2000 standards requirements, particularly ISO 9001:2000.

Why apply for accreditation?

29.10 Gaining TickIT accreditation will give the business an accepted certification for European requirements regarding accredited quality systems – all government departments in the UK recognise the accreditation.

Who should apply for accreditation?

29.11 TickIT accreditation is relevant to all businesses which involve software development including:

- In-house developers producing software that significantly affects the quality of the business product.
- Embedded software developers.

How is accreditation gained?

29.12 The procedure for applying for accreditation is the same as for ISO 9000:2000 – the quality management system must be put in place, and then evaluated by a TickIT auditor, who will issue a certificate if the system meets the requirements of the standard. The certificate will allow the business to state that it is ISO 9001:2000 accredited, endorsed by TickIT.

Other accreditations

29.13   Besides TickIT, for the software industry, businesses should investigate the relevant accreditations available to their own industry. Obtaining accreditation can give a business a significant competitive advantage, and may be a requirement for some types of work – particularly government-related work and/or business in the medical sector.

For example, the following accreditations are not optional to businesses in the relevant industry – they must be achieved and maintained in order to obtain a licence to manufacture medicinal products.

GMP – good manufacturing practice

29.14   This is a quality assurance accreditation that ensures that medicinal products are produced and controlled to an appropriate quality standard.

GDP – good distribution practice

29.15   This is a quality assurance accreditation that ensures that products are consistently stored, transported and handled under suitable conditions.

General Taxation Issues   **30**

OBJECTIVE

- This chapter provides a general overview of UK taxation, in particular:
  - The basis of UK taxation.
  - Income tax.
  - Capital gains tax.
  - Corporation tax.
  - Capital allowances.
  - VAT.
  - Stamp duty.

Warning

- **This chapter is not intended to provide you with detailed knowledge of the tax system. It is intended to provide an overview to help management teams identify potential areas of tax risk and to help them understand the background to the advice they may receive from their professional tax advisors. Any tax calculations undertaken in order to assess a potential tax exposure, estimate the tax implications of a transaction, or for submission to the Inland Revenue or HM Customs and Excise, should be discussed with professional advisors.**

Introduction

30.1

'Taxation is the art of plucking a goose in such a way that you get the most feathers for the least amount of hissing' (Jean-Baptiste Colbert, Advisor to Louis XIV)

One of the key areas often overlooked, particularly when a business starts up, is tax planning. The compliance issues are usually noted and followed. However, the decisions made when planning the business can have a major impact on the tax burden of that business later on. Whilst tax minimisation should not be the overriding motivation in a business plan it is generally worthwhile ensuring that the development of the business will not eventually be impeded by tax concerns.

For example, if it is anticipated that the technology developed is eventually to be sold to a company that is likely to be outside the UK, it may be worthwhile considering placing the intellectual property relating to that technology in a lower-tax country at an early stage, so that it does not attract UK capital gains tax when it is eventually sold. Such moves require early planning, to ensure that they are effective.

♦ **This chapter is not intended to provide you with a complete guide to UK taxation and cannot replace a professional advisor – it aims to give an overview of the areas which need to be considered and the questions and concept which should be kept in mind.**

Basis of taxation

30.2 In general, the UK taxes the income and gains of UK resident individuals and businesses, as well as the UK profits of non-UK businesses with a UK taxable presence. In some cases, individuals who are ordinarily resident or domiciled in the UK may be subject to UK tax.

Individual residence

30.3 There are a number of ways in which an individual can be affected by UK taxation – in general, they must be resident or ordinarily resident in the UK, or domiciled in the UK.

Residence

30.4 Despite the importance of the concept to UK taxation, there is no statutory definition of residence – instead, case law has developed a series of tests. Essentially, a person is resident in the UK if they have been present in the UK for more than 183 days in the year of assessment (days of arrival and departure are ignored).

Residence status generally applies for a full year of assessment however, by concession, the Revenue will split the year for people leaving or coming to the UK on a full-time basis. For example, an individual who takes up employment in the US will be taxed in the UK up to the point at which he leaves for the US; he is then subject to US taxation. Without the concession, the individual would have been liable to UK taxation on his US income for the rest of that year of assessment; ie the US income would have been taxed in both the UK and the US.

Ordinary residence

30.5 As with residence, there is no statutory definition. It is generally regarded as habitual residence and, as with residence, case law has developed some tests. These are not absolute but, in general, a person who is in the UK for at least three months a year for a period of more than four years will be considered to be ordinarily resident in the UK from the fourth year.

Dual residence

30.6 Dual residence can give rise to dual taxation; most tax treaties will limit the amount of tax which an individual has to pay in that situation, but it is still a complex issue that is best avoided as far as possible.

Domicile

30.7 A person's domicile is generally where they have their permanent home; this need not be a physical home. It is considerably harder to change domicile than it is to change residence or ordinary residence; both residence and ordinary residence are concerned with physical location in a country. Domicile is concerned with intention as well as physical location.

Domicile has two principal forms:

- domicile of origin; or
- domicile of choice.

A domicile of origin is the domicile acquired at birth; usually the domicile of the father. A domicile of choice is established by an individual who takes up permanent residence in a country and intends to remain there, displacing the domicile of origin. Proving that intention can be difficult.

A domicile of choice may be abandoned by permanently leaving that country; if a new domicile of choice is not established, the domicile of origin is re-established automatically. It is not possible to have more than one domicile, unlike residence.

Corporate residence

30.8 A company will be treated as resident in the UK if it is either:

- incorporated in the UK; or
- managed and controlled from the UK.

The management and control test is not clearly defined but, in practice, several factors will be taken into consideration when deciding whether a non-UK company is managed or controlled here. These include:

- Where the board meetings are held.
- Where the majority of directors are resident.
- Where decisions regarding overseas matters are made.
- Where contracts are concluded.

If, for example, a non-UK subsidiary of a UK company is not to be considered UK resident for tax purposes, care needs to be taken over all these issues – in particular, the subsidiary cannot be dictated to by the UK company; the UK company may make recommendations as to action, but these should be considered independently by the local directors.

Income tax

30.9 Income tax is charged on the income received by an individual (as opposed to a company) in a year of assessment. Income is not defined in tax law; instead, the distinction between income and capital is a question of fact.

Broadly speaking, payments are income if they are received for services performed or are received for the use of an asset which is retained by the recipient of the payment. There are numerous exceptions, and these are discussed in Chapter 31 which deals with the specific tax issues relating to intellectual property, as it is a key issue which needs to be addressed when dealing with intellectual property payments – received or made.

Who is assessable?

30.10 In general, UK income tax is charged on the worldwide income of UK residents, subject to any overriding provisions in tax treaties. It may also be charged on the UK income of people who are ordinarily resident in the UK.

Year of assessment

30.11 A year of assessment runs from 6 April to 5 April the following year. Income tax is due on 31 January in the year following the 5 April in the year of assessment.

For example: for the year of assessment 2000-2001, which runs from 6 April 2000 to 5 April 2001, tax is due on 31 January 2002.

Payments may be due on account in two instalments in advance – on 31 January in the year of assessment, and on 31 July following the end of the year of assessment. Payments on account only need to be made when the tax due for the year on January 31 is over £1,000.

In the example above, tax would be due on 31 January 2001 and 31 July 2001 – these advance payments would reduce the amount due on 31 January 2002.

For employees, most of their tax is collected via the PAYE system leaving little – if anything – to be paid on 31 January. Consequently, no payments on account will be needed unless the employee has another source of income which is not subject to PAYE.

Computation

30.12 Income tax is assessed in different schedules; for example, rental income is Schedule A income whereas employment income is Schedule E; income from a trade is dealt with under Schedule D, as are most forms of investment income. The different schedules have slightly different rules as regards, for example, what expenditure can be deducted from the income to calculate the taxable total for the schedule – the details of these are outside the scope of this book.

Charges on income

30.13   Certain types of expenditure are not deducted from the relevant income as part of the schedule calculation but, instead, are deducted from the aggregate income received under all schedules ('statutory income') – this type of expenditure is a *charge on income* and is particularly relevant in the case of intellectual property; patent royalties cannot be deducted from specific income but can only be deducted as a charge on income from statutory income.

This is not usually an issue – the overall tax charge remains the same – but certain tax regulations apply to statutory income rather than net income and, in these cases, the amount which needs to be taken into consideration is higher than it would have been if the royalties had been deducted from schedular income rather than from statutory income.

Pro-forma computation	
Income	£
Schedule A (income less allowable expenses)	X
Schedule D (Cases I-VI) (income less allowable expenses)	X
Schedule E (income less allowable expenses)	X
Schedule F (income less allowable expenses)	X
Statutory Income	X
Less	
Charges on income	(X)
Other annual payments	(X)
Net Income	X
Less	
Allowances and reliefs	X
Taxable Income	**X**

Capital gains tax

30.14   Capital gains tax is charged on the gains which arise when a chargeable asset is disposed of during a year of assessment. A gain must not be liable to income tax for any reason; income tax takes priority over capital gains tax.

This is less of an issue since income tax and capital gains tax rates are the same, but it has historically been useful to be able to categorise a payment as one or the other.

However, for individuals with trading losses or capital losses, it may still be useful to be able to classify a payment as capital instead of income (to use capital losses) and vice versa. Intellectual property payments are not always clearly income or capital – see the discussion in Chapter 31 on taxation of intellectual property for more details on the issue. In the end, it is usually a question of fact as to whether a payment is capital or income.

Who is assessable?

30.15   Capital gains tax is charged on the gains of individuals who are resident or ordinarily resident in the UK.

UK resident companies are not subject to capital gains tax; instead, corporation tax is charged on gains. Non-UK resident companies may be subject to capital gains tax if they have a branch in the UK.

Assets

30.16   All forms of property are assets for the purposes of capital gains tax, regardless of where they are located. Besides tangible assets – physical assets – capital gains tax is also chargeable on gains relating to intangible assets, such as options and intellectual property. It may also be charged on any form of property created by the person disposing of it, or which is owned without having been acquired (eg a right which has arisen).

This is a very broad definition – case law has tested the boundaries of what may be classed as an asset, but the definition remains very wide. For example, a court has ruled that the right to receive compensation is capable of being an asset for capital gains tax purposes.

Essentially, almost anything which is capable of being owned may be an asset for capital gains tax purposes.

Exemptions

30.17   Certain types of asset are exempt from capital gains tax; the most relevant to high-technology businesses are:

*   Wasting assets – assets with a useful remaining life of less than 50 years (including copyright acquired more than 20 years after the author's death).
*   Assets for which the acquisition cost is less than £6,000.

Disposal

30.18   A disposal can occur in a number of ways, not just on the sale of an asset. Essentially, when the beneficial ownership of an asset changes, a disposal has taken place. A disposal can also be deemed to occur in various circumstances, such as when an asset is destroyed or where a capital payment is derived from the asset – for example, when damages are received for infringement of copyright.

Computation

30.19   A chargeable gain is calculated by deducting expenditure incurred on the asset from the proceeds received. Any available capital losses are then deducted from the chargeable amount. Capital gains tax is then charged as though it was an additional slice of income – the rate of tax will depend on the amount of income which the individual has in that year of assessment. Capital gains are not reduced by trading losses.

Proceeds received

30.20   The proceeds received is usually the sum received for the disposal (whether an actual disposal or a deemed disposal). However, where the asset is disposed of to a connected person (for example, a family member), the market value of the asset will be substituted for the actual proceeds (if any) for capital gains tax purposes.

Expenditure incurred

30.21   Expenditure incurred on an asset includes any initial acquisition costs, together with any payments to improve the asset. Additionally, for assets which have been owned since before April 1998, an indexation allowance can be deducted – this allows for changes in the value of the asset due to inflation.

Acquisition costs can include stamp duty and professional fees, together with any transport costs. Expenditure to improve an asset will be deductible if the improvement is still reflected in the asset when it is sold – normal maintenance and repair work costs are *not* deductible.

Note that where the asset was originally acquired from a connected person, as described above, the acquisition cost will be the market value at the date of acquisition, not the amount actually paid.

Taper relief

30.22   For disposals after 6 April 1998 a new form of relief has been introduced; in place of indexation allowance (a relief which reduced the taxable gain by effectively uplifting the cost to reflect increases in the retail prices index), a tapering relief is given on the chargeable gain. This is intended to encourage people to hold onto assets rather than sell them. The rate of relief depends on whether the asset is a business asset or a personal asset; business assets taper much more quickly than personal assets. The details of taper relief on personal assets are outside the scope of this book.

Business assets are:

- Shares or securities in qualifying companies.
- Assets (not shares) owned by an individual but used in a business that is carried on either:
  (i)   by the individual; or
  (ii) by qualifying companies.
- Assets (not shares) owned by an employee but used for the purposes of that employment by an employer who carries on a trade.

Companies which qualify will, in principle, be trading companies – or the holding company of a trading group; for these companies, any holding will qualify for business assets taper relief. In addition, a holding in a non-trading company which is not a material interest will also qualify.

A material interest is one where the individual has the right to more than 10% of the:

- shares; or
- voting rights; or
- income; or
- assets available on winding up.

For business assets disposed of after 6 April 2000, taper relief is available as follows:

Length of time asset owned	Amount chargeable
Less than 1 year	100%
1–2 years	87.5%
2–3 years	75%
3–4 years	50%
More than 4 years	25%

This is often quoted as an effective tax rate such that a 40% taxpayer selling after holding the asset for more than four years suffers tax at an effective rate of only 10% (25% of the 40% rate they would normally pay).

Capital losses

30.23 When an asset is disposed of for less than the expenditure incurred on that asset, the resulting loss can be set against other gains made in that year of assessment or carried forward against future capital gains. Capital losses cannot generally be set against income to reduce income tax.

Reducing the capital gains tax bill

30.24 There are a number of reliefs and exemptions which are available to reduce capital gains tax; for businesses, the most useful are:

- *Rollover relief* – this allows a capital gain on the disposal of a business asset to be 'rolled' into a new replacement asset, within certain time limits. When the new asset is eventually sold, the capital gain on the old asset crystallises and becomes chargeable together with any gain that has arisen whilst the new asset has been owned (although, if another replacement asset is acquired, both gains can be rolled over again).
- *Incorporation relief* – when a business is transferred to a company, as a going concern in exchange for shares, any capital gain on the business assets is rolled into the shares acquired in the company. When the shares are eventually sold, the capital gain on the business crystallises and becomes chargeable together with any gain that has arisen whilst the individual has owned the shares.
- *Gift relief* – where an individual gives a business asset to a company, the capital gain on the asset can be taken on by the company and rolled into the asset. When the company eventually disposes of the asset, the capital gain on gift crystallises and becomes chargeable together with any gain that has arisen whilst the company owns the asset.

Corporation tax

30.25 In general, UK resident companies pay corporation tax on their worldwide income and gains. Income, in this context means both income from business activities and other income such as interest. The type of income will determine when and how it is taxed, and what can be set against it to reduce the final tax bill.

Non-UK companies

30.26 Non-UK companies are generally not subject to UK corporation tax. However, if the company is carrying on trade in the UK through a branch or agency, it will be subject to UK corporation tax on any profits or gains in the UK which are attributable to the branch or agency.

Trading

30.27 One of the key questions for a business, particularly a technology business, is whether or not the company has yet started to trade. This is particularly important when considering how expenditure is dealt with for tax purposes; a company which has not yet started to trade cannot set off expenditure against, for example, interest earned on cash in the company's bank account.

In that situation, the expenditure is not lost: the Inland Revenue allows the company to carry forward pre-trading expenses until trade actually starts. When the trade starts, all the pre-trading expenses are treated – for tax purposes – as having been incurred on the day that trading starts. At that point, they are available to reduce the income of the company on the tax return.

Whether a company is trading is a matter of fact, rather than law. There is no specific definition set out in the tax laws which must be fulfilled before a company is classified as trading. Instead, the Inland Revenue will consider various factors, none of which need be conclusive. In particular, it is not necessary for a company to be making sales in order to be treated as trading. For example, biotechnology companies may take a decade before they are in a position to receive income from a product being developed; nonetheless, they are generally treated as trading.

Computation of profits and gains

30.28 The starting point for a company's tax position is the accounts; the UK does not completely follow accounting standards when dealing with tax issues, but increasingly the tax regulations and the accounting standards are converging.

In general, a company is taxed on its chargeable profits – these include both income and gains, reduced by allowable expenditure. A detailed description of the calculation of a company's chargeable profits is outside the scope of this book; it is a complex process with a multitude of legislation, case law and concessions which all need to be taken into account.

Basis of assessment

30.29 Unlike individuals, who are taxed on the basis of a year of assessment from each 6 April to 5 April, companies pay tax on the basis of their accounting period. The accounting period may straddle two financial years (which run from 1 April to 31 March for corporation tax purposes) and, if so, the profits are apportioned between the financial years in order to calculate tax. Certain allowances, for example, may be different in different financial years.

An accounting period starts when either:

- the previous financial year ended; or
- when the company first becomes chargeable to UK tax – generally, when it starts to trade, or becomes UK resident.

An accounting period will end when:

- 12 months have elapsed; or
- the company ceases to trade.

Long periods of account, where the accounts are made up for more than 12 months, are apportioned into two accounting periods for tax purposes: one of 12 months and one of the remaining time. The income and expenses of the company are time-apportioned to those periods although the Inland Revenue may apportion them differently if there is a more appropriate basis.

Chargeable gains

30.30 The chargeable gains of a company are calculated in the same way as those of an individual, although the calculation is done on the basis of the accounting period of the company rather than for a year of assessment.

Deductible expenses

30.31 There is no specific rule which determines what expenditure can be deducted from turnover for tax purposes; instead, there are a series of statutory prohibitions which define expenditure that *cannot* be deducted for tax purposes. In general, if the expenditure can be justified under normal accounting principles then it can be deducted for tax purposes. It must be incurred 'wholly and exclusively' for the purposes of the trade – expenditure which is partly for personal reasons cannot be deducted.

Revenue expenditure – that is, expenditure which is incurred in the ongoing business of the company – is deducted from income; capital expenditure – generally that relating to the assets of the company is not deductible against income. Capital expenditure is deducted, instead, when the asset is sold in order to reduce the chargeable capital gain.

The distinction between capital and income recurs throughout intellectual property – payments in respect of intellectual property are a relatively grey area in this context. It is not always straightforward to determine the character of a payment. This is discussed further in Chapter 31 on taxation of intellectual property.

Trading losses

30.32 Trading losses for an accounting period can be set against chargeable gains made in the same accounting period; if there are not enough gains to absorb the losses, then the loss can be relieved either by being carried forward against future trading profits or, in some circumstances, by being carried back against past profits.

Carried forward trading losses

30.33 A loss can be carried forward indefinitely as long as the company carries on the trade in which the loss arose, until it is absorbed by trading profits.

Carried back trading losses

30.34 A loss can be carried back against the three accounting periods which ended immediately before the accounting period in which the loss arose – the company must have been carrying out the same trade in those years.

Capital losses

30.35 Capital losses can be offset against capital gains in the accounting period in which they arise or, if not absorbed, can be carried forward indefinitely against future capital gains until they are absorbed.

There is no requirement that the company continue in the same trade to be able to use capital losses, unlike trading losses. The losses can also be set against gains on assets bought for investment as well as against assets used in the trade.

Charges on income

30.36 Charges on income (such as patent royalties) are the last thing to be deducted from profits before tax is calculated; if the available profits do not absorb the charges, then charges which are paid wholly and exclusively for the purposes of the business can be carried forward and treated as a trading loss to set against future trading income. Non-trade charges on income cannot be carried forwards.

Groups of companies

30.37 There are a number of tax rules which apply specifically to groups of UK resident companies. A group relationship generally exists where one company owns at least 75% of the ordinary share capital of a third, or where two or more companies are at least 75% beneficially owned by a third company. Note – different rules apply for VAT and stamp duty purposes. Some reliefs also impose additional ownership tests.

The most useful rules for groups of companies include:

Asset transfers

30.38 Assets can be transferred between group companies without triggering either a chargeable gain or a balancing charge in respect of capital allowances if both group companies are UK companies. The acquiring company takes on the asset with, in effect, the taxable history of the asset – any chargeable gain or balancing charge is not crystallised unless the asset finally leaves the group, either by sale of the asset or by sale of the acquiring company.

Losses

30.39 Losses can be surrendered from one group company to another, to reduce the tax liability of the second company. There are restrictions on the amount of losses which can be transferred, particularly if the companies have not been in the same group for all of their respective accounting periods, or do not have corresponding accounting periods. For this reason, most groups ensure that the accounting periods of companies in the group are aligned.

Rollover relief

30.40 For the purposes of rollover relief, all the trades carried on by a group of companies are treated as a single trade, so the capital gain on the disposal of an asset by one group company can be rolled over into the acquisition of an asset by another group company within the appropriate time limits.

Foreign subsidiaries

30.41 A group with foreign subsidiaries needs to be aware of some additional issues: where there are foreign companies within a group there is the potential for the loss of tax income for the Inland Revenue. As a result, some tax rules have been put in place to ensure that, as far as possible, that potential loss is minimised. The two principle areas covered are controlled foreign companies and transfer pricing.

Controlled foreign companies (CFCs) are companies which are controlled by UK residents. Essentially, where a UK resident company has more than a 10% interest in an overseas company, it may be liable to UK tax on a proportion of the overseas company's income.

CFCs are considered in more detail later in this chapter.

Transfer pricing

30.42 Transfer pricing rules are used to ensure that companies cannot export profit; the rules impose an arm's length requirement when accounting for tax purposes on dealings with associated companies overseas.

Transfer pricing is considered in more detail later in this chapter under *International tax.*

Capital allowances

30.43   Capital allowances are given for capital expenditure; they are the tax equivalent of the depreciation charges in a profit and loss account. Both individuals and companies can claim capital allowances on qualifying expenditure.

Categories of allowances

30.44   The expenditure must fall into one of the specific categories for capital allowances, or no relief can be given.
   Allowances may be given, amongst other things, for:

- Industrial buildings or structures.
- Plant and machinery.
- Agricultural buildings – note: this is generally only available for expenditure in connection with producing food for human consumption. Expenditure on buildings etc for rearing (for example) animals which produce biotech products will not qualify for this allowance.
- Research and development (this is discussed further in Chapter 31 on taxation of intellectual property).

Available allowances

30.45   Capital allowances are available in various types, depending on the allowance given and the type of company claiming the allowance.

Initial allowances

30.46   100% initial allowances are available on industrial buildings in enterprise zones; there are a number of conditions attached but, essentially, the entire expenditure can be written off in the first year.

First year allowances

30.47   A first year allowance is given on capital expenditure on new (or second-hand) machinery and plant. The amount of the allowance can vary, as can the types of expenditure that qualify. At the moment, small- and medium-sized businesses can claim 100% first year allowances on purchases on computers, software, mobile phones and certain other telecommunications devices. More information related to research and development is included in Chapter 31.

Writing-down allowance

30.48   This is the standard allowance. For industrial buildings, it is a straight-line percentage allowance – the same amount is deducted each year that the building is owned and in use until the allowances given equal the overall expenditure.

For plant and machinery, a reducing balance allowance is given; the allowance is a percentage of the balance outstanding after previous years' allowances have been deducted.

Balancing allowance and charge

30.49   When an asset is disposed of, having qualified for capital allowances, the value after deduction of the allowances is compared with the proceeds of sale.

If the proceeds are less than the written-down value, then a balancing allowance can be deducted in the accounting period – this is equal to the difference between the proceeds and the written-down value.

If the proceeds are more than the written-down value, then a balancing charge is made in the accounting period – the difference between the proceeds and the written-down value is chargeable to tax in the accounting period. If the proceeds are more than the original cost of the asset, capital gains may also be charged.

Procedure for claiming

30.50   For individuals, capital allowances are claimed on the self-assessment return, usually by treating the allowance as trading expenditure for that period. Balancing charges are treated as trading receipts of the period.

Companies claim capital allowances by adjusting profits for the accounting period; allowances are treated as trading expenditure and balancing charges are treated as trading receipts.

VAT

30.51   Value Added Tax (VAT) is a form of sales tax introduced in the UK as part of the UK's membership of the European Union. It is a tax on the supply of goods and services; generally, the effect of VAT will be on the end-user, the consumer, rather than a tax on profits – businesses are usually able to recover VAT which they have been charged. VAT is collected through the supply chain, with businesses accounting to Customs & Excise for the difference between any VAT they have incurred and any VAT charged. The chain stops with any person (individual or business) who is not registered for VAT and is unable to reclaim VAT incurred.

VAT is charged on:

- the supply of goods and services in the UK; and
- on the acquisition in the UK of goods from other European Union member states; and
- on import to the UK of goods from outside the European Union.

A taxable business is required to charge VAT ('output VAT') on all taxable supplies, but can recover most of the VAT paid by the business ('input VAT').

Registration

30.52   A business is required to register for VAT when either:

- the gross taxable turnover of the business in the previous 12 months exceeds the threshold currently set at £54,000 – this is measured on a rolling basis, from month to month, not on the basis of the accounting period; or
- there are reasonable grounds to believe that the total value of taxable supplies to be made in the following 30 days will exceed the threshold.

Note that only taxable turnover – that which would be liable to VAT (even if zero-rated) – is taken into account in calculating whether the limit has been, or will be, reached. Both tests are ongoing and need to be kept in mind as a business approaches the limit; registration is required:

- Within 30 days of the 12 month turnover test being met, and the business will become VAT registered from the first day of the month following the month in which a liability to register arose.
- In the case of the 30 days test, registration is required immediately and is effectively from the beginning of the month.

A business can also register voluntarily, before the turnover limits have been reached. Whilst this means that the business has to charge VAT on its supplies – increasing the cost of those supplies by 17.5% – it also means that the business can recover any VAT which it has had to pay out. The requirement to charge VAT is only a disadvantage for businesses dealing directly with the public; businesses which supply only, or mainly, other businesses will not be disadvantaged as business customers will usually be able to recoup the VAT charge.

Supply

30.53   The type of supply – goods or services – affects the VAT treatment, and in particular, can affect the place in which the supply is made. Supplies are subject to VAT at the standard rate of 17.5% in the UK unless:

- there is a non-standard rate which applies (eg fuel for domestic use, charged at 5%); or
- the supply is zero-rated (ie charged with VAT at 0% – eg books); or
- the supply is exempt from VAT (eg postal services); or
- the supply is outside the scope of VAT (eg the supply of goods outside the European Union).

Business

30.54   A supply must be made 'in the course of business' – there is no statutory definition of what counts as 'business', but the interpretation has been wide. In effect, it covers all organisations that carry on activities that can be interpreted as business. There are some exceptions – political and religious organisations, for example, are generally not considered to be carrying on a business. Charities, however, may be carrying on business and therefore may be required to register and account for VAT on some of their activities.

Supply of goods

30.55 A supply of goods is made when legal title to the property is transferred to another person – the transfer does not have to be of the whole of the legal title; long leases of property can be subject to VAT, for example, even though the freehold title is not transferred.

Supply of services

30.56 Anything done for a consideration, which is not a supply of goods, is a supply of services for the purposes of VAT. A free supply of services is therefore outside the scope of VAT.

Certain supplies have been deemed to be a supply of goods, where they might have fallen within the supply of services definition (and vice versa). For example, the supply of power is a supply of goods rather than a supply of services.

Time of supply

30.57 VAT on goods and services becomes chargeable at a particular point – the tax point. The tax charged is the rate in force at the tax point, and the supplier has to account for VAT in the accounting period in which the tax point falls.

The basic tax point is when the goods are made available to the customer, or when the services are completed.

The basic tax point can be overridden by, for example, issuing a tax invoice before the basic tax point or within 14 days after the basic tax point.

Invoices

30.58 A VAT-registered business which makes a standard-rated taxable supply to another taxable business *must* supply a tax invoice; there is no requirement to supply a tax invoice to customers which are not taxable, or for zero-rated supplies. Note that the invoice must be supplied to the business which pays for the order, not to the recipient of the goods or services.

The invoice must contain the following information:

- VAT registration number.
- Number identifying order.
- Date of supply.
- Date of issue.
- Supplier's name and address.
- Purchaser's name and address.

- Type of supply.
- Description, including the rate of tax and amount payable ex-VAT.
- Gross amount payable.
- Details of cash discounts.
- Total tax chargeable at each VAT rate.
- Total VAT chargeable.

VAT recovery

30.59 VAT paid by a business ('input VAT') is recovered by setting it against any VAT which the business has charged its customers ('output VAT'); if the business has paid more VAT than it has charged in a VAT accounting period, it will receive a refund from Customs & Excise.

VAT can be recovered on goods and services which have been supplied to the business *and* which will be used by the business to make taxable supplies. A tax invoice relating to the purchase is also required.

VAT cannot be recovered on payments for goods and services which are used for non-business related activities such as private purposes, for example.

Imports and exports

Imports from outside the EU

30.60 VAT is due on all goods imported into the UK which would be charged with VAT in the UK. The VAT due is paid either in cash at the point of import (ie at the airport or docks), or is settled by the shipping agent. If a business makes a lot of imports it can also set up a deferment facility with Customs, which allows the business to account for import VAT on a regular basis rather than on each individual import.

VAT paid on imports can be recovered in the same way and on the same basis as if the goods had been purchased in the UK.

Exports outside the EU

30.61 Generally, exported goods are zero-rated – usually some documentation is needed to convince Customs that the goods have been exported, such as an order from the overseas customer.

EU imports and exports

30.62 Imports and exports relating to EU businesses are dealt with under a system known as the 'reverse charge'.

No VAT is charged on goods imported into the UK by a VAT registered business where the purchasing business's VAT registration number is quoted on the invoice. If no registration number is quoted, the local rate of VAT in the supplier's country must be charged.

Where a registration number is on the invoice, the UK business accounts for any appropriate VAT on its next VAT return as though the UK business had made the supply (ie as output VAT). The VAT accounted for can be deducted (if it related to the activities of the business) as input VAT paid by the business in the same accounting period – the effect is neutral to the business.

Similarly, supplies by a UK business are zero-rated when made to an EU business which supplies a VAT registration number. If the purchaser does not supply a registration number, VAT must be charged at the appropriate rate – in the same way that it would be charged to a UK customer.

Additional reporting requirements are imposed on businesses which make regular EU imports or exports and which exceed the reporting threshold (currently £150,000).

Stamp duty

30.63 Stamp duty is paid on documents transferring property, not the transactions itself – if a transaction can be done without a document (eg by oral contract) no stamp duty is due. If a stampable document has not been stamped with duty paid, it cannot be produced in court and may not be able to be registered – for example, transactions in land cannot be registered at the Land Registry unless they have been appropriately stamped.

Stamp duty is payable on:

* documents executed in the UK which relate to:
  (i)   property in the UK; or
  (ii) a matter or thing which is to be done in the UK.

Not all documents are liable to stamp duty – the legislation specifically exempts certain types of document. Essentially, stampable documents are those which transfer shares and other securities, land and buildings (including the grant and assignment of certain leases) and certain types of business property (such as goodwill).

Rates of stamp duty

30.64 Stamp duty is generally charged as a percentage of the value of the transaction, as follows:

* Shares – 0.5% of the value, rounded up to the nearest £5.
* Land/buildings and business property:

  (i)   £0 to £60,000 – 0%
  (ii)   £60,001 to £250,000 – 1%
  (iii) £250,001 to £500,000 – 3%
  (iv)   Over £500,000 – 4%

* Leases – the stamp duty on leases is complex, relating both to the length of the lease, the rent payable, and any premium payable. It is an area outside the scope of this book.

Payment of stamp duty

30.65 Stamp duty is due within 30 days of the date on which the document was executed; the document must be sent to the Stamp Office for signing together with the appropriate form and payments.

Documents which carry 0% stamp duty (generally transfers under £60,000) must still be sent to the Stamp Office – it will be stamped, so that the document can be produced in court, or registered as appropriate. To get the benefit of the reduced rate, the document must include a certificate to confirm that the value of the transaction is below £60,000. A similar certificate is also required to claim the lower rates of stamp duty for transactions below £250,000 and £500,000.

It is not possible to avoid stamp duty simply by executing a document outside the UK – if it relates to property in the UK, or something to be done in the UK, stamp duty must be paid on the document within 30 days of the execution of the document.

International tax

30.66 The advent of the Internet has made global business accessible to businesses that would not have previously considered it – the IBM e-business television advert featuring an Italian grandmother exporting her olive oil across the world is not entirely fictional.

For technology businesses, the Internet opens up the possibility of global research and development – 24-hour development, following the sun, to win the race to market with a new product; the ability to bring together two research teams on opposite sides of the planet, to create new ideas through collaboration.

With this opening up of the global markets comes international tax – the full complexities of international taxation are outside the scope of this book, but there are some areas that need to be highlighted, as they need to be taken into account from the start.

Transfer pricing

30.67 International groups of companies trade within their groups – they exchange technology, intellectual property, physical assets, management skills and other know-how. Without some restraint, these transactions could easily be used to move profit around the group to the most tax-advantageous location. Tax authorities are, understandably, not inclined to encourage such actions.

DEFINITION

Transfer pricing is a mechanism which tries to ensure that profits are not skewed between the countries within which a group operates. Instead, companies are required to account (for tax purposes) for intra-group transactions as though they were made at arm's length. In effect, treat them as though they were made between independent companies. The value of the transaction should generally reflect a reasonable – not excessively large or small – profit.

The UK requires companies to record international group transactions on an arm's length basis for tax, and report accordingly on the company's self-assessment tax return. The Inland Revenue can, and will, query whether the transfer pricing is appropriate, to check whether it does in fact reflect arm's length pricing and terms. Companies are required to keep documentation to show how they arrived at their transfer pricing policy.

Controlled foreign companies

30.68 Where a UK company has control over an overseas company (either alone or with others), it may be taxed on a proportion of the income of that company. The purpose of the controlled foreign companies (CFC) legislation is to prevent UK companies from setting up structures to accumulate income outside the UK at a low rate of tax. The rules do not apply where the overseas company is quoted on a recognised stock exchange.

There are a number of ways in which the UK company can avoid being taxed on the income of the overseas company. These include:

- Ensuring that the overseas company is located in one of a number of approved locations – if located in these countries, the CFC rules do not apply
    - Generally, the CFC rules will not apply in countries which have a similar rate of tax to the UK – where the tax liability of the overseas company is at least 75% of the tax which would be payable if it was located in the UK.
- Ensuring that the overseas company carries on an exempt activity – most forms of trading which involve some risk will be exempt.
    - Companies which exist only to hold intellectual property will not be exempt, nor will companies which are used as a delivery centre for the group, or for the UK business.
- Ensuring that the company distributes to its shareholders (for example, by way of a dividend) at least 90% of its profits (if an investment company) or 50% of its profits (if a trading company).
    - Such distributions will generally satisfy the Revenue that the overseas company is not being used to divert income which would otherwise be taxable in the UK.

Taxing Intellectual Property **31**

OBJECTIVES

- To explain the tax aspects of creating intellectual property.
- To explain the tax aspects of selling or exploiting intellectual property.
- To explain the tax aspects of acquiring intellectual property.
- To explain the tax aspects of damages and compensation received in respect of intellectual property.

♦ **This chapter is not intended to provide you with a complete guide to taxing intellectual property, and cannot replace a professional advisor. Instead, this chapter aims to give an overview of the areas which need to be considered and the questions and concepts which should be kept in mind. Any taxation matters relating to intellectual property should be discussed with your professional tax advisors.**

Taxing intellectual property – an overview

31.1 Intellectual property is one of the more haphazard areas of UK taxation; the rules and regulations governing the application of tax to intellectual property have arisen over decades and centuries in a piecemeal way. Generally, rules have been created to deal with specific issues as they arise, rather than as part of a more holistic approach. That should begin to change soon, as the Government has issued a consultation paper looking at the taxation of intellectual property overall. As that paper is only at the preliminary stages of consultation at the time of writing of this book, the following chapter discusses the taxation issues currently applicable to intellectual property, not least because the consultation paper suggests that the current regime may well continue to apply to existing intellectual property. Any new rules and regulations enacted may apply only to new intellectual property created after the legislation has been put in place.

Intellectual property is generally taxed when something is done with it – when it is sold, licensed or otherwise disposed of. Unlike real estate, there are no taxes relating to the ongoing existence of intellectual property – there are no business rates, for example.

However, tax issues arise throughout the life cycle of the intellectual property – from creation to destruction.

Creating intellectual property

31.2 The general issues relating to deduction of expenditure from taxable profits, as described in Chapter 30, will apply to the expense incurred in creating intellectual property. However, there are some specific allowances available in respect of intellectual property.

Research and development

31.3 The UK government has long been interested in promoting research and development by UK companies; tax support for this has historically been in the form of Research and Development Allowances, which allowed for the immediate deduction of all R&D related capital expenditure against income.

A new tax-based support for R&D came into force for company accounting periods ending on or after 1 April 2000: R&D *tax relief* and *tax credits*. These complement the capital allowance and can boost the cashflow of small- and medium-sized companies ('SMEs') involved in R&D. Note: these rules do not apply to scientific research associations ('SRAs') or payments to SRAs, universities, colleges, and other such institutions – different tax rules apply, and continue to apply, to these.

Additionally, we now have a definition of 'Research and Development' for tax purposes; previously, there was no statutory definition.

The tax *relief* now available means that SMEs can deduct from their taxable income 150% of their expenditure on qualifying R&D: for every £100 spent, they can deduct £150. This will either reduce taxable profits or increase losses.

If the SME is not yet profit-making, that £150 relief can either be carried forward as losses to set against future income of the company, or a *credit* can be repaid on application. The credit available will result in the repayment to the company of £24 for every £100 of R&D expenditure. In contrast, if the relief is carried forward against future profits instead of a repayment being made, the company will eventually get £30 of relief for every £100 of expenditure (at the 20% corporate tax rate).

However, from that £30, to make a true comparison, a deduction should be made to reflect the cost of capital used to fund the business whilst the losses are being carried forwards – repayments do not impact the capital of the business as they are immediately available to fund the ongoing business. Using the relief to offset future profits may appear more valuable but, overall, it may in fact be more beneficial to the business if a repayment is taken. This is a situation that needs to be considered on a company-by-company basis; the funding arrangements for companies differ and it is not possible to make a general recommendation as to whether it is better to carry forward the losses or take the repayment.

DEFINITION

The new definition of '*Research and Development*' is based on the definition for accounting principles in SSAP 13 which is discussed in more detail in Chapter 33; it must also fall within the Guidelines developed by the DTI and the Inland Revenue. In essence, to qualify as Research and Development, the activity must involve creative or innovative work in the areas of science or technology – generally, it must aim to break new ground or resolve uncertainties. Purely theoretical 'blue sky' research could qualify, as could applied research and development aimed at producing a particular product. However, commercial development without such scientific/technological investigation – or development carried out after uncertainties have been resolved – will not qualify.

R&D tax relief

31.4 Where the company carrying out the R&D is owned by a consortium (broadly, a group of companies each owning less than 20% of the company carrying out the R&D) the company cannot surrender losses which contain R&D tax relief *unless* the company to which they are surrendered is an SME.

The claims for relief and repayment must be made within six years of the end of the accounting period for which the claim is made (except in the case of companies which are not yet trading, where the claim must be made within two years.)

DEFINITION

A company is a small- or medium-sized enterprise ('SME') if it, considered together with any company in which it owns 25% or more of the voting rights, meets certain criteria:

- less than 250 employees; and
- annual turnover below Euro 40million (around £25 million); and/or
- annual balance sheet total (equating to net assets) is less than Euro 27million (around £17 million).

Additionally, a company cannot be an SME if more than 25% of its voting rights are owned by one or more companies which are not SMEs (ownership or rights by venture capital companies, investment funds, etc or public investment corporations which do not exercise control over the company will not affect the status of the company).

Qualifying conditions

31.5 The research/development undertaken must fulfil certain conditions before relief can be given:

- The claimant must be a company – individuals and partnerships cannot claim either relief or repayment. Companies which enter into joint ventures to carry out research and development need to ensure that the joint venture entity is a company, if relief/repayment is envisaged as part of the business plan.
  - However, if two companies simply collaborate on a project, each company (if it qualifies) can claim R&D relief on its qualifying expenditure as long as it owns or co-owns the intellectual property created.
- The company must own any intellectual property created by the research/develvopment.
  - Licensing any product of the R&D does not disqualify the company from claiming relief for any further research, as long as it continues to own the intellectual property in the product.
- The expenditure qualifying for relief must be at least £25,000 each year (pro rata for short/long accounting periods).
- The expenditure cannot be funded by a third party; this includes projects funded in whole or in part by state aid such as Government grants. Even if only part of the cost of the project is met by the state aid, none of the expenditure qualifies for R&D relief.

Qualifying expenditure

31.6 The expenditure against which tax relief/credit can be claimed is as follows:

- Staff costs for staff directly and actively involved in R&D (scientists, technical support and managers; costs incurred in respect of remoter staff, such as clerical staff, do not qualify).
  - The costs which can be deducted are: all payments such as salaries, wages, fees, bonuses, etc, but not benefits-in-kind. The amount that can be deducted is the amount before deduction of PAYE, NIC and items such as season-ticket loans.
  - Also deductible are employer's Class 1 National Insurance Contributions and payments to a pension scheme.
- As long as a staff member spends 80% or more of their time on R&D, the full cost in respect of that person can be deducted. Where the time spent is less than 20%, none of the cost may be deducted. The costs in respect of staff who spend between 20% and 80% on R&D may be deducted in proportion to the amount of time spent on R&D.
- Consumable stores used in R&D.
- Payments to subcontractors.
  - (i)   The company paying the subcontractor must own any intellectual property developed by the R&D.
  - (ii) The subcontractor cannot claim any R&D tax relief.
  - (iii) If the subcontractor is connected to the company then tax relief is available on the lower of:
    - the amount payable to the subcontractor; or
    - the subcontractor's expenditure on staff costs and consumable costs incurred in performing the R&D.

(iv) If the subcontractor is *not* connected to the company, then the company can claim relief on 65% of the payments to the subcontractor.

Note: the company and subcontractor can jointly elect for the 'connected parties' treatment described above. The election has to be made within two years of the end of the accounting period of the claiming company to which the claim for relief applies.

Pre-trading expenditure

31.7 Normally, expenditure incurred before a company begins to trade is treated as incurred on the day the company actually starts trading. However, where the company is carrying out research and development in the pre-trading period, the Inland Revenue now allow the company to elect for R&D relief on the expenditure and to treat it as a trading loss of the company. The usual rules for trading loss relief will then apply, so that the loss can be set against other profits of the period (such as bank interest) or carried back against profits of the preceding 12 months (as long as the company would have been able to claim R&D relief in the preceding 12 months).

Alternatively, the loss may be surrendered by group relief, or cashed in for the R&D tax credit. If no action is taken, the losses are carried forward until trade commences, when they can be set against profits.

The election for this treatment must be made within two years of the end of the accounting period for which the claim is made. The election must be made for the whole of the R&D expenditure; part-claims are not possible. Additionally, unsurprisingly, once an election has been made the expenditure cannot be treated as incurred on the date trading begins.

R&D tax credits

31.8 An R&D tax credit can be claimed when the company is making losses; the losses for which the credit is paid are treated as surrendered to the Treasury in return for the payment.

Maximum loss claim

31.9 A company can claim the lower of:

- 150% of the qualifying R&D expenditure (as above).
- The total loss of the trade for that accounting period, less
  - Any claim which could be made (regardless of whether it was actually made) to reduce the loss by setting it against other profits or gains of the same accounting period.
  - Any other relief actually given in respect of the losses, including losses carried back to earlier accounting periods or surrendered by way of group relief or consortium relief.

In either case, the total repayment cannot exceed the total PAYE and Class 1 National Insurance Contributions paid by the company for each of the periods ending on the fifth of the month within the accounting period. Where a company has opted to pay PAYE and NICs quarterly, the repayment is restricted to the payments made for the quarterly periods that end within the accounting period. This amount is the total paid for all staff employed by the company, not just those whose costs qualify for R&D relief.

The total amounts for PAYE and NICs ignore any deductions for:

- Working Families Tax Credit (PAYE & NIC)
- Disabled Persons Tax Credit (PAYE & NIC)
- Statutory Sick Pay (NIC)
- Statutory Maternity Leave (NIC)

Method of claim

31.10 The repayment is claimed on the company's corporate tax self-assessment return; the speed with which a repayment is made depends, therefore, on how quickly the company can complete its tax return. The claim can be made, amended or withdrawn at any time up to one year after the date on which the return is filed.

Research and Development allowances

31.11 All companies – regardless of size – can claim R&D allowances on capital expenditure on assets used for, or used to provide facilities for, R&D.

Expenditure

31.12 The expenditure incurred must be related to the trade being carried on by the company – either to lead to or facilitate the trade. Exceptionally, the expenditure can be incurred on medical research which is specifically related to the welfare of workers in that trade (generally, research into relevant occupational diseases).

The expenditure must be directly incurred on R&D. Assets which have previously been used for other purposes do not qualify for the allowance, although they may continue to qualify for other capital allowances (such as plant and machinery, or industrial buildings allowances).

As with the R&D tax relief and tax credit, expenditure which is met by a third party or state aid does not qualify for the allowance. However, expenditure met by certain regional development grants will still qualify.

Qualifying expenditure

31.13 Most capital expenditure will qualify, except expenditure on land. Any expenditure on buildings, structures, fixed plant or machinery will need to be apportioned to exclude any element that relates to land.

Where an asset is used for both R&D and non-R&D purposes (for example, a building which contains both offices and research facilities), the cost should be apportioned to reflect the R&D usage. The allowance can be claimed on the element which relates to R&D.

The allowances are only given to trading companies; companies which have not yet commenced trading cannot claim the relief. Qualifying expenditure for these companies will be considered to have been incurred on the date they actually start trading and, at that point, the allowances may be claimed.

The trade being carried on may be solely research and development; a group company set up to carry out R&D for the rest of the group, for example, will be able to claim allowances on all qualifying capital expenditure as they will be used for, or provide facilities for, R&D.

The allowance may be claimed for R&D carried out directly by the company, or for R&D carried out by a third party for the company. In the latter case, there must be a contractual or agency arrangement between the parties; the mere fact that the R&D has been carried out is not enough to entitle the company to claim the allowance.

Allowance

31.14 The allowance given is 100% of the qualifying expenditure; once the R&D allowance has been given, no other allowances can be claimed on the expenditure (eg industrial buildings allowances etc). The company has the choice of which allowance to take, where the expenditure qualifies for another allowance as well as R&D.

The allowance is claimed in the Corporate Tax Self-Assessment Return, and is given as a deduction against profits.

Balancing adjustments

31.15 Where an allowance has been given and the asset later ceases to belong to the company, any receipts on that cessation are treated as taxable trading receipts of the company.

Cessation of ownership includes sale, gift, or destruction. On destruction, the asset is deemed to have been sold immediately before it is destroyed. The receipts will include the net money received on sale, or insurance proceeds in the case of destruction, plus anything received for the scrap. In other cases, such as gift, it will be the open market value of the asset.

VAT issues

31.16 Where capital expenditure qualifies for the R&D allowance then 100% of the cost to the company will be allowed; if the company is able to recover VAT then it is the VAT-exclusive cost that is allowed, otherwise it is the VAT-inclusive cost.

If the asset is one to which the VAT Capital Goods Scheme applies, then any additional VAT incurred by the company whilst the asset still belongs to the company also qualifies for R&D allowances. Similarly, any VAT rebates received under the Scheme are treated as trading receipts.

Selling or licensing intellectual property

31.17 The key question that needs to be considered is the nature of the transaction and, once the nature of the transaction is established, how any payment received should be treated.

Payments – capital or income

31.18 The payment for an IP right may be taxed in a number of ways, depending on how the income is classed. A particular distinction needs to be made as to whether the payment is profit (income) or capital gains in the hands of the owner of the IP. It affects not only how the payment is taxed, but also what reliefs may be available to reduce the tax on the payment.

In particular, if a payment is considered to be income it may be necessary to deduct withholding tax if it is being paid to someone outside the UK.

Because of the way in which intellectual property tax law has developed, it is not always easy to distinguish between income and capital payments. For example, payments under a licence are usually income but, depending on the terms of the licence, may be considered to be instalments of a capital payment. Each transaction needs to be assessed on its own facts. When planning for the future, consider how any intellectual property is likely to be exploited, and how the business is best benefited – it may be possible to structure disposals or licences to ensure that the most favourable outcome is achieved.

Certain payments are specifically defined as either capital or income in the tax legislation but, for all other payments, it remains a question of fact rather than law as to which type of payment is being made – the terms used in any contract describing the transaction will be helpful, but not absolute, evidence in determining the nature of the payment.

The complete disposal of an IP right will generally be treated as being made in exchange for a capital payment, even if the payment is made in instalments. In contrast, if the owner retains any of the IP rights then the payment is more likely to be treated as income.

In general, payments to a business are likely to be considered income if the payment is connected to the business, even if the payment is made in a single sum – for example, payments to a computer software developer in respect of transactions involving the software developed by the business will usually be treated as income, even if the whole of the IP right is disposed of.

Other factors should also be considered when deciding whether a payment is capital or income – exclusive licences, for example, are more likely to result in a capital payment whereas non-exclusive licences are more likely to result in an income payments. Payments which are defined on a royalty basis (relating to the use of the asset), rather than as simple payments, are more likely to be treated as income payments.

Licences

DEFINITION

31.19   The most common transaction relating to intellectual property is the grant of a licence. The owner of the IP will grant a licence to a third person, allowing them to use the copyright, patent or other IP, but will retain ultimate ownership of the IP rather than selling it to them outright.

A licence is, in effect, a contract between the owner and the exploiter in which – for payment of a fee – the owner agrees not to enforce its monopoly rights over the IP. The extent of the licence depends on the contract – it may be limited as to time and/or geography, and may or may not grant the licensee an exclusive licence in respect of that time or geography. If the licence is not exclusive, the owner is free to grant licences to others within the same time frame and/or in the same geographical area. The licence may also be revocable, allowing the owner to reclaim the IP rights granted under the licence.

For certain types of transaction, there are particular tax rules which will apply. These are discussed in more detail below.

Copyright

31.20   Acquirers of copyright are taxed under the general rules when they sell or licence the copyright; it will be necessary to consider each sale or licence in the context of the trade (if any) to determine whether a payment is a capital or income receipt. A lump sum payment – whether capital or income – will be taxed in the year of receipt.

In contrast, for individuals who create copyright material, single payments in respect of assignments and licences can be spread over several years of assessment if certain conditions are fulfilled; this can reduce the tax burden by – for example – taking the taxable income creator below the upper-rate tax band.

In both cases, the gross income is spread over the years of assessment; any deductible expenses incurred in creating the copyright are deducted as usual in the year(s) in which they are incurred.

Retrospective spread of payments

31.21   When a licence is granted for a single payment, that payment may be spread over a three year period if the following conditions are met:

- the payment for the licence would normally be included in the taxable profits for a single year of assessment; and
- the work took more than a year to create.

The following payments are covered:

- A lump sum payment.
- A non-returnable advance on royalties.
- Any royalties received, or receivable, in the first two years of the licence.

If the work took less than two years to create, the payment is spread by treating it as though it had been received in two equal parts, half received on the date payment was actually received and half treated as though received 12 months before that date.

If the work took more than two years to create, the payment is spread by treating it as though it had been received in three equal parts, in the three years up to and including the year in which it was actually paid.

FOR EXAMPLE:

If on 1 September 2001 a creator licences a piece of software which took 3 years to create for a single payment of £90,000, then that payment of £90,000 will be treated for income tax purposes as follows:

Received 1 September 2001, assessable in 2001–2002 – £30,000

Received 1 September 2000, assessable in 2000–2001 – £30,000

Received 1 September 1999, assessable in 1999–2000 – £30,000

If the software had taken only 18 months to create, instead of 3 years, then the payment could only be spread back 12 months and would be treated for tax purposes as follows:

Received 1 September 2001, assessable in 2001–2002 – £45,000

Received 1 September 2000, assessable in 2000–2001 – £45,000

In order to spread the payment backwards, a claim is needed within 12 months of 31 January following the year of assessment in which the payment is received.

Design rights and registered designs

31.22 A similar claim can be made for payments in respect of design rights and registered designs.

Forward spread of payments

31.23 An alternative way to spread single payments is also available in some circumstances; this allows the creator of a copyright to spread a single payment over up to six years. The payment is treated as received in equal instalments – the first instalment is treated as received on the date the full payment is actually received.

The conditions for the spreading provisions to apply are:

- the assignment or licence of the copyright (in whole or in part) must be more than ten years after the creation of first publication of the copyright work; and
- the assignment or licence of the copyright must be for more than two years; and
- the payment would normally be assessed in full as income of the copyright creator in the year in which it is received.

If the assignment or licence is for less than six years, the payment is spread over the period of the assignment or licence.

FOR EXAMPLE:

If on 1 September 2001 a creator licences a piece of software which was first published in 1985, for a period of 4 years and for a single payment of £120,000, then that payment of £120,000 will be spread over the 4 years of the licence and treated for income tax purposes as follows:

Year 1 Received 1 September 2001, assessed in 2001–2002 – £30,000

Year 2 Received 1 September 2002, assessed in 2002–2003 – £30,000

Year 3 Received 1 September 2003, assessed in 2003–2004 – £30,000

Year 4 Received 1 September 2004, assessed in 2004–2005 – £30,000

If the software had been licensed for 7 years, the payments could be spread over the maximum 6 years for income tax purposes and would be treated as follows:

Year 1 Received 1 September 2001, assessed in 2001–2002 – £20,000

Year 2 Received 1 September 2002, assessed in 2002–2003 – £20,000

Year 3 Received 1 September 2003, assessed in 2003–2004 – £20,000

Year 4 Received 1 September 2004, assessed in 2004–2005 – £20,000

Year 5 Received 1 September 2005, assessed in 2005–2006 – £20,000

Year 6 Received 1 September 2006, assessed in 2006–2006 – £20,000

As with the retrospective spreading provisions, a claim has to be made to receive the benefit and must be made within 12 months of 31 January following the year of assessment to which it relates.

Patents

31.24 As with copyright, a patent may be sold or licensed; the tax treatment may be affected by the type of transaction.

In general, *royalty payments* for patents – ie payments for restricted use of the patent, whether the restriction is as to time or quantity – are treated as income. As such, they will be taxed in the year of receipt.

Election to spread royalties

31.25 It is possible to elect to have the royalty taxed as though it had been received in instalments over six years. The conditions required for the election to be available are:

- The royalty must be paid in respect of the use of a patent.
- The use of the patent must be for six years or more.

Where the use of the patent is for less than six years but more than two years, an election may be made to spread the royalties in equal instalments over the same number of years as the use of the patent. This election is available to both the first owner and any subsequent acquirers of a patent.

Other payments, such as payments for exclusive use or for the outright sale of the patent, are generally treated as capital.

Capital payments treated as income

31.26 However, payments in respect of patents may be treated as income even though they are technically capital payments. These payments will be spread for tax purposes over a period of up to six years, unless the licensor (and this is not restricted to the creator of the patent) elects to have the payment taxed in full in the year it is received. This is in contrast to copyright, where the default is taxation in the year of receipt and an election is required to spread the payments. This election is available to both the first owner and any subsequent acquirers of a patent.

An election to have the payment taxed in the year of receipt must be made within one year of 31 January following the year of assessment (for individuals) or within two years of the end of the accounting period in which the payment was received (for companies).

Sale of a patent by a non-UK resident

31.27 Where a UK patent is owned by a non-UK resident, payments received on the sale of the patent rights (whether sold in full or licensed) will be taxed in the year of receipt, unless an election is made to spread them over up to six years – this is effectively the opposite treatment to that for sales by UK residents.

An election to spread the payment in instalments must be made within 12 months of 31 January following the year in which the payment is received.

Costs of acquisition

31.28 Although capital payments in respect of patents may be treated as income for tax purposes, the capital cost of acquiring the patent (where the person selling or licensing the patent is not the original creator) may still be deducted from the payment.

Trademarks and registered designs

31.29 Payments for trademarks are assessed under the general rules – the usual capital gains tax, income tax and corporation tax rules apply, once the payments have been established to be either capital or income. There are no specific reliefs for creators of trademarks.

Know-how

31.30 Payments received for the sale of know-how are generally taxed as income – they are considered to be trading receipts of the business.

The exception is where know-how is sold as part of the *sale of the business as a whole*; in that case, the payment is treated as though it is a payment for goodwill. Payments received for goodwill are taxed as capital, rather than income.

Where the sale of know-how is treated as the sale of goodwill, and therefore as capital, it is possible to make an election to have the payment treated as income instead. The election has to be made jointly by the purchaser and the seller of the know-how within two years of the sale.

This election is usually made where the seller has trading losses available, rather than capital losses. Electing to have the payment for the know-how treated as income means that the payment can be set off against those trading losses, rather than taxed as capital. The overall tax paid on the sale of the business is then lower.

Restrictive covenants

31.31 If the vendor of know-how gives any restrictive covenants as part of the sale of that know-how (for example, a covenant not to compete in the same market sector for a number of years), any payment received for that covenant is treated as a payment for know-how for tax purposes. This applies even if the covenant is not legally enforceable.

Stamp duty

31.32 There is no stamp duty charged on documents transferring intellectual property – copyright, registered designs, design rights, trademarks and patent rights, etc were previously considered property for stamp duty purposes and therefore stampable, but the Budget in March 2000 removed all stamp duty for intellectual property.

Note, however, that although know-how is exempt from stamp duty, it can be difficult in practice to distinguish know-how from business goodwill, which *is* property and which therefore attracts stamp duty on transfers.

However, any goodwill of the business which is specifically associated with intellectual property (other than know-how) is exempt from stamp duty in the same way as the intellectual property itself.

VAT

31.33 VAT can be a not-insignificant element of any intellectual property transaction; at 17.5% in the UK, it is essential to ensure that the VAT elements of any transaction are considered carefully to make sure that the business strategy is not affected by unexpected VAT costs.

The general rules regarding VAT are discussed in Chapter 30; the following relates those general rules to intellectual property in particular.

Copyright, trademarks and patents, etc

31.34 The licence or sale of intellectual property (including copyright, design rights, patents, registered designs, trademarks and know-how) by a UK resident is treated as a supply of services and, for VAT purposes, the supply is made where it is received.

If the licensee/purchaser is UK resident, then the standard UK VAT rate of 17.5% will apply.

If the licensee/purchaser is resident anywhere else in the European Union, then the local rates will apply – if the licensee/purchaser is VAT registered (ie can provide a VAT registration number) then no VAT needs to be charged on the licence/assignment. Instead, the licensee/purchaser must account for VAT under the reverse charge procedure. If the license/sale of the copyright is not made to a VAT-registered business, then the licensor/seller must charge VAT at the UK standard rate of 17.5%.

If the licensee/purchaser is not resident in the European Union, then the supply is outside the scope of VAT because the place of supply is not within the European Union.

Withholding tax

Payments to UK residents

31.35 When:

* paying patent royalties; or
* making payments to someone holding copyrights, trademarks etc as an investment,

to a UK resident, careful consideration is needed to ensure that the payer is not left out of pocket. These payments are not deductible as trading expenditure; instead, they are deducted as a charge on income before calculating tax.

Individuals

31.36 The tax regulations allow an individual to deduct basic rate tax from these payments. The payer is not required to make the deduction, but usually will.

The payee cannot dispute the deduction, if one is made, but can either:

- deduct the amount withheld against his own tax liability; or
- reclaim the payment from the Inland Revenue if not in a tax-paying position.

Companies

31.37 A corporate payer is *required* to deduct basic rate tax from these payments – there is no option to absorb the deduction as there is with individuals. Any UK resident through whom a payment is made – if the company does not make the payment directly – is also required to deduct basic rate tax in the same way.

Companies are required to account for such payments on a quarterly basis.

Payments to non-UK residents

31.38 Payments by UK residents to non-UK residents represent a potential loss of tax to the Inland Revenue – the UK resident making the payment can (usually) deduct the payment from pre-tax profits, to reduce the tax due on profits that year. This deduction is balanced – for Inland Revenue purposes – by the fact that a UK recipient of the payment will (usually) have to include the payment in pre-tax profits and hence pay tax on it. Although there is not always a balance – the payer and recipient may pay tax at different rates, or the recipient may be loss-making in which case any balancing tax income to the Revenue is deferred – in general, the two sides of the transaction balance to leave the Inland Revenue in a neutral position.

Where a payment is made to a non-UK resident, that balancing tax does not benefit the Inland Revenue; instead, any tax on the payment will go to the local tax authority. If the non-UK resident is in a tax haven, the payment may not be taxed at all.

To reduce this potential loss, in certain circumstances UK residents are required to deduct *withholding tax* at the basic rate of tax from payments to *non-UK residents*. This withholding tax is then paid to the Inland Revenue.

However, it is possible to make payments without deducting withholding tax if a claim is made; the recipient will need to show that they will have to pay tax in their own country. If the Inland Revenue is satisfied that tax will be paid in the recipient's country then the payer can make the payment without deduction of tax.

Withholding tax is *not* deducted from payments to someone who is tax-resident in the UK.

Double tax treaties

31.39 Even where there is an apparent requirement to deduct withholding tax, a double tax treaty between the UK and the recipient's country may override that requirement or reduce the amount of withholding tax that must be deducted.

The OECD Model Tax Treaty, on which most modern treaties are based, provides that royalties should be exempt from withholding tax so that they are taxed in the country in which the owner is resident, unless the owner has a taxable presence in the other country.

However, each tax treaty has its own requirements, and it is beyond the scope of this book to discuss each treaty individually – in addition, tax treaties continue to be re-negotiated and the rates of withholding tax may change.

When buying a licence or buying intellectual property outright, it is good practice to try to ensure that the licence or transfer document permits the licensor/seller to deduct withholding tax from payments to a non-UK resident; if the document does not include such a provision, the licensor/seller may find that withholding tax payments which must be made to the Inland Revenue cannot be recovered from the licensee/purchaser.

Copyright

31.40   Where copyright royalties are paid to someone who is *not* UK resident, the payer (or anyone through whom the payment is made, such as an agent) must deduct tax at the basic rate from the payments.

Patents

31.41   When a UK resident buys patent rights from a non-UK resident then tax must be withheld on the payment, where it is a capital payment and not income.

This is an issue that is often overlooked; the tax regulations generally treat capital payments for patent rights as income and, accordingly, there is a specific provision which requires that tax be withheld from the payments.

Acquiring intellectual property

31.42   A person who does not create intellectual property but, instead, acquires it by licence or purchase will – usually – want to be able to deduct expenditure on that intellectual property. The amount which can be deducted, and the way in which it can be deducted, depend on the type of intellectual property acquired and the status of the person who has acquired it.

Trading in intellectual property

31.43   Where intellectual property is acquired by a business that trades in that property – in effect, an intellectual property broker – the expenditure on the intellectual property will be treated as trading expenditure. Conversely, receipts will be trading receipts rather capital.

Acquisition of an asset

Copyright and design rights

31.44   Expenditure will either be capital or revenue (income of the recipient), depending on the facts (see the section on 'selling copyright', above).

If the expenditure is revenue then the deductibility will depend on the general principles – it must be wholly and exclusively for the purposes of the trade. If the expenditure is in the form of royalties to a non-UK resident, or making payments to someone who owns the copyright as an investment, always check whether tax needs to be withheld from the payment as well (see 'withholding tax', above, for more information).

If the payment is to someone holding the copyright as an investment, the payment is not deductible when calculating taxable profits – it is, instead, deducted as a charge on income.

If the expenditure is capital, then capital allowances will generally be available against the expenditure over time.

In general, it is more useful to try to structure the acquisition to ensure that acquiring copyright results in revenue, rather than capital, treatment. This will allow the acquirer to get 100% deduction for the expenditure in the year of acquisition, rather than relying on capital allowances.

Companies may be able to claim capital allowances on expenditure on acquired copyright – the allowances given will depend on whether or not the copyright is a wasting asset (ie has a useful remaining life of less than 50 years).

At present, for small- and medium-sized companies, the question of whether an acquisition is for income or capital is irrelevant in respect of *computer software* – a 100% deduction in the year of acquisition is available via capital allowances, so the treatment for tax purposes is effectively the same.

Patents

31.45   As with copyrights, expenditure on patent rights may be either revenue or capital depending on the circumstances.

Revenue expenditure will be patent royalties which are *not* deductible when calculating taxable profits of a business; they are treated as a charge on income instead – the effect is that the deduction is made from profits, rather than in calculating the profits; this can affect certain reliefs and allowances that refer to the calculated profit before charges on income.

Where capital expenditure is incurred in buying patent rights, there are specific allowances given which are similar to capital allowances.

A 25% allowance is given (on a reducing balance basis) on the excess of *qualifying expenditure* over any *disposal value* in respect of patent rights owned in a year of assessment.

DEFINITION

Qualifying expenditure is the aggregate of:

- any capital expenditure on patent rights in the year of assessment; and
- 75% of the amount on which the allowance was calculated in the previous year.

The 'disposal value' is the net proceeds of sale received in the year of assessment for any patent rights sold; this disposal value is capped so that it cannot exceed the capital expenditure paid out on the acquisition of the patent rights (ie where the patent rights are sold for a profit).

There are some anti-avoidance provisions which limit the allowances that can be claimed where the purchaser and seller of patent rights are connected, or where the transaction took place solely to get a tax benefit.

Trademarks and registered designs

31.46 The general rules relating to the deductibility of expenditure apply to trademarks; there are no additional allowances or reliefs available.

Royalties in respect of trademarks and registered designs will generally be revenue expenditure, and deducted as a normal business expense when calculating taxable profits. However, check whether basic rate tax needs to be deducted from the payment when making a payment either to a non-UK resident or when making a payment to someone who holds the trademark or registered design as an investment.

In the latter case, the expenditure will also be deducted as a charge on income rather than as normal business expenditure.

Lump sum payments will generally be treated as capital expenditure; the trademark or registered design is then carried as an asset of the business. Capital gains tax (or, in the case of a company, corporation tax) will be chargeable on any gain made on the eventual sale of the asset. The exception to this is where the trademark or registered design is held as part of the trading stock of the business – this will not be the case for most businesses, only those which deal in intellectual property.

Know-how

31.47 Where know-how is acquired for use in an existing trade, or to be used in a trade which begins after the know-how is acquired, allowances similar to those available for patents can be deducted in calculating taxable profits.

When acquired for other purposes – for investment, for example – the expenditure will generally be deductible as a business expense.

Damages and compensation

31.48 As intellectual property rights are generally monopoly rights, damages and/or compensation can be claimed if those rights are infringed; there are additional legal remedies such as injunctions and criminal penalties, but those do not generally create tax issues for the owner of the intellectual property as no payment is received which is connected with the intellectual property. Damages may also be claimed where a licence is broken.

Compensation payments may be made on, for example, early termination of a licence.

Types of compensation

31.49   Damages are payments which attempt to put the owner of the intellectual property in the same position as would have been the case if there had been no infringement; an alternative compensation payment is an account of profits – the infringer accounts to the owner for all profits made from the infringement. This may be preferable where the infringer has made a significant profit, but is usually more complicated to assess. It is also a discretionary payment, unlike damages.

Capital or income?

31.50   Where damages or compensation payments are made, they may be taxable as income or capital – as with other payments, the distinction will depend on the circumstances. For example, a recurring payment may be treated as income. A single payment may be a capital payment which, as it is derived from an asset, will be a chargeable gain.

In general, damages for infringement of copyright or a trademark will result in the payment of damages being income, as it represents profits which the owner could have made. Damages for breach of contract – where a licensee has broken the terms of the licence – will also generally be income.

Damages will be treated as capital payments in circumstances where the intellectual property is effectively destroyed – for example, where a breach of licence is such that the underlying intellectual property is effectively worthless as a result.

Termination payments may be capital if the terminated licence is important to the business; if the licence is an ordinary part of the business, it is more likely that a payment will be income, treated as replacing the revenue that would have been expected to arise from exploiting the licence.

Payments in exchange for an agreement not to enforce intellectual property rights may be capital or income; the distinction depends on the terms of the payment. In general, if the contract is short-term and not particularly restrictive, the payment is likely to be income – replacing profits – whereas payment for a long term agreement is more likely to be capital. The more the agreement resembles an exclusive licence, the more likely it is that payments will be treated as capital.

Layouts of Accounts

32

OBJECTIVES

- To explain the three principle accounting statements.
- To provide illustrations of the standard layouts for the statements.

The three principle accounting statements

32.1 The three principle accounting statements that appear in published company accounts are:

- The profit and loss account
- The balance sheet
- The cash flow statement

The profit and loss account and the cash flow statement cover a financial period. The balance sheet is a snapshot of the business at the end of the period.

DEFINITION

A *financial period* is the period between two specific dates. For most companies the normal financial period for which accounts are drawn up and sent to shareholders and the Registrar of Companies is a year with each financial year ending on the same date. Internally financial periods are often months for management accounts or, as is normal in some industries, 13 periods of 4 weeks to give better comparability.

The formats for the profit and loss account and the balance sheet are laid down in the Companies Act 1985. There are two balance sheet formats and four profit and loss account formats allowed in the legislation. However, only one balance sheet format and two of the profit and loss account formats are commonly used. The choice of format relates to the nature of the business and the directors need to think about which one to adopt as changing is not a minor activity.

Profit and loss account

32.2   This statement shows the value of the revenues generated by the business in the period and against that the costs incurred in generating those revenues. The net of the revenues and the costs is the profit or loss of the company.

Balance sheet

32.3   This statement summarises the assets and liabilities of the company in the top half and the share capital, retained profits or losses and other reserves in the bottom half. The totals of the two halves are equal.

Cash flow statement

32.4   This statement is, in many ways, a reconciliation between the profit and loss account and the balance sheet. Starting with the operating profit it adjusts for the differences in accounting between the profit and loss account/balance sheet and cashflows to show where cash has been generated and what it has been spent on.

Assets and liabilities

32.5   Assets and liabilities are hard to define: definitions of them tend to be rather limiting in their scope. For UK Generally Acepted Accounting Principles (GAAP) purposes they are defined by the Accounting Standards Board's *Statement of Principles for Financial Reporting* as follows:

- Assets are rights or other access to future economic benefits controlled by an entity as a result of past transactions or events.
- Liabilities are an entity's obligations to transfer economic benefits as a result of past transactions or events.

So an asset will give rise to a benefit in the future while a liability is an obligation to provide a benefit to another.
   Assets come in two broad types:

- Fixed assets, which are assets that are held to be used in the business in the long term.
- Current assets, which are all assets other than fixed assets.

Liabilities tend to be classified firstly by the time period until they have to be fulfilled, so within one year and after one year is the first cutoff point, and then by type as to whether they have been invoiced for by the third party (creditors) or it is known that they will be invoiced as the benefit has been gained by the purchaser (accruals).
   Within liabilities there are certain items where the obligation is certain but one or both of the timing or the quantum are uncertain. In these cases an estimate is included in the accounts which is referred to as a provision. The timing and/or quantum of the provision will be updated in future sets of accounts as the uncertainty crystallises into a known position.

The standard layouts

32.6 The following is an example of the standard layout for each of the three principle statements together with the accompanying standard notes. They are not intended to be comprehensive examples but to set out the sort of categories that would normally be seen in a set of accounts.

Consolidated profit and loss accounts

Years ended 30 June

	Note	*1999* *£000*	*2000* *£000*
Turnover	i	3,147	4,052
Cost of sales		(126)	(287)
Gross profit		3,021	3,765
Selling and distribution costs		(158)	(212)
Administrative expenses – normal		(2,737)	(3,075)
– impairment		–	(473)
		(2,737)	(3,548)
Operating profit		126	5
Bank interest receivable		7	6
Finance lease and hire-purchase interest		(8)	(12)
Bank interest on loans and overdrafts		(8)	(2)
Profit/(loss) on ordinary activities before taxation		117	(3)
Tax on profit on ordinary activities	ii	(57)	3
Retained profit on ordinary activities after taxation		60	–

All amounts relate to continuing activities.

Statement of total recognised gains and losses

Years ended 30 June

	1999 £000	2000 £000
Profit for the financial year	60	–
Foreign exchange gain/(loss) on consolidation	2	(38)
	62	(38)

Alternative format profit and loss accounts

Years ended 30 June

	Note	1999 £000	2000 £000
Turnover		3,147	4,052
Change in stocks and work in progress		–	27
Raw materials and consumables		(261)	(492)
Staff costs		(1,797)	(2,390)
Depreciation and amortisation		(283)	(300)
Impairment of goodwill		–	(473)
Other operating charges		(680)	(419)
Operating profit		126	5
Bank interest receivable		7	6
Finance lease and hire-purchase interest		(8)	(12)
Bank interest on loans and overdrafts		(8)	(2)
Profit/(loss) on ordinary activities before taxation		117	(3)
Tax on profit on ordinary activities	ii	(57)	3
Retained profit on ordinary activities after taxation		60	–

[Note: this is a true alternative, only one of the formats from this or the previous page can be adopted.

This version is often used by research based companies where there may not be a clearly identifiable 'cost of sale' related to turnover – for example where intellectual property is licensed to a series of customers.]

Group balance sheets

As at 30 June

	Note	1999 £000	2000 £000
Fixed assets			
Intangible assets	iii	1,000	327
Tangible assets	iv	140	714
Investments	v	35	322
		1,175	1,363
Current assets			
Stock	vi	51	78
Debtors	vii	819	1,296
Cash at bank and in hand		482	78
		1,352	1,452
Creditors: Amounts falling due within one year	viii	(706)	(718)
Net current assets		646	734
Total assets less current liabilities		1,821	2,097
Creditors: Amounts falling due after more than one year	viii	(67)	(58)
Deferred income		(471)	(745)
Net assets		1,283	1,294
Capital and reserves			
Called up share capital	ix	1,011	1,022
Share premium account	x	365	403
Profit and loss account	x	(93)	(131)
Shareholders' funds	xi	1,283	1,294

Consolidated cash flow statement

Years ended 30 June

	Note	1999 £000	2000 £000
Reconciliation of operating profit to net cash inflow from operating activities			
Operating profit		126	5
Depreciation charge		83	100
Amortisation		200	200
Profit on sale of fixed assets		–	(1)
Impairment of goodwill		–	473
Loss on exchange		–	(42)
Increase in stock		–	(27)
Increase in debtors		(650)	(477)
Increase in creditors		269	63
Increase in deferred income		224	274
Net cash inflow from operating activities		252	568

Cash flow statement

	Note	1999 £000	2000 £000
Net cash inflow from operating activities		252	568
Returns on investments and servicing of finance	xiii	(9)	(8)
Taxation		(8)	(48)
Capital expenditure and financial investment	xiii	(80)	(860)
Net cash in/(out)flow before financing		155	(348)
Financing	xiii	(85)	(59)
Increase/(decrease) in cash		70	(407)
Reconciliation of net cashflow to movement in net debt			
Increase/(decrease) in cash		70	(407)
Cash outflow from decrease in net debt	xiv	85	108
Changes in net debt resulting from cash flows		155	(299)
New finance leases		(51)	(99)
Translation difference		1	3
Decrease/(increase) in net debt	xiv	105	(395)

Notes to the financial information

i) Turnover by final destination

| | Years ended 30 June | |
	1999	2000
	£000	£000
United Kingdom	651	696
Europe	524	908
USA	1,972	2,448
	3,147	4,052

ii) Taxation

| | Years ended 30 June | |
	1999	2000
	£000	£000
Corporation tax at 1999: 26%, 2000: 20%:	54	1
Under/(over) provision in previous periods	1	(5)
Overseas taxation	2	1
	57	(3)

iii) Intangible fixed assets

	Goodwill
	£000
Cost	
At 1 July 1999 and 30 June 2000	1,237
Amortisation	
At 1 July 1999	237
Charge for the year	200
Impairment charge	473
At 30 June 2000	910
Net book value	
At 30 June 1999	1,000
At 30 June 2000	327

In accordance with FRS 11, the directors have reviewed the carrying value of goodwill in the balance sheet and, for certain of the underlying businesses, impairment reviews have been carried out to compare their recoverable amounts with their carrying values. Where the carrying value exceeds the recoverable amount, a provision has been made to write down the goodwill to the recoverable amount of the relevant asset. The recoverable amount is the greater of the market value and value in use of an asset. In establishing the value in use, a discount rate of 15% has been applied to the pre-tax cash-flows.

iv) Investments

	Investment in own shares
	£000
Cost	
At 1 July 1999	35
Additions	287
At 30 June 2000	322

The Company owns 100% of the issued share capital of X Inc., X Australia (Pty) Ltd and X Belgium NV/SA, all of which have the same principal activity as the Company.

v) Tangible fixed assets

	Short term leasehold improvements	*Computer equipment and software*	*Office equipment, fixtures and fittings*	*Total*
	£000	*£000*	*£000*	*£000*
Cost				
At 1 July 1999	8	258	48	314
Additions	250	389	46	685
Disposals	–	(24)	(2)	(26)
Foreign exchange translation difference	–	2	–	2
At 30 June 2000	258	625	92	975
Depreciation				
At 1 July 1999	4	152	18	174
Charge for the year	3	71	26	100
Disposals	–	(13)	(1)	(14)
Foreign exchange translation difference	–	1	–	1
At 30 June 2000	7	211	43	261
Net book value				
At 30 June 1999	4	106	30	140
At 30 June 2000	251	414	49	714

Included in fixed assets are assets held under finance leases and hire-purchase contracts. The net book value of such assets at 30 June 1999 was £72,927 and at 30 June 2000 was £108,269 and the depreciation charge in the year ended 30 June 1999 was £42,385 and in the year ended 30 June 2000 was £32,273.

vi) Stock

	As at 30 June	
	1999	*2000*
	£000	*£000*
Work in progress	27	45
Finished goods	24	33
	51	78

vii) Debtors

	As at 30 June	
	1999	*2000*
	£000	*£000*
Trade debtors	735	1,146
Other debtors	29	34
Prepayments	55	116
	819	1,296

viii) Creditors
Amounts falling due within one year:

	As at 30 June	
	1999	*2000*
	£000	*£000*
Bank loans and overdrafts	33	25
Trade creditors	195	306
Net obligations under finance leases	44	52
Corporation tax	54	3
Tax and social security	28	23
Accruals	352	309
	706	718

Secured creditors included in the above are as follows:

	As at 30 June	
	1999	*2000*
	£000	*£000*
Bank loans and overdrafts	33	25
Finance lease obligations	44	52

Amounts falling due after more than one year:

	As at 30 June	
	1999	2000
	£000	£000
Bank loans	28	–
Net obligations under finance leases	39	58
	67	58

All these amounts are payable by instalment between two and five years. Secured creditors included above are as follows:

	As at 30 June	
	1999	2000
	£000	£000
Bank loans and overdrafts	28	–
Finance lease obligations	39	58

Security provided

The bank loans and overdrafts are secured by a fixed charge over the subsidiary's book debts and by a floating charge over the assets of the subsidiary. The finance lease obligations are secured on the assets concerned.

ix) Share capital

	As at 30 June	
	1999	2000
	£000	£000
Authorised		
2,000,000 Ordinary shares of £1 each	2,000	2,000

	As at 30 June	
Allotted, called up and fully paid		
1,022,000 (1999: 1,011,000) Ordinary		
shares of £1 each	1,011	1,022

[Details of share option arrangements are omitted from this example to save space and as they have limited impact on, for example, projections.]

x) Reserves
Profit and loss account

	As at 30 June	
	1999	2000
	£000	£000
Balance at beginning of the year	(155)	(93)
Retained profit for the year	60	–
Exchange gain/(loss) on consolidation	2	(38)
Balance at end of the year	(93)	(131)

Share Premium

	As at 30 June	
	1999	*2000*
	£000	*£000*
Balance at beginning of the year	365	365
Arising on issue of shares	–	38
Balance at end of the year	365	403

xi) Reconciliation of shareholders' funds

	As at 30 June	
	1999	*2000*
	£000	*£000*
Balance at beginning of the year	221	283
Retained profit for the year	60	–
Exchange gain/(loss) on consolidation	2	(38)
Share capital issued	–	49
Balance at end of the year	1,283	1,294

xii) Operating lease commitments

The Group had the following annual lease commitments under non-cancellable operating leases:

	30 June 1999		30 June 2000	
	Land and Buildings	*Other*	*Land and Buildings*	*Other*
	£000	*£000*	*£000*	*£000*
Expiry date				
Within one year	33	4	2	–
Between two and five years	28	5	53	–
Over five years	–	–	11	–
	61	9	66	–

xiii) Gross cash flows

	Years ended 30 June	
	1999	*2000*
	£000	*£000*
Returns on investments and servicing of finance		
Interest received	7	6
Interest paid	(8)	(2)
Interest element of finance lease rentals	(8)	(12)
Net cash outflow from returns on investments and servicing of finance	(9)	(8)

Capital expenditure and financial investment

	1999 £000	2000 £000
Payments to acquire fixed assets	(45)	(586)
Receipts from sale of fixed assets -	–	13
Investment in own shares	(35)	(287)
Net cash outflow from capital expenditure	(80)	(860)

Financing

	1999 £000	2000 £000
Issue of ordinary share capital	–	49
New borrowings	–	25
Repayment of borrowings	(38)	(61)
Capital element of finance lease and hire-purchase repayments	(47)	(72)
Net cash inflow from financing	(85)	(59)

xiv) Analysis of changes in net debt

	At 1 July 1999 £000	Cash flows £000	Other non-cash changes £000	30 June 2000 Total £000
Cash at bank and in hand	482	(407)	3	78
Debt due within one year	(33)	8	–	(25)
Debt due after one year	(28)	28	–	–
Finance leases	(83)	72	(99)	(110)
		108		
Net funds/(debt)	338	(299)	(96)	(57)

Accounting policies

32.7 In order to assist readers of accounts in understanding how certain numbers in the accounts have been derived one of the requirements of a set of accounts is that they include the accounting policies adopted. Most companies have very similar policies but there are areas in which policies can vary giving rise to differences between sets of accounts. These include:

- Depreciation rates – the period or rate at which tangible fixed assets are written off to the profit and loss account.
- Amortisation rates – the period or rate at which intangible fixed assets are written off to the profit and loss account.
- Recognition of turnover.
- Method adopted for accounting for long-term contracts.

Chapter 33 addresses the issues of revenue recognition and Chapter 34 accounts for intangible assets.

The accounting policies for the set of accounts set out above are as follows:

'The principal accounting policies, which have been applied consistently throughout each of the two years ended 30 June 2000 were as follows:

(a) Basis of accounting

32.8   The financial statements are prepared in accordance with the historical cost convention and applicable accounting standards.

(b) Basis of consolidation

32.9   The financial information consolidates the financial statements of the Company and its subsidiary undertakings drawn up to 30 June each year. The results of the subsidiaries acquired during the year are included in the consolidated profit and loss account from the date of their acquisition.

(c) Goodwill

32.10   Goodwill arising on consolidation represents the excess of the fair value of the consideration paid over the fair value of the identifiable net assets acquired and is amortised through the profit and loss account over its useful economic life. For each acquisition, the directors review the economic life of the associated goodwill and amortise this over a period of 6 years.

Provision is made for any impairment in the carrying value of the goodwill to the extent that an asset's recoverable value in use is reduced below its carrying value.

(d) Fixed assets

32.11   Depreciation is provided at the following rates in order to write off the assets over their estimated useful lives.

Computer equipment and software   33% straight line
Office equipment, fixtures and fittings 33% straight line
Short leasehold improvements   over the remaining period of the lease

Provision is made for any impairment in the carrying value of the fixed assets to the extent that an asset's recoverable value in use is reduced below its carrying value.

(e) Investments

32.12 Investments are capitalised at historical cost. Provision is made for any impairment in the carrying value of the investments to the extent that its recoverable value is reduced below its carrying value.

(f) Pension costs

32.13 The Group contributes to a group personal pension plan. The amount charged against profits represents the contributions payable to the scheme in respect of the accounting period.

(g) Stock and work in progress

32.14 Stocks are included at the lower of cost and net realisable value. Net realisable value is based on estimated selling price less any further costs expected to be incurred to disposal.

Work in progress is valued at the lower of cost and net realisable value less any payments received on account. Cost includes materials, labour and other expenses incurred on the contract at the date of the balance sheet.

(h) Turnover

32.15 Turnover represents the amounts (excluding value added tax) derived from the provision of goods and services to customers for the year. Income from maintenance contracts is deferred over the period to which it relates.

(i) Deferred taxation

32.16 Deferred taxation is provided on material timing differences, arising from the different treatments of items for accounts and taxation purposes, which are expected to reverse in the future, calculated at rates at which it is estimated that tax will arise.

(j) Leases

32.17 Rental costs under operating leases are charged to the profit and loss account in equal annual amounts over the periods of the leases.

Assets held under finance leases are capitalised and depreciated over their useful lives. The corresponding lease obligation is treated in the balance sheet as a liability. The interest element of rental obligations is charged to the profit and loss account using the sum of digits method or in equal amounts over the period of the leases.

(k) Foreign currencies

32.18 Assets and liabilities of the subsidiaries in foreign currencies are translated into sterling at rates of exchange ruling at the end of the financial year and the trading results of the subsidiaries are translated at the average exchange rate for the year. Differences on exchange arising from this translation are taken to reserves.

Other profit and loss account transactions in foreign currencies are translated into sterling at the exchange rate in operation on the date of the transaction or where appropriate at contracted forward rates of exchange. Other assets and liabilities denominated in foreign currencies are translated into sterling at the closing rates. Differences on exchange arising from these translations are taken to the profit and loss account.

(l) Research and development

32.19 Research and development expenditure is written off in the year in which it is incurred.'

Management accounts formats

32.20 Internal management accounts may use a different format to statutory accounts although they will, in general, simply provide either more detail on the face of each statement or different analyses of costs and revenues in order to give management the information it needs to judge the performance of departments and the business as a whole.

The other key area where management accounts may differ is the area of Key Performance Indicators.

SUMMARY

32.21 This chapter is intended solely as an overview of the format of the accounts. This format will be useful when it comes to drawing up financial projections to show to investors.

No matter what format is adopted for management accounts it should be possible without too much work to reconcile from the management accounts format to the statutory formats as illustrated here.

Revenue Recognition and R&D Accounting

33

OBJECTIVES

- To provide an overview of the accounting issues around revenue recognition.
- To provide an overview of the accounting issues around research and development costs.
- To highlight pitfalls.
- To identify potential changes.

Revenue recognition

33.1   Accounting for revenues always sounds like an easy subject. Sales are made and that is that, or so it appears at first sight. For a lot of businesses that is true and revenue recognition is not too much more of a problem than working out whether the sale is recognised when the invoice is raised or when the cash is received.

For technology companies, however, the problem can be much more difficult and the process of deciding when to recognise sales as revenue is complex and, in parts, rather esoteric.

Some basic background

33.2   There are a series of concepts that underpin the way that accounting works. One of those is the concept of matching (referred to by FRS18 as the *accruals concept*) which states that costs and directly related revenues should be recognised in the same period. The practicalities of that statement are that:

- If costs are incurred in one period and the related revenues in the next then the costs should be carried forward in the balance sheet at the end of the first period and set against the revenues in the next period.
- If invoices are issued at the start of a process then the revenues should be spread across periods so as to match the costs as they are incurred.

Revenue recognition therefore becomes a two part process which involves identifying both the quantum of the revenue and the timing of its recognition.

Quantum

33.3   Not all revenue is easy to quantify. Invoices for fixed sums are obvious enough but other arrangements such as funded research, milestone payments based on levels of functionality (for example speed of action), or royalty arrangements may be more difficult to identify.

Likewise, on projects where the revenue recognition is spread over a number of periods the difficulty can be in working out how much revenue to recognise in each period. Indeed, on long-term contracts the revenue recognised will be an estimate right up to the period of completion and even beyond that if there are system performance or other criteria in the contract.

Timing

33.4   Timing is the element that creates the biggest headache for accountants. The matching concept seems reasonable enough but, in practice, the relationship between costs and revenues may not be that clear. An example is maintenance or other support arrangements. The contract may run for a number of years with fixed amounts payable by the customer but the associated costs will not be clear until the end of the period. A simple application of the matching concept is therefore difficult as, without a known cost, how can the costs and revenues be matched?

One answer in this case is to spread the revenues evenly over the period of the contract and to recognise the costs as they arise. However, if the profile of costs is known or can be estimated with reasonable certainty then the revenue should be spread so as to evenly match the costs.

A more fundamental issue can arise with the simple question: what triggers the revenue anyway? This is generally an area that gives rise to commercial disputes between customer and supplier as well and some industries have set up or accepted practices to address the problem. The construction industry, for example, has a system whereby a qualified Quantity Surveyor signs off on the work done at different stages and this sign-off forms the basis of the invoicing. Other industries do not have such well-defined systems.

Technology businesses tend to fall into this second category. The major exception is the drug development sector. Here the external approval process forms the basis of contractual terms and hence revenue timing. For example, the licence agreement between a biotech company and a pharmaceutical business for a compound to be used in a particular disease area will often include milestone payments to be made to the biotech company. These may well be tied to regulatory milestones such as approval to move into the next clinical trials phase or successful completion of a clinical trials phase.

Other technology businesses, such as the software industry, attempt to use similar milestone approaches but these can still lead to dispute as there is no independent third party involved in the assessment process.

Accounting policies

33.5   These issues are addressed by the adoption of a standard accounting policy by the company that is intended to provide the rules for recognising both quantum and timing. The combination of legal requirements, chiefly in the Companies Act 1985 (as revised), accounting standards and other pronouncements, such as those of the UK Accounting Standards Board's Urgent Issues Task Force, sets out the framework into which the accounting policies and the accounting treatments must fall. This combined weight of regulation and standard setting is referred to as Generally Accepted Accounting Practice or GAAP for short.

GAAP varies from country to country. There are three major sets of GAAP:

- International – based on the developing set of International Accounting Standards produced by the International Accounting Standards Committee.
- US GAAP.
- UK GAAP.

Each has its own philosophy of reporting based, in the case of UK and US GAAP, on historical practice and local legislative frameworks.

Historically UK GAAP has been the most accommodating on revenue recognition. This has lead to some companies adopting relatively aggressive accounting policies.

DEFINITION

An *aggressive accounting policy* is one where any benefit is recognised early and any downside is deferred to be recognised in the future. Whilst this may seem short-termist in outlook, for public companies – with more than half an eye on their share prices – adopting an aggressive accounting policy may be tactically important *now* – for example as part of a defence against a takeover.

The range of available approaches can lead to confusion and certainly does not assist in comparing different companies' financial performance.

US GAAP has tended to be more restricting and regulatory in the way it has approached revenue recognition. Certain sectors, such as the software industry, have even gone so far as to work with organisations like the American Institute of Certified Public Accountants to draw up Statements of Position on revenue recognition areas.

The Statement of Position (or SOP for short) on software revenue recognition has undergone a number of revisions over time. The most recent version was issued in 1997 and is known as SOP 97-2. The SOP sets out, for a variety of different scenarios relating to the underlying service or product or combination of services and products being supplied, how the revenue should be recognised.

The previous incarnation of the rules in SOP 91-1 was particularly fierce on performance issues and one of the changes in SOP 97-2 was to recognise that certain items of performance on a contract do not call into question the completion of the underlying contract itself. For example, under SOP 91-1 the requirement in the contract to require training to be provided could have meant that *no* revenue could be recognised on a contract until all the training had been provided. The latest practice takes a more practical view that if the software systems are in and working, and training has commenced that revenue can be recognised on all but the element that relates to that training.

Addressing the issue

33.6 This is a problem that standard setters have recognised for some time and there are moves afoot in the UK to develop a standard to address the issues around revenue recognition. At present the Accounting Standards Board has issued a discussion paper for comment.

Between now and the finalisation of any guidance, there will doubtless be a refinement (and possibly a rewrite) based on comments from industry and the accounting profession, but some of the effects of the proposals as they currently stand are set out below as they form what is probably the best UK guidance currently available on the subject.

♦ **However, readers should, as ever with these technical issues, seek advice from their advisors on the application of GAAP to specific situations. It is further stressed that the comments that follow are based on an ASB discussion document and therefore do not necessarily represent either current practice or the final requirements that may appear in a new accounting standard.**

What is revenue?

33.7 The basis of accounting for revenue is not going to change significantly, however, the role of the underlying contract between supplier and customer is emphasised, and underpins the proposed approach.

When can you recognise it?

33.8 Building on the importance of the contract the driver for recognition becomes: has the (selling) company performed its duties under the contract?

As ever this appears to be a simple question. However, below are just some of the potential pitfalls:

• Completion of the contract is yet to occur – as in a long-term development arrangement or any form of contract which falls into two or more accounting periods.
• Rights of return and options.
• Linked services.
• Valuation/measurement.

Performance is an obvious starting point for considering recognition and has underpinned practice for a long time. The basic rule is that simply entering into a contract is not enough to be a revenue event. Similarly, settlement of the consideration by the buyer does not necessarily indicate when the seller has actually provided benefit to the other party – for example an up-front rent payment does not of itself show that the tenant has gained an economic benefit of the lease.

Incomplete performance

33.9   The problem here is: has enough been done for part of the revenue to be taken? The answer given is that some benefit needs to have accrued to the customer. Again the construction industry approach with the involvement of a Quantity Surveyor contrasts with arrangements such as a bundled hardware and software sale.

Two basic situations arise: supply of a non-task specific system and installation of a bespoke package. A further question arises as to whether any associated hardware sale could be recognised before the software is fully installed. For a non-task specific system, it is relatively easy to break the contract into distinct parts and recognise revenue on completion of the hardware installation before the whole contract is complete.

The second scenario presents a more difficult problem. If the components are inextricably linked (and they would probably include training), can they really be separated? Alternatively, is there another approach to calculating the quantum of revenue to be recognised? Reliable valuation of revenues is going to be difficult but the discussion paper does allow for a portion of revenue to be taken during the contract. That said, if the contract requires full performance before payment then the accounting treatment will need to follow in the same way.

Compared to the US, the UK Accounting Standard's Board proposals still allow a little more flexibility.

Right to return

33.10   EU Distance Selling regulations enshrine a consumer's right to return goods bought within seven days. This could have a significant influence on e-tailers and others selling over the Internet, such as software download sites. For the seller, this presents the problem of identifying the point of sale.

Most companies expect that the majority of sales will not result in a return. However, legally the purchase could be avoided by the customer for one week. The discussion paper takes a prudent view and suggests the current practice of making some provision for future returns is sensible.

Multiple part contracts

33.11   Internet Service Providers and telecoms companies, amongst others, often charge connection fees at the start of a supply contract. This contract would then require future services to be provided by the seller.

Currently, an aggressive but probably allowable policy would be to take the connection fee as revenue immediately. The proposed treatment suggests that the future services are conditional on the connection fee, likening the initial fee to a call option for future services. If the connection is for a specified period, then the proposal is that revenue should be spread over the contract term. Difficulties arise when the contract is open-ended, as is often the case with telecoms companies. In such a case, the revenue should be spread over an estimate of the probable term. Measures of customer churn could therefore become quite important in the calculation of revenue in any one period.

Of course, costs will need to be considered carefully in this. Where significant costs are incurred in connecting a customer, consideration ought to be given as to whether benefit has passed to the customer at the point of connection. If it has, then revenue could be taken, but contract terms may need to be reviewed and careful thought will be required in reaching a conclusion on the timing of revenue recognition.

Licences

33.12 In contrast to connection charges, the proposal for software licences appears to treat them in a counter-intuitive manner. For example, a fee for a five year licence could be recognised up front and not spread over the term. This assumes there are no ongoing support requirements as part of the licence (as these are probably dealt with in a separate arrangement).

The reasoning behind such a treatment is that the seller, beyond granting the licence, does not then have a further obligation to the customer. Why, therefore, should it show a liability in its balance sheet in the form of deferred revenue?

Access fees and advance royalties

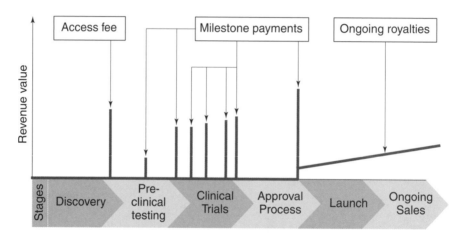

Figure 33.13 – illustrative revenue profile during the development of a biotech product with a partnering big pharma company

Source: PKF

33.13 Companies such as those in the biotech sector often receive payments during the development phase of projects. These vary in contractual nature but, where fees are for access to review a technology and milestone payments on the achievement of certain goals, current practice of taking the revenue on receipt of the cash appears appropriate.

One of the main reasons for this is the level of risk involved in development. The nature of long-term development projects such as those in the biotech area is such that any real surety of success is only gained at the very last stage. Hence, it is sensible and prudent only to recognise the milestone payments at the earliest when they have been agreed by the development partner (in this case the big pharma company) if not when the cash is safely in the bank.

An important point to address as a result of this is the setting of milestones – in order for the revenue to be clearly earned and the cash clearly due and payable the milestones must be easily measurable. Performance against these milestones will therefore always relate to a historical event at the time of payment.

For advance royalties, it is harder to determine a single standard treatment as the contract is key to understanding the benefits delivered at the time of the payment and those that are to be delivered after the payment has been made. However, assuming advance royalty payments are really that – in that they are non-refundable but do result in a real reduction of future, potential royalties – then an element of the payment received will need to be deferred until such time as that future performance is either achieved or reasonably certain to be avoided, through failure of the project, for example.

Valuation

33.14 A common theme running through most of these examples is calculation of quantum or more simply valuing the revenue to be recognised. Where elements of a contract require assessment for revenue recognition purposes, estimates will probably be needed. Unlike the construction industry it is doubtful that there is an industry recognised valuation methodology for most scenarios.

As is becoming the norm in financial reporting, fair values are the suggested solution for measurement problems, with an acknowledgement that these can be difficult to establish.

DEFINITION

A *fair value* is basically the value that the open market would place on the item.

Hence, judgement will still play a part in setting the policy and doing the calculations.

Conclusion

33.15 The overriding theme in all of this is the importance of the contract, and performance against it. The opportunity should be taken now to consider revenue streams, particularly new ones, and the policy adopted in recognising them. For new revenues, adopting an appropriate policy now could avoid the need for a future restatement of results and the investor uncertainty and confusion that could follow.

Further, as happened in the US with the introduction of accounting requirements such as those set out in SOP 91-1, licences and other agreements may change in form. As the contract is becoming more and more the arbiter of revenue recognition it follows that companies, sensitive to their reported financial results, will attempt to adjust their contracts to provide the best outcome.

Interestingly, for presentational purposes this may not be to allow early recognition but may err more towards allowing a spreading of revenue over time. Spreading revenues helps to avoid the peaks and the often accompanying troughs in revenue and hence profitability, that disorient and disconcert investors.

As stated earlier, revenue recognition is an area of developing practice for UK GAAP and one where advice on an ongoing basis will be required from accountants and, if changes to contractual terms for future deals are involved, lawyers as well. Further, it is important to understand the implications of the final standard for your business to ensure that you can explain the position and any impact on period results to staff, investors and your bank.

Research and Development

33.16 Research and Development is a term used to cover a wide range of activities. Accounting for them is covered by Statement of Standard Accounting Practice (or SSAP) number 13 *'Accounting for Research and Development'* which was issued in 1977 and updated in 1989 and, for small companies, by the Financial Reporting Standard for Smaller Entities (or FRSSE for short) which was issued in 1997 and amended in 2000.

SSAP13 adopts the three definitions of the different types of research and development activity used by the Organisation for Economic Co-operation and Development for the purposes of collecting data world-wide:

- *Pure (or basic) research*: experimental or theoretical work undertaken primarily to acquire new scientific or technical knowledge for its own sake rather than being directed towards any specific aim or application.
- *Applied research*: original or critical investigation undertaken in order to gain new scientific or technical knowledge and directed towards a specific practical aim or objective.
- *Development*: use of scientific or technical knowledge in order to produce new or substantially improved materials, devices, products or services, to install new processes or systems prior to the commencement of commercial production or commercial applications, or to improving substantially those already produced or installed.

The standard recognises that the point where each of these activities stops and the next one begins is often indistinct. It also states that particular costs incurred by a business may have characteristics of more than one category, particularly when new offerings pass from research and development to production, when the activities may have characteristics of both development and production.

Innovation is cited as the key element in identifying research and development activities. The SSAP states that 'if the activity departs from routine and breaks new ground it should normally be included [as research and development expenditure]; if it follows an established pattern it should normally be excluded'.

SSAP 13 includes the following as examples of activities that would normally be included in Research and Development:

- Experimental, theoretical or other work aimed at the discovery of new knowledge, or the advancement of existing knowledge.
- Searching for applications of that knowledge.

- Formulation and design of possible applications for such work.
- Testing in search for, or evaluation of, product, service or process alternatives.
- Design, construction and testing of pre-production prototypes and models and development batches.
- Design of products, services, processes or systems involving new technology or substantially improving those already produced or installed.
- Construction and operation of pilot plants.

On the other hand the following activities are given as examples of those that would normally be excluded:

- Testing analysis of either equipment or product for purposes of quality or quantity control.
- Periodic alterations to existing products, services or processes even though these may represent some improvement.
- Operational research not tied to a specific research and development activity.
- Cost of corrective action in connection with break-downs during commercial production.
- Legal and administrative work in connection with patent applications, records and litigation and the sale or licensing of patents.
- Activity, including design and construction engineering, relating to the construction, relocation, rearrangement or start-up of facilities or equipment other than facilities or equipment whose sole use is for a particular research and development project.
- Market research.

Accounting treatment

33.17   The Standard requires that pure and applied research costs are written off to the profit and loss account as they are incurred. There is a threepart logic to this:

- Research is by nature uncertain and therefore it would not be prudent to carry the costs forward as no economic value may arise from the expenditure.
- The concept of matching would require the carried forward costs to be written off so as to match related revenues but the timing of revenues is often uncertain both in terms of timing and total quantum and therefore it would be impractical to try and calculate the periods that were benefiting from the research work. Indeed, it might not even be possible to clearly link any one piece of research work to a revenue stream as the research may be at such a fundamental and low level that the development work effectively makes it invisible in the final product.
- The recognition of pure or applied research is specifically disallowed by the Companies Act 1985.

Development activities are considered to be easier to identify and relate to actual or potential future revenues. Indeed SSAP 13 states that 'expenditure on such development is normally undertaken with a reasonable expectation of specific commercial success and of future benefits arising from the work, either from increased revenue and related profits or from reduced costs.'

This is a basis for arguing that, under the matching concept, the costs should be carried forward and offset against the revenues as they arise in future periods. However, there are still a number of hurdles to consider before such a treatment is allowed under the Standard, starting with the reasonably simple points that:

- there has to be a clearly defined project; and
- the expenditure of the project is separately identifiable.

The matching concept works from the assumption that known costs are matched against known revenues. The idea of carrying development costs forward to offset against future revenues is simply an extension of this. It takes the logical view that, as the right costs have to be matched against the right revenues, development costs should logically be carried forward. That works fine when the quantum of the revenues and their very existence is not in doubt. However, with development work there are still areas of doubt relating to features of a project such as:

- its technical feasibility; and
- its ultimate commercial viability considered in the light of factors such as:
  (i)   likely market conditions (including competing products or services);
  (ii) public opinion;
  (iii) consumer and environmental legislation.

The Standard therefore requires that each of these elements is evaluated and some comfort is available on a positive outcome for each before costs can be carried forward.

Furthermore the Standard states that 'a project will be of value:

- only if further development costs to be incurred on the same project, together with related production, selling and administrative costs, will be more than covered by related revenues; and
- adequate resources exist, or are reasonably expected to be available, to enable the project to be completed and to provide any consequential increases in working capital.'

The process of deciding whether costs can be carried forward is therefore not a simple one and requires the involvement not only of accountants but more importantly of members of the management team who can make *objective* judgements about the:

- Technical viability of the project.
- Commercial viability of the project.
- Financial viability of the project.

The directors in the first instance and the company's auditors during the audit have to be comfortable about the existence and value of future benefits from the development work before any costs can be carried forward.

This leads to the position where, because of the accounting concept of prudence, carrying development costs forward is unusual. To technologists this approach can appear either unduly cautious or, at worst, downright unsupportive and insulting as it carries with it the suggestion that the development work will fail.

> **DEFINITION**
>
> In fact this is not the case but simply the implication of *prudence* – the concept that it is better to recognise the costs related to any risk up front rather than have to take the hit for them later. In the same way prudence leads to the deferring of the recognition of revenue where it is not certain to be received.

From a non-accountant's point of view it may help to look at the position this way: if the costs of the work are written off as the project progresses then if the worst does occur and the development does not lead to a commercial offering then at least the full cost does not hit the results all in one go – the impact is therefore less noticable and the failure less public. However, if the development succeeds then the profitability of the offering after launch will be that much greater as the revenues do not have the carried forward costs offset against them.

Not much comfort for the hours of hard work that appear to be regarded as purely a cost but, maybe, some consolation.

Exceptions and oddities

33.18   As with so many of the accounting rules there are a couple of exceptions to the rules on development costs being carried forward. These relate to occasions where companies enter into a firm contract:

- to carry out development work on behalf of third parties with all of the costs being guaranteed to be reimbursed; or
- to develop and manufacture at an agreed price calculated to reimburse expenditure on development as well as on manufacture.

On these occasions any expenditure which has not been reimbursed at the period end is carried forward and referred to as contract work-in-progress.

There is one further oddity in the accounting for research and development activities and that relates to capital equipment and other assets acquired or built in order to provide facilities for research and/or development activities. Because these assets are generally used for a number of accounting periods they meet the Companies Act's definition of fixed assets and are therefore capitalised (that is treated as long-term fixed assets in the balance sheet) and depreciated over their expected useful lives.

Web-site development costs

33.19   The Urgent Issues Task Force (or UITF for short) is responsible for providing guidance, and mandatory accounting treatment opinions, on issues that arise where the acounting treatment cannot easily be determined from the Companies Act or the existing UK financial reporting and accounting standards. One area that has attracted the UITF's attention recently is the accounting treatment of the costs of web-site development.

UITF Abstract 29 on the subject of accounting for web-site development costs was issued in February 2001. In that Abstract it identifies the costs of developing a web-site as including:

- *'Planning costs* – including, for example, the costs of undertaking feasibility studies, determining the objectives and functionalities of the Web-site, exploring ways of achieving the desired functionalities, identifying appropriate hardware and Web applications and selecting suppliers and consultants.
- *Application and infrastructure development costs* – including the costs of obtaining and registering a domain name and of buying or developing hardware and operating software that relate to the functionality of the site (for example, updateable content management systems and e-commerce systems, including encryption software, and interfaces with other IT systems used by the entity).
- *Design costs* – expenditure to develop the design and appearance of individual Web-site pages, including the creation of graphics.
- *Content costs* – expenditure incurred on preparing, accumulating and posting the Web-site content.'

The same basic approach is taken to these costs as is applied to research and development costs under SSAP 13. On this basis, planning costs should be written off as they are incurred as they do not, of themselves, generate any future economic benefits to the business.

The other costs can be capitalised and treated as fixed assets if 'the relationship between the expenditure and the future economic benefits is sufficiently certain.'

Even here, however, given the uncertainty over the viability and useful life of a web-site the UITF invoked the test of whether the costs will give rise to 'an enduring asset' that will give rise to future economic benefits that, in total, would exceed in value the cost of developing the site. Hence, the UITF's view is that 'this would be the case only if the Web-site was capable of generating revenues directly, for example by enabling orders to be placed.'

As for research and development costs there are a series of tests that need to be applied to the potentially capitalisable costs before they are carried forward. The Abstract puts it as follows:

'Design and content development costs should be capitalised only to the extent that they lead to the creation of an enduring asset delivering benefits at least as great as the amount capitalised. This will be the case only to the extent that

- the expenditure is separately identifiable;
- the technical feasibility and commercial viability of the Web-site have been assessed with reasonable certainty in the light of factors such as likely market conditions (including competing products), public opinion, and possible legislation;
- the Web-site will generate sales or other revenues directly';
- 'there is a reasonable expectation that the present value of the future cash flows (ie future revenues less attributable costs) to be generated by the Web-site will be no less than the amounts capitalised in respect of that revenue-generating activity; and
- adequate resources exist, or are reasonably expected to be available, to enable the Web-site project to be completed and to meet any consequential need for increased working capital.'

With regard to what constitues relevant revenues the UITF is of the opinion that: 'revenues that can be regarded as arising directly from the Web-site could include those attributable to orders placed via the Web-site, amounts paid by subscribers for access to information contained on the Web-site or advertising revenues obtained by selling advertising space on the Web-site.'

However, 'if a web-site is used only for advertising or promotion of the entity's own products or services, it is unlikely to be possible to provide sufficient evidence to demonstrate that future sales or revenue will be generated directly by the Web-site.'

As with development costs, if these tests cannot be met with a reasonable degree of certainty then the costs should be written off as they are incurred. Further, the costs of operating and maintaining the Web-site, once developed, are also to be charged against profits as they are incurred.

Revisiting the position

33.20 Sometimes development costs and, probably more frequently website costs, will be carried forward and written down against profits over a number of financial years. In these cases at the end of each financial period when audited or publicly released numbers are being drawn up, the status of the projects needs to be re-assessed.

This involves, effectively, revisiting the position and asking all the same questions that were asked when the cost was carried forward initially. Where the position has changed, so that the costs would not be carried forward given current circumstances, the remaining costs should be written off to the profit and loss account straight away.

SUMMARY

33.21 Revenue recognition and accounting for research and development costs are two areas that give rise to significant disagreements and can have significant impacts on reported financial results. As such, it is important that they are considered as part of the day-to-day running of a business. It is not unusual to involve your in-house accountant or your advisors in discussions on matters like contract terms and the nature of projects to ensure that, at the end of the period, the accounting reflects the activities you expect it to reflect – at least, you understand where the differences lie.

Brands, Intangible Assets and Acquiring Goodwill

34

OBJECTIVES

- To introduce the accounting concepts for intangible assets.
- To explain the differences between the types of intangibles.
- To outline the accounting treatment for the different types of intangible asset.

Brands, other intangibles and goodwill

34.1 Generally Accepted Accounting Practice (or GAAP for short) has recognised the existence of intangible assets for some time. They do, however, cause difficulties from an accounting viewpoint in that:

- They have no physical substance and cannot always be easily verified.
- Their useful life is not always easy to ascertain.
- They are difficult to define in a way that brings in real and valuable intangibles but excludes superficially valuable but actually ephemeral ones.
- They can be extremely difficult to value.
- They can be very difficult for a non-technician to understand.

Three specific groups of intangibles have been identified by the accounting theoreticians and treatments have been put forward, and largely agreed, for each type. The types are:

Type	Characteristics
Brands	Explain the premium pricing or customer loyalty that a product or business has attached to it.
Regulated intangibles	Items requiring some form of registration or where intellectual property status is granted automatically by law including: • Patents • Copyright • Design rights • Licences • Quotas • Franchises
Goodwill	Explains the difference between the overall value of a business and the sum of its assets less the sum of its liabilities as recognised in the balance sheet.

Of these, brands tend to fall into the more ephemeral category while goodwill is really only visible if a business is either publicly traded (it is then the difference between the market capitalisation and net assets).

Development of an accounting standard

34.2   As the number of technology companies increased during the 1980s and 1990s and, as the valuations put on companies by the stock markets became less and less related to their underlying assets, the discussions about accounting treatment for intangibles developed. Certain of the big accounting firms began undertaking brand valuations for clients and those businesses whose raison d'être was the creation of premium priced branded goods began to clamour to be allowed to carry the value of those brands on their balance sheets.

The reasoning was in part that the historical cost approach to accounting was clearly failing to keep up with the value of businesses in the real world but also that, by carrying brands at value on the balance sheet, a company could strengthen the appearance of that balance sheet substantially – after all, it would be recognising significant assets in the net asset statement and a nice revaluation reserve in shareholders' funds.

However, many standard setters were concerned about this trend and about the potential for the system to be abused. A current cost accounting standard had been issued in 1980 but it quickly became obvious that the methods of valuation needed for current cost were either confusing, conflicting, deeply subjective or too expensive to be practical. It was withdrawn in 1988 but it took the best part of ten years before the current standard on accounting for intangible assets, Financial Reporting Standard (or FRS) 10 was issued in December 1997.

The discussion papers and drafts of FRS 10 caused considerable debate and consternation in the accounting fraternity, particularly over the proposed treatment of goodwill. Indeed, in a most unusual move one of the members of the Accounting Standards Board, Raymond Hinton, voted against its approval. His dissenting view, with his reasons, are included as an appendix to the FRS.

Why was there such a fuss?

34.3   The major reason lies in the FRS's required treatment for goodwill: this is to recognise it as an asset and carry it on the balance sheet with a profit and loss account charge for each period of its useful life. This was a significant change from the standard practice of the time which was to write off goodwill in full direct to reserves at the date of acquisition.

The concern arose on two fronts: that goodwill does not have the same nature as other assets in that it is not easily separable from the business such that it could be sold without the business and, secondly, that the useful life of goodwill is very hard to estimate. In the dissenting view appendix this view is expanded with the statement that 'purchased goodwill is incapable of being separately measured in the years after purchase and inevitably wanes, only to be replaced in whole or in part by new goodwill arising from current expenditures and events.'

This is important as the amortisation reduces reported profits; yet it is hard to see how this fits in with the matching concept in that the amortisation can be seen as a cost but with no directly related revenues. Elsewhere in GAAP the treatment of such items would be to write them off as they arose.

Interestingly, analysts now tend to add back the amortisation charge relating to goodwill in order to calculate the true underlying profit of the business for a period and the earnings per share. More and more companies are now providing this information in their accounts by way of additional earnings per share figures or the inclusion of EBITDA *(Earnings Before Interest, Tax, Depreciation and Amortisation)* data.

Further the Standard does not allow purchased intangibles to be revalued. This is slightly strange in that the Standard does allow them to be recognised on purchase thereby implying that there are valid measures of valuation for intangibles.

The requirements of the Standard

34.4 The Standard deals with goodwill separately from intangible assets (both brands and regulated intangibles).

Goodwill

DEFINITION

Goodwill is defined as being the difference between the fair value of the price paid for a business and the aggregate of the fair values of its assets and liabilities. *Fair value* being the amount for which an asset or liability could be bought or sold in a normal arm's length transaction (in other words not a forced sale as might happen in an insolvency situation).

There are two types of goodwill:

- Positive goodwill occurs when the price paid exceeds the fair value of the net assets acquired.
- Negative goodwill occurs when the fair value of the net assets exceeds the price paid for the business.

Treatment of goodwill

34.5 Internally generated goodwill (which is in effect the goodwill figure but based on an estimate of the value of the business were it to be sold) cannot be recognised in the balance sheet.

Both positive and negative purchased goodwill are recognised on the face of the balance sheet from the date of acquisition of the business. Positive goodwill as a fixed asset and negative goodwill as a form of negative asset (it is actually recorded in the fixed asset section but as a negative figure).

It should be noted that negative goodwill does not arise often as it is an indication that the business is worth less than net asset value. The implication is that the vendors would potentially have done better to sell the assets and pay off the creditors than to sell the business as a whole.

It is particularly rare in the technology arena where net asset totals can be quite small or even negative with initial period losses relating to research and development costs.

Goodwill should be amortised through the profit and loss accounts in the periods expected to benefit from the purchase of the business. This is based on a presumption that the premium over net assets that would be paid now will diminish over time. For some businesses that may not be true but in the technology sector it generally is, as it is unlikely that a business with what is currently a leading piece of technology will be worth as much in, say, five years time if all it has then is the same piece of technology.

Estimating the useful economic life of goodwill is highly judgmental. A number of factors have to be taken into account such as:

- The nature of the business.
- The stability of the industry.
- Comparable lives of products in the sector.
- The extent to which the acquisition overcomes market entry barriers that will continue to exist.
- The expected future impact of competition on the business.

Taking these factors into account, goodwill arising on technology company acquisitions can often be written off over a relatively short period of time such as 5 to 10 years. For some acquisitions it can be even shorter than that. Either way there is a rebuttable presumption set out in the FRS that the economic lives of goodwill and intangible assets are limited to 20 years. This does not, however, imply that 20 years is the default period. The exercise set out above has to be undertaken to estimate the life of goodwill.

Intangible assets

> **DEFINITION**
>
> **34.6** *Intangible assets* are described as being non-physical in substance but identifiable and clearly controlled by the company through legal rights or by custody. Identifiable assets are defined by legislation as being those that can be disposed of without selling the entire business. Control indicators include franchises, licenses, trade marks or patents where a legal right exists to use the intellectual property. Custody is more difficult in that it relates to privately held intellectual property of a technical or other nature.
>
> Excluded from the definition are things such as the value of staff knowledge or customer lists. Here, because there are no long-term legal rights to the revenue streams from the staff (who could leave) or the customers (who could buy from someone else), the view is that there is not adequate control to recognise them as separable assets.

Interestingly software development costs relating to the development of systems for internal use (such as accounting and management information or knowledge management systems) are not included as separate intangible assets. They are deemed to be part of the cost of the system and are therefore included with the cost of the hardware as tangible fixed assets.

Accounting for development work on software that will be, or be part of, an offering should be accounted for in the same way as other development costs, as set out in the previous chapter.

Treatment of intangibles

34.7   Intangibles arise in three ways:

Arising	Treatment
Through direct purchase (such as a licence or a quota).	Recognise at cost and write off over the expected useful life of the asset.
As part of the acquisition of a business.	If its value can be reliably measured it should be recorded at its fair value separately from goodwill and written off over the expected useful life of the asset (see note below).
	The value attributed to the intangible is further limited by the rule that recognition of an intangible cannot turn positive goodwill into negative goodwill or increase negative goodwill.
	If the value cannot be reliably ascertained then the intangible should not be separately recognised but should be treated as being an element of the goodwill.
Internally generated.	Should only be recognised if they have a readily ascertainable market value. Basically, as most intangibles are unique, this effectively means that internally generated intangibles are not recognised.

Note: Generally fair values of intangible assets are estimated by taking the replacement cost. The FRS states categorically that it is not possible to identify market values for unique intangibles such as brands or publishing titles and that replacement costs may be similarly difficult to calculate. However, it may be possible where experts, who are used to valuing similar intangibles for sale, have developed techniques to place value on the intangible. The question then arises of how reliable those valuation methods really are.

In practice this approach means that companies find it hard to justify recording any intangibles other than purchased intangibles in their balance sheets. Specifically, without directly prohibiting it, the required treatment effectively rules out recognising the value of self-generated brand values on the balance sheet.

Chapter 27 on valuation looks in more detail at techniques that are used to value intangibles and the issues involved.

Amortisation periods

34.8   As noted above the value of the intangible asset is amortised over its useful life. The process of estimating useful life is very similar to that for goodwill. There are, however, certain features of intangibles that can at least give a useful starting point. One of these is a natural in-built expiry date such as the ending of patent protection.

As with goodwill, however, it cannot simply be assumed that the useful economic life of an intangible asset is the period of intellectual property protection. The useful life may well be shorter than that if there is a reasonable expectation that the technology will be superseded.

Reviews of useful economic life and impairment reviews

34.9 FRS 10 states that the useful economic life of both goodwill and intangibles needs to be reviewed at the end of each reporting period. This is to check that market or other conditions have not turned against or in favour of the business or the technology. If it is considered that the remaining useful life is now different than was originally anticipated the remaining life should be reassessed and the amortisation adjusted to spread the remaining cost over the new estimate of useful life.

FRS 11 formalised the concept of impairment reviews. These reviews are undertaken if it is suspected that the carrying value of an asset, such as goodwill or intangibles exceeds its continuing value to the business. This can occur if circumstances have changed in the industry or at the company. The estimation of an impairment provision that is needed to write the carrying value down is as follows:

$$\text{Provision} = \begin{array}{l}\text{Current carrying value less the higher of}\\ \text{Recoverable Amount and Value in Use}\end{array}$$

DEFINITION

Recoverable Amount equates to the current market value of the asset in its current condition and *Value in Use* is calculated as the net present value of future cash flows, including estimated disposal proceeds, from future use of the asset.

Impairment provisions were initially quite rare. However, in 2001 a number of high profile companies have had to provide for impairment relating to investments in dotcom or telecoms related businesses they acquired in 1999 or 2000. The reason for this is the sharp adverse movement of market sentiment in these sectors. In 1999 and 2000 these sectors were seen as being exciting prospects with significant future values. However, issues encountered in both the sectors around customer take-up and future potential led to the premium values placed on businesses in 1999 and 2000 not being sustained in 2001. The fall in the market capitalisations of quoted companies in this sector has led to the likelihood of impairments and some very large provisions being put in place.

The example accounts included in Chapter 32 include just such an impairment provision. The provision was calculated on the value in use basis discounting the cashflow at 15% per annum.

These impairment provisions, which are a charge to the profit and loss account, have given rise to dramatic falls in profitability or increases in losses for a number of high profile companies. The interesting thing is that the provisions can often relate solely to market sentiment. The need for a provision does not, of itself, infer that the initial acquisition of the business or technology was wrong. Indeed, some companies have needed to make impairment provisions even when the businesses they acquired are meeting or exceeding their budgeted performance.

This may seem counter-intuitive but the Standard is trying to ensure that carrying values do not exceed market values to avoid the readers of company accounts being misled about the real underlying net asset value of a company. In sectors such as technology where companies may be making losses as they develop the technology, the underlying net asset position is important from an investor's point of view as it should set the baseline for valuation.

SUMMARY

34.10   After nearly a decade of debate FRS 10 and FRS 11 set out the mandatory treatment of intangibles and goodwill. The treatment, if not always logical, is at least consistent. There are, however, a number of areas of judgement still involved in the process and the implications of these judgements can make interpreting company accounts complicated.

Unfortunately, there is probably no single practical answer to overcoming these issues due to the varied nature of businesses and intellectual property.

Index

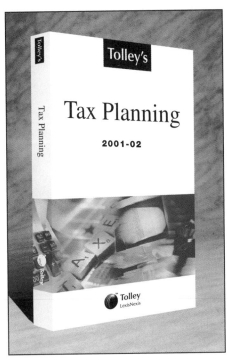

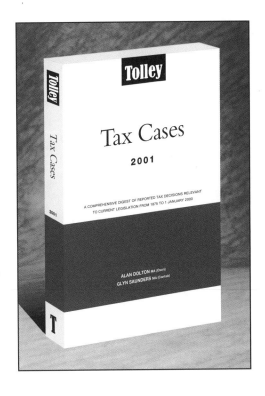